D0991089

John Quincy Adams
and
American Global Empire

John Quincy Adams and American Global Empire

WILLIAM EARL WEEKS

THE UNIVERSITY PRESS OF KENTUCKY

Copyright © 1992 by The University Press of Kentucky
Scholarly publisher for the Commonwealth,
serving Bellarmine College, Berea College, Centre
College of Kentucky, Eastern Kentucky University,
The Filson Club, Georgetown College, Kentucky
Historical Society, Kentucky State University,
Morehead State University, Murray State University,
Northern Kentucky University, Transylvania University,
University of Kentucky, University of Louisville,
and Western Kentucky University.

Editorial and Sales Offices: Lexington, Kentucky 40508-4008

Library of Congress Cataloging-in-Publication Data
Weeks, William Earl, 1957-
    John Quincy Adams and American global empire / William Earl Weeks.
      p.   cm.
    Includes bibliographical references and index.
    ISBN 0-8131-1779-8
    1. Florida—History—Cession to the United States, 1819.
2. Spain. Treaties, etc. United States, 1819 Feb. 22.   3. Adams,
John Quincy, 1767-1848.   4. United States—Foreign relations—Spain.
5. Spain—Foreign relations—United States.   I. Title.
F314.W44   1992
973.5'5'092—dc20   91-39022

To the memory of
Professor Armin Rappaport

Contents

Maps

Acknowledgments

I would like to thank the following people for their assistance during the evolution of this project from a gleam in my mind's eye to a book:

Professors John S. Galbraith and Alexander DeConde, for their gracious support of an orphaned graduate student.

Professors H. Stuart Hughes, Earl Pomeroy, David Luft, Howard Kushner, Steven Hahn, Michael Parrish, Robert C. Ritchie, and Michael J. Hogan, all of whom influenced my development as a historian.

Mark and Marilyn Merrell, Jack and Michele Winn, Suzanne Kryder, Judy Warnock, Robert McDonell, Andrea Hattersley, Alice Green, Jeannie Whayne, Gail Shatsky, Jim Crosswhite, Bonnie and Gunnar Biggs, and Babar, friends who buoyed my spirits over the years.

Lucille Duvall, for rescuing me countless times from the graduate school bureaucracy.

Patricia and David Mendenhall, for allowing me to share a piece of ranching paradise.

Muriel Jones Weeks, my mother, and Susan, Nancy, and Elizabeth, my sisters.

Deborah Small, for her love and support over the years.

And finally, the late Armin Rappaport, who inspired my entry into the field of history and who first stimulated my interest in John Quincy Adams. May this work stand as a small tribute to his memory.

Quotations from the Adams Papers are from the microfilm edition by permission of the Massachusetts Historical Society.

Introduction

This is a story about a man, a treaty, and a nation. The man is John Quincy Adams: son of a president, congressman, president and the greatest secretary of state in American history. The treaty is the Transcontinental Treaty of 1819, which acquired Florida, secured a western boundary extending to the Pacific Ocean, and, I argue, represented the first determined step in the creation of an American global empire. The nation is the United States, the most powerful nation-state in world history and a country in whose growth and development Adams perceived himself destined to play a crucial role.

Samuel Flagg Bemis writes that "the historical figure of John Quincy Adams stands behind that of Abraham Lincoln in the history of this Union."[1] Given Adams's lifetime of service and achievement, Bemis's judgment is sound. Yet Adams's historical significance is not limited to a recitation of his remarkable public accomplishments. Of equal and perhaps greater significance are the peculiar circumstances of his life, which unfolded in parallel to that of the nation. A child of the nation's preeminent revolutionary couple, Adams watched the Battle of Bunker Hill from his mother's knee,[2] suffered a personal crisis during the "critical period" of the drafting and ratification of the Constitution, found himself in the middle of the controversy surrounding the Louisiana Purchase, and wrestled throughout his life with the moral and practical dilemmas presented by black slavery. These and other aspects of Adams's life resonate strongly with the history of the nation. When he died at the climax of the Mexican War, the nation knew that an era had passed with him. This is "great man" history, although not in the traditional sense in which the term is used. Adams's historical significance may be seen less in his public achievements than in the ironies that characterized his life. Perhaps more than anyone of his time, John Quincy Adams lived at the intersection of the personal and the public; in a very real sense, the story of his life is the story of a nation.

I examine in detail Adams's greatest contribution to the American nation: the Transcontinental Treaty of 1819. A major event in a year that saw the beginning of the Missouri debates and the Panic of 1819,

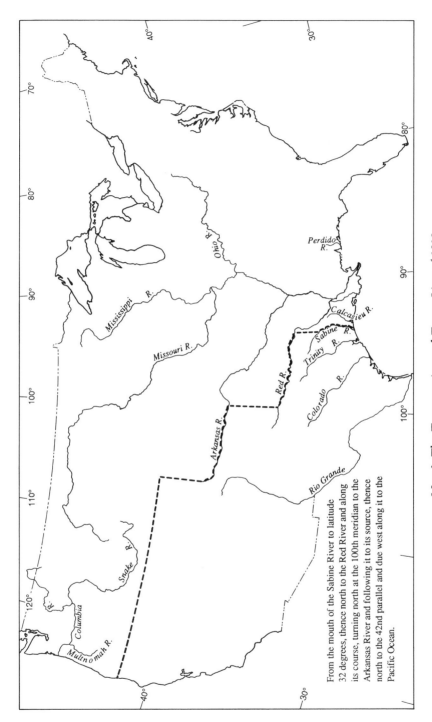

From the mouth of the Sabine River to latitude 32 degrees, thence north to the Red River and along its course, turning north at the 100th meridian to the Arkansas River and following it to its source, thence north to the 42nd parallel and due west along it to the Pacific Ocean.

Map 1. The Transcontinental Treaty Line of 1819

its significance has been underestimated by historians. The acquisition of Florida with which it is most often associated was in fact secondarily important to the transcontinental claim it secured and the global vision that informed its negotiation. The Transcontinental Treaty (along with the policies pursued during its negotiation) was the foundation of Monroe's "doctrine" of American hemispheric dominance. Moreover, the acquisition of a claim to the Oregon territory in exchange for a claim to Texas established a dynamic that would determine the course of American expansionism until the Civil War. Adams's brilliant diplomatic achievement deserves renewed explication: his conduct of foreign affairs in the perilous circumstances of 1817 improved the nation's position so as to allow Monroe to declare the Western Hemisphere off limits to further European colonization by December 1823. It is the skill with which Adams transformed the nation's international position from one of relative weakness to one of relative strength which merits for him the title of "America's greatest secretary of state." His vision of empire persisted in the policies of William Seward and John Hay.

During the conduct of the negotiations with Spain, Adams confronted the dilemmas that divided the nation and ultimately broke it apart. The interrelated problems of slavery, sectionalism, and impending financial crisis which influenced the outcome of the treaty forced Adams to compromise his personal integrity in ways that his personal myth forbade. In so doing, he gradually realized that the Founders' dream of a virtuous republic in which the common good took precedence over individual self-interest was itself compromised and that the nation faced inevitable civil war.

This study is informed primarily by three areas of American historical scholarship. First, as a contribution to the history of American foreign relations, it seeks to occupy a place between Alexander De-Conde's *This Affair of Louisiana* and Norman Graebner's *Empire on the Pacific.* DeConde's keen insights regarding the imperialist impulse behind the Louisiana Purchase have been a point of departure for my understanding of the treaty. Graebner's thesis that the expansionism of the 1840s can be understood as motivated by a desire for Pacific ports has been extended backward in time. In this regard the Transcontinental Treaty can be understood as a prelude to "Polk's aggressive diplomacy." In addition, William Appleman Williams's landmark article "The Age of Mercantilism" has suggested a framework within which to explain the foreign policy of the Monroe administration.

Second, during the last quarter-century the influence of a classical

republican tradition on the revolutionary generation has been docu-
mented by Bernard Bailyn, Gordon Wood, J.G.A. Pocock, Joyce
Appleby, and others. Their work emphasizes that generation's perception that the survival of the American republican experiment depended on the virtue of its citizens. A republican people had to resist
the temptations of personal ambition, self-interest, and faction if the
republic was to withstand the disintegrative effects of time. The
Adams family can be considered "classical republicans": for three
generations, public service was the axis around which the family
oriented its existence. John Quincy Adams was groomed from early
childhood to occupy what was assumed to be his destined role of
leadership. His moral, religious, and educational training were all
intended to create the ideal republican leader, one whose personal
integrity matches the purity of his public vision. Adams acted out the
myth of the classical republican, so much so that late in life he
identified with the Roman statesman Cicero. Adams steadfastly asserted an ethic holding that process is as important as result, that
public service must not be tainted by private ambition. Yet he lived in
an era in which ambition and self-interest were becoming the motive
forces in American society. This basic tension in his life forced him to
choose between adhering to his ideals and realizing his appointed
destiny. In the end, Adams opted for diplomatic and electoral success
at the cost of his sense of virtue. By so doing, he demonstrated the irrelevance of classical republican notions of public service in the nineteenth century. In this sense, Adams's life bore witness to the truths
contained in the predictions of republican disintegration and collapse.

Third, although the sheer size of the Adams Family Papers (605
reels of microfilm, more than 150 for John Quincy Adams alone)
prohibits a comprehensive reexamination of his life, I have closely
examined the record of the period from late 1817 to early 1819, during
which Adams negotiated the treaty with Spain. I attempt to chronicle
this moment, so crucial to both the life of Adams and the history of
the nation. Then, using the work of his numerous biographers, I seek
to contextualize my understanding of this critical time in Adams's
life within the broader perspective of both his career and the nation's
history. Brooks and Henry Adams's perception of their grandfather is
the starting point for this analysis; of near-equal importance is the
two-volume biography of Adams by Samuel Flagg Bemis.

My research has confirmed Brooks and Henry Adams's perception
of the tragic nature of their grandfather's life. Raised to believe that a
loving God exercised His will in rationally ascertainable ways and

that the United States was an agent of divine will, Adams discovered during the course of his life the inscrutable nature of divine providence and the unlikelihood that the nation he had served so faithfully could be an agent of that providence. He realized that his destiny (and that of the Adams family) was not to lead the nation but to serve as a symbol for all that Jacksonian America rejected. In an attempt to be the "man of the whole nation," Adams had (as Brooks put it) "ministered to the demon" of Jacksonianism and slavery. His "second career" as a member of the House of Representatives can, in large part, be understood as a repudiation of the achievements of his first career as a national leader. Like John C. Calhoun, Adams evolved from staunch nationalist to fiery sectionalist, one who anticipated and encouraged the breakup of the Union.

I have quoted extensively from Adams's diary (both published and unpublished), letters, and public writings in order to reveal the pungent eloquence of his expression. This is not to suggest that Adams's words are coterminous with the "truth." His famous diary, kept almost daily for more than half a century, is better understood as epic American literature than as an "objective" view of the world. His rich and voluminous expression suggests multiple meanings; Henry Adams's dictum that "no one means all he says, and yet very few say all they mean, for words are slippery and thought is viscous" holds true for his grandfather.[3] The interpretation advanced here is by no means the only plausible one. Yet I hope the reader will perceive the tormented soul that emerges from the profusion of words that defined John Quincy Adams's life. For Adams, words ultimately proved a trap that obscured as much as they illuminated the reality he inhabited. It is a lesson to be heeded by scholars of the Western tradition.

ONE

Destiny

Oh! God, my only trust went there
Through all life's scenes before
Lo! At the throne again I bow,
New mercies to implore.

Grant active power, grant fervent zeal;
and guide by thy controul;
and ever be my country's weal
the purpose of my soul.

Extend, all seeing God, thy hand
In memory still decree
And make, to bless thy native land
An instrument of me.

From John Quincy Adams's diary,
21 September 1817

Fifty years old in 1817, John Quincy Adams stood at the crossroads of an already remarkable life. Returning from his post as United States minister to Great Britain, he prepared to assume the office of secretary of state in the new administration of James Monroe. The appointment represented both an opportunity and a risk for Adams; all his previous accomplishments would count for little if he failed in his new job.

No American had been better prepared to be secretary of state. Adams's entire life had led to this end; if he failed, it would not be for lack of experience. His diplomatic career had begun at age twelve, when he accompanied his father to Paris to serve as his secretary in the negotiations to end the War of Independence. George Washington, acting as a patron to the young Adams, appointed him to his first diplomatic post in 1794 as United States minister to the Netherlands. At The Hague, Adams received his mature introduction to European diplomacy. It proved a strategic spot from which to watch the balance of the French Revolution unfold. Adams's reports home told of the extensive influence of Jacobinism in the nominally independent Netherlands. His experiences there reinforced what became a lifelong hostility to the French Revolution and a suspicion of revolutions generally.[1]

From The Hague, in 1795 Adams went to London, where he assisted in the final exchange of ratifications of Jay's Treaty. Though not entirely successful in his mission, he had the opportunity to deal face to face with some of the most skilled diplomats in Europe. It proved an educational if chastening experience.

Adams's first important diplomatic assignment came in 1797 when his father, now president, appointed his son to be the first United States minister to Prussia. In Berlin he negotiated his first treaty, an agreement outlining commercial relations between the United States and Prussia. The most important issue concerned the maritime rights of neutrals, a cause Adams championed the rest of his life. The negotiations gave him his first opportunity to bargain by diplomatic note; he later became a master of this technique. A keen and tireless observer of people and events, Adams found his four years in Prussia an invaluable part of his education as a diplomat.[2]

After a brief and uninspiring interlude practicing law in his native Massachusetts, Adams returned to public life in 1803 as a United States senator. Nominally a Federalist, he pursued an independent political course that resulted in his siding frequently with the Republicans. He was the only Federalist from New England in either house to support the Louisiana Purchase; moreover, he strongly supported Jefferson's embargo, a policy that was anathema to most New Englanders.[3] Adams paid a price for his principled stands, being recalled from office prior to the end of his term. Yet he had established a reputation as a powerful spokesman for expansion and nationalism.

Rebuked by his own party, Adams formally switched allegiance to the Republicans in 1808. Not long after, President James Madison rewarded his support by appointing him minister to Russia. Adams stayed in St. Petersburg from 1809 to 1814 and developed a cordial relationship Tsar Alexander I. The two men went on long walks together, during which Adams gained further insight into the intricacies of European balance-of-power politics.[4] The dazzling court life of St. Petersburg enlightened but did not beguile him; the soirees permitted him to observe and study the European diplomatic corps. Adams's most important achievement in Russia concerned a conflict over the northwest coast of North America: he instinctively refused a Russian offer that would in effect have recognized the Russian right to fur trading posts in the region. This turned out to be the first step in a long strategy that eventually resulted in the formal statement prohibiting further European colonization in the Western Hemisphere—the Monroe Doctrine.

From St. Petersburg, Adams went directly to the city of Ghent in Belgium, where he chaired the American peace comission negotiating an end to the War of 1812. Here he had the opportunity to duplicate the peacemaking achievements of his father. Many of the issues in dispute were the same as those in 1782: boundaries, fishing rights, and the status of the native peoples of North America. At first, a favorable settlement seemed unlikely; however, a shift in battlefield fortunes and the determined work of the American commissioners salvaged an agreement based on the *status quo ante bellum.* In light of the circumstances, it was a formidable diplomatic accomplishment.

For Adams, the triumph at Ghent opened the door to the preeminent position in the American foreign service—minister to Great Britain. The rising diplomat made the most of his opportunity. He participated in the negotiation of the Anglo-American Commercial Convention of July 1815, having been at his post less than a month. He laid the foundation for the Rush-Bagot Agreement of 1817, a pact limiting Anglo-American naval forces on the Great Lakes. Most important, he worked diligently to cultivate good relations between the United States and Great Britain.

British Foreign Secretary Lord Castlereagh joined Adams in the quest for closer Anglo-American ties. Though of very different personalities, the two men were like-minded when it came to the necessity of ending hostilities between the two nations. The dawn of the post-Napoleonic era made clear the interest each nation had in peace, trade, and expansion. The alignment of forces making possible the Monroe Doctrine began to evolve at this time; Castlereagh and Adams played a central role in that evolution.[5]

In sum, John Quincy Adams had led a life of distinguished achievement. His career to a remarkable degree mirrored that of his father, yet he had not reached the presidency, the post for which all previous accomplishments had been mere preparation. Adams had spent seventeen of the previous twenty-three years abroad, establishing an enviable reputation in European courts from St. Petersburg to London. Now it was time to assume a position of leadership at home and perhaps a place in history on a par with the near-mythical figures of the previous generation. To Adams it must have seemed that in some ways his career was only beginning.

It is therefore not surprising that Adams suffered from anxiety and self-doubt in the weeks and months before his return to America. Plagued with sleeplessness and physical ailments, he toyed with the idea of turning down the offer to head the Department of State. Even before Monroe offered the position, Adams wrote to William Eustis, a family friend, that he had "several strong, personal motives" for not accepting and that "the pros and cons [are] so nearly balanced that I willingly postpone the decision until there shall be a certainty that it will be called for."[6] Formal nomination to the post did not end his indecision; he wrote to his mother on 23 April 1817 of his "very serious doubts" as to his competency for the job. He feared that he could not "conciliate" his self-respect and "spirit of personal independence" with the subordination the job would require. Ultimately, as he did so often in times of crisis, Adams relied on his faith in God to assuage his uncertainties; he wrote his mother that "the disposer of every gift can alone enable me faithfully and acceptably to perform my duties."[7] In retrospect, Adams's doubts as to his competency seem more coquettish than sincere. No American had more reason for confidence about his ability to discharge the duties of secretary of state.

Yet no American bore a greater burden of history and destiny than John Quincy Adams. Success for him was measured in terms far grander than for other men. The Founding Fathers had taken an active interest in him from the time he assisted his father in Europe. George Washington (after whom Adams named his firstborn) had launched his diplomatic career. Thomas Jefferson played a large role in his personal development: John Adams once wrote to the Sage of Monticello that John Quincy "appeared to be as much your boy as mine."[8] Finally, there was the example of his father—peace negotiator, vice-president, president—a giant among giants, constantly held up to the young boy as the personification of virtue and wisdom. Against this backdrop of immortality, John Quincy Adams hesitantly approached his term as secretary of state, unsure of his ability to measure up to his father's generation yet compelled by his family to try.

Indeed, he has the distinction of being, as Samuel Flagg Bemis observed, the only national leader whose parents planned his life for him that way.[9] John Quincy Adams bore the responsibility of extending the fame of a family convinced of its role as an agent of national destiny—a responsibility made greater by the alcoholism and dissipation of his two brothers. For Adams, success required extending the achievements of his father's generation. Anything less would be failure. Abigail Adams continually reminded her eldest son of his special destiny as "a guardian of the laws, liberty, and religion of your country, as your father . . . had already been."[10] She stressed the heritage of previous generations and the need for their work to be continued: "Glory my son in a country which has given birth to characters, both in the civil and military departments, which may vie with the wisdom and valor of antiquity. As an immediate descendant of one of these characters, may you be led to an imitation of that disinterested patriotism and that noble love of country, which will teach you to despise wealth, titles, pomp, and equipage, as mere external advantages, which cannot add to the internal excellence of your mind, or compensate for the want of integrity or virtue."[11] The emphasis was on service, integrity, and, most important, a conformity between one's personal values and public actions.

John Adams, despite his long absences from home (he was away for all but six months of the years between 1774 and 1781), took an active interest in the upbringing of his children. His letters to Abigail continually stress that she must be attentive to the moral, religious, and educational training of their brood. He urged her to "mould the minds and manners of our children. . . . teach them not only to do virtuously but to excell." Abigail was to "train them to virtue, habituate them to industry, activity, and spirit. Make them consider every vice, as shameful and unmanly." He feared his absence would hinder the educational and moral development of his children. "Truth, sobriety, and industry" were to be "perpetually inculcated upon them."[12] The lessons were of the utmost importance, for John Adams believed that the survival of the republic depended on "a small number of the ablest men" serving their nation virtuously and unselfishly.[13] John Quincy Adams was from birth groomed to be one of these men.

While both his parents envisioned John Quincy as a future leader, it was Abigail who did the most to mold his mind. During her husband's long absences she formed an especially close attachment to John Quincy. One historian writes that "she attended to every aspect, from his appearance to his soul."[14] Her precocious son provided sorely needed conversation and companionship during John's absences.[15] From his early teens she treated John Quincy as an adult, referring to him from time to time as "young Hercules."[16] Ardently interested in the success of her husband, Abigail deemed John Quincy the heir to greatness. She groomed him for future responsibilities, admonishing him at age twelve that "nothing is wanting from you but attention, diligence, and steady application. Nature has not been deficient."[17]

Abigail and John knew that destiny, in order to be fulfilled, had to be prepared for. The success of the United States as the redeemer nation required that it be led by virtuous and learned men. Consequently, religion and education became the cornerstones of John

Quincy Adams's world. Abigail wrote to him in 1780: "The only sure and permanent foundation of virtue is religion. Let this important truth be engraven upon your heart."[18] She cultivated in her son a belief in an infinitely wise, just, and good God who held out the promise of eternal life to those who lived on earth the principle of the Golden Rule, thus reinforcing the relationship between right conduct and earthly reward. Moreover, she stressed to him that "you are accountable to your Maker for all your words and actions."[19] John Quincy took to heart his mother's religious instruction. Christian belief guided his life more than that of any other American political leader of his age. Adams read the Bible daily upon arising, believing it to be divine revelation. As an adult he read it in French and German translations.[20]

John Quincy Adams came to rely heavily on his faith in God to surmount the frequent crises he faced. His belief in the power of human reason did not prevent him from appreciating the essentially unknowable nature of the universe. In this vein he wrote: "That same God who in one person exacts the punishment, in another person sustains it [and] thus makes his own mercy pay the satisfaction to his own injustice—this is not reason—it is mystery."[21] Religious faith provided Adams with a justification for life's sufferings that his rationalist philosophy could not.

Education served as the other cornerstone of John Quincy Adams's life, the second means by which one prepared to serve destiny. Bemis writes that his parents "prescribed his education to a degree that would stagger a modern psychologist."[22] As a toddler, the first book he read was *Giles Gingerbread: A Little Boy Who Lived upon Learning*, which taught that "merit and industry may entitle a man to any thing." The stories in the book stressed the importance of familial duty, rigid adherence to moral precepts, piety, hard work, and a love for learning. In later years Abigail fondly recalled John Quincy's learning the lessons of Giles Gingerbread by heart.[23] By age ten he had read most of the works of Shakespeare and Pope. His travels with his father gave his education a strongly European flavor. After attending prep schools in Paris and Amsterdam (and gaining the benefits of his father's tutoring), he enrolled for a while at the University of Leyden. By his teenage years he had mastered French, Latin, German, and Dutch; he would later acquire Greek and a rudimentary knowledge of Spanish. His fluent French allowed him to serve at age fourteen as interpreter on Francis Dana's mission to Russia.

Reading "the great books" proved a major source of enlightenment and enjoyment for John Quincy Adams throughout his life. At age seven he began to read excerpts from Charles Rollin's *Ancient History* to his mother.[24] He had a thorough knowledge of both English and French literature and history. He was an expert on the literature of classical Greece and Rome, reading as a teenager the works of, among others, Cicero, Suetonius, Livy, Herodotus, Aristotle, and Plutarch in their original Latin and Greek. He translated Virgil's *Aeneid* and the works of Tacitus.[25] Such was his love for the writings of Tacitus and Cicero that later in life he declared that to be deprived of their wisdom would be akin to the loss of a limb.

John Quincy Adams's intense study of the ancient world was not solely for academic purposes. The works particularly of the classical historians, representing the accumulated experience of the ages, served as invaluable guides to the present. Abigail wrote to sixteen-year-old John Quincy: "It is instructive to trace the various causes, which produced the strength of one nation, and the decline and weakness of another; to learn by what arts one man has been able to subjugate millions of his fellow creatures . . . sometimes driven by ambition and a lust of power; at other times, swallowed up by religious enthusiasm, blind bigotry, and ignorant zeal; sometimes enervated with luxury and debauched by pleasure, until the most powerful nations have become a prey and been subdued by these sirens, when neither the number of their enemies, nor the prowess of their arms, could conquer them."[26] Hence the modern lessons of the evils of luxury and the necessity of virtue received ancient confirmation. Throughout his life John Quincy Adams relied on the experience of the past to serve as a lens through which to evaluate the issues and events of his own day.[27]

While it was Abigail who did the most to shape John Quincy during his formative years, the influence of John Adams cannot be underestimated. Abigail's political philosophy mirrored that of her husband. The necessity of mixed government, the limits of egalitarianism, and the use of history as a tool for learning were all axiomatic to John and were faithfully passed on via Abigail to John Quincy.[28] This similarity in political philosophy between father and son later prompted Joseph Addison of the London *Spectator* to remark, "Curse on the stripling, how he apes his sire."

In addition to his impressive knowledge of languages, literature, and history, John Quincy Adams became, during the course of his life, well-schooled in the sciences. In the tradition of Franklin and Jefferson he was a meticulous observer of the natural world. He kept a daily record of the temperature and became an amateur horticulturalist.

His investigation of weights and measures proved a classic in the field.[29] His work on behalf of the Smithson bequest was essential to the establishment of the Smithsonian Institution. Awestruck by the heavens, Adams developed a thorough knowledge of celestial objects. His advocacy of the development of observatories in the United States earned him a place as one of the fathers of American astronomy.[30] Bemis writes: "No one save Franklin had done so much to advance the cause of science in America."[31]

John Quincy Adams envisioned education as the natural complement to religion. He believed that God's laws could be discerned by scientific investigation and that, once learned, these laws could be used for the improvement of humanity.[32] Therefore, he pushed for federal suport of education and science, including the establishment of a national university, long before it became acceptable to do so.[33] Adams's belief in the power of learning and of the potential for human improvement through education is an interesting counterpoint in the life of a man often described (with some justice) as puritanical.

While stressing the importance of education for cultivating the mind and of religion for ministering to the soul, Abigail and John did not overlook the physical aspect of existence. John urged Abigail to augment the mental and moral training of their children with exercise: "Without strength and activity and vigor of body, the brightest mental excellencies will be eclipsed and obscured."[34] Abigail was more direct. She informed John Quincy that "our bodies are framed of such materials as to require constant exercise to keep them in repair, to brace the nerves and give vigor to the animal functions."[35] Again, their son took the advice of his parents to heart. Physical exercise became almost as much a part of his daily life as did reading the Bible. Historians have long noted his habit of swimming in the Potomac, a practice he continued into his late seventies. In Washington he routinely walked to his office and also took long solitary strolls as a means of relaxation from the stresses of official duties. John Quincy Adams's exercise regimen and naturally resilient constitution gave him an awesome capacity for work: for years he was known as the hardest-working, most indefatigable person in Washington.[36]

Although Abigail and John worked endlessly to make their prized son appreciate the importance of piety and learning, all the encouragement, prodding, and lessons in the world would have been fruitless had not he been so receptive to their admonitions. From his earliest days he sought to seek his parents' approval by fulfilling their hopes for him. Undoubtedly, John Quincy Adams's love for his mother and his desire to show his devotion to her fueled his intense efforts to please. He loved his mother more than he loved anyone else during his long life. Brooks Adams later wrote that Adams's "love and veneration for his mother . . . even passed the adoration of Catholics for the Virgin."[37] To fulfill her hopes, to live up to her expectations, became paramount to him at an early age. Thus when Abigail wrote to ten-year-old John Quincy that "I would rather you should have found your grave in the ocean you have crossed, or that any untimely death crop you in your infant years, then see you an immoral, profligate, or graceless child," it profoundly effected the future statesman.[38] Abigail pleaded with her eldest son to "preserve your innocence and pure conscience. Your morals are of more importance, both to yourself and the world, than all languages and sciences. The least stain upon your character will do more harm to your happiness than all accomplishments will do it good."[39] In short, John Quincy Adams's lifelong determination to lead a principled, moral life can be understood as the natural result of an upbringing that conditioned his happiness, his success, and even his salvation on doing so.[40]

While religion and education were meant to prepare John Quincy Adams for leadership, destiny was to be fulfilled by selfless service to the nation and devotion to the ideals on which the republic had been founded. Abigail and John believed that the fate of the nation depended on the willingness of its wise and virtuous members to take an active role in civic affairs. They saw the United States as the manifestation of divine will; to serve the republic was to serve both God and the cause of humanity. Abigail continually held up to John Quincy the image of his father as the embodiment of patriotic virtue. Indeed, she stressed that the greatness of the nation (like the salvation of its citizens) depended on the virtue and morality of its leaders. No family in American history has more personified the ideal of service to the nation than the Adamses; and no members of that family devoted more of themselves to the country than did John Quincy.[41]

Adams bore the burden of extending the fame of his family as well as that of the nation. He knew that to be anything less than extraordinary in his achievements meant a betrayal of the family. One historian terms this ethic the "Adams family myth."[42] Inculcated unconsciously as well as consciously, it taught that political power could be attained only by moral and educational superiority; moreover, it stressed that the reward for such superiority must be freely bestowed rather than sought. To grasp for power, to actively seek the approbation and support of one's fellow citizens, was as serious an offense as to ignore one's public duties entirely. In short, personal ambition was an egregious moral failing.

The "Adams family myth" created severe tension in the mind of John Quincy Adams. It demanded personal striving for success yet denied that it might be done for personal satisfaction. The myth stressed achievement but condemned personal aggrandizement. Adams was to emulate the accomplishments of his father but was prohibited from doing so in any way that smacked of selfishness or personal ambition. At times it must have seemed an unbearable burden for him. It is little wonder that his brothers Charles and Thomas, raised under similar injunctions, found comfort in alcohol.[43]

Indeed, the myth the Adams family created for itself was a burden for all its members. Deeply distressed by her husband's long absences, Abigail rationalized them as necessary sacrifices for the common good and the progress of the nation. She found the strength to go on in the belief that "the honour of my dearest friend, the welfare and happiness of this wide extended country, ages yet unborn, depend for their happiness and security, upon the able and skillful, the honest and upright discharge of the important trust committed to him."[44] Although these lines seem exaggerated, time has demonstrated that Abigail's personal sacrifices were indeed necessary for the good of the country.[45] She wrote to her husband: "All domestick pleasures and injoyments are absorbed in the great and important duty you owe your country 'for our country is as it were a secondary God, and the first and greatest parent'. . . . Thus do I suppress every wish, and silence every murmur, acquiescing in a painful separation."[46] For three generations the Adamses served their country at the cost of long familial separations.

During his late teens and early twenties, John Quincy Adams balked at the role that had been prescribed for him. He did not choose to be a man of destiny; destiny (through the agency of his parents) had chosen him. He suffered from frequent depressions as he tried to reconcile in his own mind what was important in life. One biographer has noted that his personal "critical years" coincided with the "critical period" of American history during which the Constitution was drafted and ratified.[47] While it might be too much to suggest, in the words of Hawthorne, that "jollity and gloom contended for an empire" in the heart of the young native of Mount Wollaston (later Quincy, and Hawthorne's Merrymount), it is clear that the years 1785-94—spent first at Harvard and then as a lawyer—were a time of anguish and indecision for John Quincy Adams. The prescription of a life of public service conflicted with his deepest yearnings to be a man of letters and a poet, the latter inclination undoubtedly derived from his mother.[48] Destiny meant the unrelenting sacrifice of personal desires without any expectation of personal reward. By late adolescence he had not yet resigned himself to such a life.

Adams struggled during this time to overcome his physical desires. At fourteen he suffered a passionate and unrequited love for a young French actress whom he never met in person. The experience engendered in him a lifelong suspicion of ladies of the stage.[49] His flirtatious encounters with the opposite sex were countered by brutal after-the-fact assessments of the objects of his fancy. At twenty-three he broke off an engagement, at the insistence of his mother, with Mary Frazier of Newburyport. Abigail feared that choosing a mate at such a young age would hinder her son's career as a statesman. Obedient to his mother's wishes, John Quincy Adams nonetheless never forgot Mary Frazier or loved another woman (with the exception of his mother) as much.[50]

The cultivation of Adams's mental powers and moral faculties came at the expense of the growth of a well-rounded personality. His childhood was anything but "normal." In his first letter (written at age six) he admonished himself, attributing his lack of progress in reading to spending "too much of my time in play." He added that "there is a great deal of room for me to grow better."[51] In his first letter to his father, the young Adams wrote: "I hope I grow a better boy and that you will have no occasion to be ashamed of me when you return."[52] He preached to his younger brothers: "We are sent into this world for some end. It is our duty to discover by close study what that end is and when we discover it to pursue it with unconquerable perseverance."[53] His long travels, disjointed education, and experiences in adult circles deprived Adams of the benefits of a peer group to grow up with. He always occupied the role of the outsider. At Harvard his long absence from the United Sates and what he perceived as the foolishness of his classmates combined to make him a solitary figure.[54]

Adams never mastered the art of social conversation. When his reticence did not render him uncommunicative, his pugnaciousness tended to make him argumentative in discussions. He recognized his shortcomings in this regard: "I went out this evening in search of conversation, an art of which I never had an adequate idea. . . . I am by nature a silent animal, and my dear mother's constant lesson in childhood, that children in company should be seen and not heard, confirmed me irrevocably in what I now deem a bad habit."[55] A man of many acquaintances, John Quincy Adams had few friends. The surface most people dealt with was austere, dour. His son Charles

Francis thought his father "the only man I ever saw whose feelings I could not penetrate. . . . I can study his countenance forever and very seldom find any sure guide by which to move."[56]

Washington's appointment of John Quincy Adams as minister to the Netherlands ended all doubts regarding his future. The beginning of his public career marked the triumph of destiny over introspection, of public service over private happiness. His yearnings for a life of philosophic repose and agricultural pursuits (such as his father had enjoyed for nearly sixty years) were thenceforth subordinated to the demands of public service, to be conjured up in moments of exhaustion in the form of self-pity.[57] Adams, for better or worse, had embraced the destiny laid out for him and the personal sacrifices that fulfilling such a destiny required. His being, like that of his mother, came to rest on the twin pillars of religious faith and patriotism.

John Quincy Adams had no doubts that the United States was the agent of God's work on earth, the vehicle by which human progress could be achieved. Unless one appreciates how deeply and how sincerely this belief motivated him, much of his life is difficult to understand. His sense of purpose as an individual hinged on his perception that America had been designated by God as the redeemer nation and that he had an essential role to play in the national mission of global redemption. The founding fathers had begun this process, and the Declaration of Independence was their holy writ. Now the torch had been passed to a new generation—and Adams saw himself as the natural leader of that generation. Given his parentage and training, it was not an unreasonable assumption.

As a leader of the nation chosen by God to redeem the world, Adams saw himself as literally an instrument of divine providence. Throughout his life he attributed his accomplishments to the inspiration and aid of providence. He struggled to subordinate his own desires, ambition, and pride to the humility and tireless sense of duty that he felt were appropriate to his role as divine servant. He viewed his destiny as a trust, a special responsibility—indeed, a heavy burden—from which he expected neither profit nor enjoyment. Although it is easy to discount Adams's pious conception of his "destiny" as a mere cover for the pursuit of personal ambition, his financial records and his diary unarguably demonstrate that he received little profit and even less joy from his long years of public service.[58] A profound sense of his own sinfulness and inadequacy for the task of leadership more than balanced any personal rewards such a destiny might have provided.

As he matured, John Quincy Adams evolved a vision of society that drew upon the ideals of Washington, Jefferson, and John Adams. It was an article of faith to him that effective leadership depended on the president's having a moral vision of the nation's future. At the center of his own vision of America's future lay an extensive system of federally built internal improvements, to be financed by the sale of public lands. Inspired by Washington's efforts to construct a system of canals and highways in Virginia, Adams's plan of internal improvements became central to his political philosophy.[59] Federally financed canals and highways would facilitate commerce, stimulate manufactures, and aid travel, thus reinforcing the bonds of union. He wrote to James Lloyd in 1822 that "the first duty of a nation . . . [is that of] bettering its own condition by internal improvements."[60] As president, he called in his inaugural address for a system of internal improvements rivaling those of ancient Rome, a gift to the future that would prompt "the most fervent gratitude . . . [of] the unborn millions of our posterity."[61] Yet this commitment did not begin with his presidency. When on 23 February 1807 he introduced in the Senate a resolution calling for a national plan of roads and canals, he became the first member of Congress to go on record in support of such improvements.[62]

Adams's vision of the role of government in the betterment of society was not confined to transport and travel facilities, however. He believed that government, as the instrument of the people (and of God), had a moral obligation to assist desirable enterprises that profit-minded entrepreneurs would not undertake; that it had a literal obligation to "establish justice," "provide for the common defense," "promote the general welfare," and otherwise ensure that the promises of the preamble of the Constitution were kept. The subsidization of education, the promotion of a favorable business climate, and even the planning of cities were to Adams all legitimate activities of government.[63] His perception that mutual obligation bound the members of society to one another and his advocacy of an activist central government reveal him to have been simultaneously behind and ahead of his time. His belief in a broad interpretation of the constitutional powers of government existed in parallel to his adamant opposition to the usurpation of individual rights by government.[64] Edward Everett noted: "It is characteristic of most men . . . to lean decidedly either to the conservative or progressive tendency. . . . In Mr. Adams's political system there was a singular mixture of both principles."[65]

Adams grafted a vision of human equality to a conception of society, at once hierarchical and organic, in which the members had

mutual bonds of obligation and responsibility. A staunch defender
of the rights of property, he equally asserted the obligation of the
stronger and wealthier citizens to take care of the needs of the poor.
Like John Winthrop's "city on a hill," Adams envisioned a society in
which all members were linked and in which the interest of the
individual was, to a certain extent, both defined and limited by the
common good.[66]

Adams ridiculed the notion that the pursuit of the unbridled self-
interest of each individual would promote the best interests of the
society. Individual self-interest untempered by a concern for the
common good would be disastrous to the social cohesion of the nation and the moral advance of both society and the individual. Such a
system would lead to the rise of a capitalistic or speculative class
presiding over a discontented and degraded mass owing no sense of
loyalty or obligation to the society.[67] In the tradition of his Puritan
forebears, he believed that liberty meant the right to do what was just
and moral, not what suited individual profit or fancy. Insofar as the
marketplace did not address social imperatives of either a material or
a moral nature, it was the function of the government, acting in the
interest of the citizenry, to step in. Adams's first message to Congress,
in December 1825, captures this aspect of his thought: "The great
object of the institution of government is the improvement of the
condition of those who are parties to the social compact. . . . Roads
and canals, by multiplying and facilitating the communications and
intercourse between distant regions and multitudes of men, are
among the most important means of improvement. But moral, political, intellectual improvement are duties assigned by the Author of
Our Existence to social no less than to individual man. For the
fulfillment of those duties governments are invested with power, and
to the attainment of the end—the progressive improvement of the
condition of the governed—the exercise of delegated powers is a duty
as sacred and indispensable as the usurpation of powers not granted is
criminal and odious."[68]

The conviction that the United States had been designated by God
to be the redeemer nation prompted Adams to become one of the
most ardent proponents of continental expansionism. He conceived
of the North American continent as the proper laboratory for the
great experiment in human freedom, and early on he determined to
devote his energies to the expansion of the nation's limits. His support of the Louisiana Purchase confirmed that if he had not fully
embraced the ideology of the Jeffersonians, he had gone beyond what
were by 1803 the sectional (and thereby limited) concerns of the

Federalists. Adams later decreed continental expansion to be a manifestation of natural law: "The world shall be familiarized with the idea of considering our proper dominion to be the continent of North America. From the time that we became an independent people it was as much a law of nature that this should become our pretension as that the Mississippi should flow to the sea."[69]

Adams just as strongly believed in the economic and moral necessity of expanding the nation's overseas commerce. Trade would be the means of uniting the diverse cultures of the world in a common interest. A thriving international trade would be the basis of a new global community, with the United States as its leader. Adams looked to a day when interstate warfare would be made obsolete by the economic interests that tied nations together. Following in the footsteps of his father, John Quincy fought throughout his professional life for the destruction of the European mercantile system and the establishment of an international trading order based on the principles of equality of commercial access, reciprocity, and freedom of the seas.[70] The creation of global sea lanes open to all nations and dedicated to the protection of neutral shipping was the international counterpart to Adams's plan for domestic internal improvements and advocated for much the same reason: to reinforce the ties of community.

Adams elevated trade to the status of moral duty. When the Chinese refused to trade with the Western powers because of their merchants' continued importations of opium into China, Adams responded irately. Describing commerce as "among the natural rights and duties of men," he argued that China's refusal to trade with the West on terms of equality and reciprocity represented a selfish, un-Christian, and "unsocial" system that hindered international progress. Adams believed it to be the "duty" of nations to trade—"not from exclusive or paramount consideration of [the one's] own interest; but from a joint and equal moral consideration of the interests of both." He denied that the cause of the opium war was the opium trade: "The cause of the war is the kowtow! the arrogant and insupportable pretension of China, that she will hold commercial intercourse . . . not upon terms of equal reciprocity, but upon the insulting and degrading forms of the relation between lord and vassal."[71] Hence John Quincy Adams was a champion of the "open door" long before the term was used to describe that basic aspect of American foreign policy.

Although Adams championed the establishment of greater commercial ties as a means of establishing international community, he just as resolutely resisted attempts to involve the United States in the affairs of other nations. While he advocated the unlimited expansion of American overseas trade, unilateralism and isolationism characterized his approach to political and military matters. Here again the influence of George Washington is clear. The role of the United States as moral leader of the world and the great example of republican government implied no obligation to assist other nations struggling for independence. Adams's steadfast opposition to the extension of material or diplomatic aid to the South American and Greek revolutions provides vivid evidence of his refusal to jeopardize American national interest for the sake of other nations. In a famous speech on 4 July 1821 he stated that the United States "goes not abroad, in search of monsters to destroy. She is the well-wisher to the freedom and independence of all. She is the champion and vindicator only of her own."[72]

When John Quincy Adams returned to the United States in 1817, he carried with him an image of himself as the "man of the whole nation," a man above party and section. For twenty-five years he had crafted a career that emphasized the interests of the nation as a unified whole. His vision of leadership was built upon the ideals of both Washington and Jefferson, Federalist and Republican. It looked back with pride on the legacy of the Founders and forward to the realization of their dreams. The office of secretary of state, traditional stepping-stone to the White House, now belonged to a man who considered the presidency to be his birthright. Destiny seemed on the verge of fulfillment.

The United States, like John Quincy Adams, had reached a critical stage of development by 1817. The bitterly divisive war with Great Britain had ended on terms far more favorable than anyone could have dared to hope for, and the full flush of peace brought a brief period of economic prosperity in 1816 and 1817. Yet the disputes that had caused the war remained unsettled, as did a festering disagreement with Spain over the nation's boundaries. In addition to these international disputes, an impending crisis of confidence in the dollar loomed, caused in part by export of U.S. silver reserves to finance a lucrative trade with the Orient. Moreover, an ever widening sectional schism was emerging between the Northeast, the South, and the trans-Appalachian West. Each region had specific economic needs and aspirations that found expression in conflicting programs to deal with the problems the nation faced. Underneath all these issues lay the question of slavery. Despite constitutional compromise, the continuation of human bondage in the presumed land of freedom drove a wedge through the middle of American society. With the end of the Napoleonic wars and the controversies they had engendered, the nation's attention focused on internal development and the settlement of the West. The manner of solving the problems with Great Britain, Spain, the dollar, sectionalism, and slavery established a dynamic that would influence the course of American history until the Civil War.

The dispute with Spain was the most pressing problem in 1817. Having its immediate origins in a disagreement over the boundaries and indeed the legitimacy of the Louisiana Purchase, the dispute actually formed but one part of a long-term struggle between the United States and Spain for dominance in the Western Hemisphere. Beginning with the formal independence of the United States in 1783, the ceaseless expansion of the new republic created friction with a Spanish government too weak to defend its far-flung possessions, yet too proud and too stubborn meekly to surrender them. Pinckney's Treaty of 1795 marked the close of the first phase of this struggle; it secured for the United States the right to navigate the Mississippi River and defined a southern border with Spanish Florida. The conflict between the two nations ended in 1898 with the complete expulsion of Spanish influence from the hemisphere in the aftermath of the Spanish-Cuban-American War. The Transcontinental Treaty of 1819 can therefore be understood as a part of an ongoing American drive to acquire or control Spain's dominions in the Western Hemisphere.

But in 1817 the debate concerned Louisiana. From the beginning, Spain had claimed the purchase of the territory from France to be illegal, for two reasons. First, the terms under which Louisiana had been retroceded to France in 1800 stipulated that the territory could not be transferred to a third party without prior Spanish consent—which Napoleon had not obtained when he instructed his ministers to sell Louisiana to the United States for $15 million. Second, Spain claimed that nonfulfillment of another of the terms of the retrocession had invalidated the transfer of Louisiana to France. The retrocession stipulated that Napoleon would place the Duke of Parma, Carlos IV's brother-in-law, on the throne of the kingdom of Tuscany. Napoleon did not do this. France, therefore, could not sell what it did not own, or so Spain's ministers argued.[73]

The United States rejected the Spanish protest. Although President Jefferson did not deny the validity of the Spanish argument, he knew that without the support of a major European power Spain could not assert its claim militarily.[74] France certainly would not come to Spain's rescue; Talleyrand argued that Spain had made the sale of the territory necessary when the Spanish intendant at New Orleans temporarily closed the port to American shipping. Even the momentary suspension of the right of deposit had created a furor in the United States, whose western states relied on New Orleans as an outlet for the produce of the Mississippi Valley region. The uncertainty regarding New Orleans had engendered talk of a war with France to settle the matter, an ominous prospect for a nation soon to be at war with most of Europe. These circumstances, said Talleyrand, necessitated the sale as a means of fostering American good will. Thus, Spain was abandoned by a nation presumed to be a close ally—an occurrence that was to be repeated.

Spain's impotence soon forced a retreat from its claim regarding the illegality of the sale of Louisiana. Then began the arduous task of defining its uncertain boundaries through negotiations with the United States. In selling Louisiana to the United States, the French had purposely left unclear the extent of the territory. When Robert Livingston, the chief American negotiator of the deal, inquired of Talleyrand as to the boundaries of the immense tract he had bought, he received a cryptic reply: "I can give you no direction. You have made a noble bargain for yourselves and I suppose you will make the most of it."[75] Make the most of it the United States did, ultimately extending the boundaries of "Louisiana" to the shores of the Pacific Ocean.

In 1803, however, discussion focused on the uncertainty surrounding the boundaries and the ownership of West Florida, or the part of West Florida west of the Perdido River. Spanish foreign minister Don Pedro de Cevallos claimed that West Florida formed no part of the territory of Louisiana, basing his assertion on the fact that Great Britain had seized West Florida from France in 1763, thereby splitting it off from Louisiana. Spain subsequently had obtained East and West Florida from Great Britain in the Treaty of Paris of 1783 as compensation for its part in the recent war. From this, Cevallos reasoned that since the terms of the Louisiana Purchase held that its boundaries were the same as when Spain had retroceded the territory to France in 1800, then West Florida could not be considered part of the purchase.[76]

In fact, French negotiator François Barbe-Marbois had informed the Americans that West Florida was not part of Louisiana. Livingston, however, chose to ignore this advice and instead referred to French maps of the early eighteenth century showing the Louisiana boundary extending to the Perdido River.[77] Although these maps predated the seizure of West Florida by Great Britain in 1763 and its subsequent transfer to Spain, they became the basis of the American claim to the region.

In response to mounting Spanish opposition to the sale of Louisiana, the Jefferson administration vigorously asserted its claim to West Florida. In February 1804 the House of Representatives passed a remarkable bill known as the "Mobile Act." Sponsored by John Randolph and encouraged by Jefferson, the legislation called for the president to establish a customs district in the Mobile Bay area and extended the legal jurisdiction of the United States to the Perdido River. In effect, the bill assumed American ownership of West Florida; implementing its provisions would invite war with Spain.[78] Jefferson increased the pressure on Spain by gaining Senate approval of a convention settling the claims of American shippers who had suffered losses in Spanish waters at the hands of the French during the "Quasi-War" of 1798-1800. Although the Spanish government had had no control over the actions of the French fleet in its waters, the convention held Spain accountable for several million dollars' worth of ship seizures. The value of these claims as a diplomatic bargaining chip overshadowed their doubtful validity.

These actions, particularly the Mobile Act, outraged the Spanish minister to the United States, Casa Yrujo. Yrujo rebutted the spoliation claims against Spain with the aid of expert American legal opinion. He described the Mobile Act as "an atrocious libel" against the king of Spain and demanded that it be annulled. He published a pseudonymous series of articles in a Philadelphia newspaper attacking Jefferson's Florida policy. He eventually proved such an embarrassment that in early 1805 the administration requested his recall to Spain.[79]

Yrujo's strong protests, as well as uncertainty over the French policy regarding West Florida, prevented Jefferson from establishing the customs district that the Mobile Act called for. Instead, he suggested in his annual message, November 1804, that Spain had misunderstood the act. This seems unlikely; every member of the House knew that Spain claimed the territory with which the legislation dealt. A more reasonable explanation is that the Mobile Act was an attempt to bully Spain into ceding West Florida by an implied threat to use military force. When Spain called his bluff, Jefferson proved unwilling to take steps that likely would have led to war.

Meanwhile, in Madrid, Charles Pinckney attempted to secure by negotiation what the House could not achieve by legislation. The opposition of France and the coarseness of Pinckney's diplomacy doomed these efforts from the start. Perhaps assuming that the Jefferson administration intended to pursue the strong course dictated by the Mobile Act, Pinckney opened the talks in May 1804 by demanding ratification of the Commercial Convention of 1802 between Spain and the United States. The Senate had taken over a year to ratify the convention, and now the steadily worsening relations of the two nations led Spain to reconsider. Foreign Minister Cevallos replied coldly to Pinckney's demands, laying down the repeal of the Mobile Act and the dropping of the spoliation claims as conditions for ratification. Pinckney then implied that refusal to ratify the convention would lead to war and threatened to ask for his passport—a threat made without authorization from Washington and one that caused embarrassment when Cevallos called Pinckney's bluff.

James Monroe arrived in Madrid in January 1805 to assist the hapless Pinckney. Monroe knew the futility of his mission, for his recent stay in Paris had revealed the strong French support for Spain's claims to West Florida. But by this time the American claim had expanded to include the entire Florida peninsula. The claim to West Florida from the first had been intended as a starting point to gain control of both Floridas. In May 1805, Monroe offered to draw the western boundary of Louisiana at the Colorado River of Texas and drop the spoliation claims against Spain in exchange for the cession of East as well as West Florida. Cevallos, by now assured of French support, rejected this offer.

The Jefferson administration's willingness to draw the western boundary of Louisiana at the Colorado River of Texas foreshadowed the eventual retreat to the Sabine River in the Treaty of 1819. During the course of the tortuous negotiations, the Texas frontier proved the one area where the United States stood ready to make concessions, first in exchange for the Floridas and finally for a transcontinental boundary. How did the boundaries of "Louisiana" come to encompass Oregon as well as Texas?

At the time of the Louisiana Purchase, Jefferson thought the "unquestioned" bounds of the territory to be roughly the lands drained by the Missouri and Mississippi Rivers, bounded on the west by the Sabine River and on the east by the Iberville River. These are the limits depicted on schoolroom maps today. But beyond these "unquestioned" claims Jefferson thought the United States held reasonable "pretensions" to lands westward to the Rio Bravo (Rio Grande) and eastward to the Perdido River—in other words, Texas and West Florida. He carefully researched a scholarly treatise that he thought provided historical documentation for this enlarged claim. The notion of a French Louisiana extending from the Rio Bravo to the Perdido was based on the explorations of the Frenchmen LaSalle and Iberville, as well as a land grant made by Louis XIV early in the eighteenth century to a nobleman named Crozat. The argument advanced in Jefferson's treatise is significant because it formed the basis of John Quincy Adams's negotiating position in 1818.[80]

While Jefferson developed his argument regarding the eastern limits of Louisiana, Meriwether Lewis and William Clark prepared to explore the territory to the shores of the Pacific Ocean, ostensibly for scientific purposes. The true motive of their expedition, however, was to develop the fur trade of the West for American interests. Jefferson admitted as much in his personal correspondence as well as in the secret message to Congress of 1803 in which he first proposed the expedition.[81] By 1808 he was convinced that Oregon formed a part of the Louisiana territory. Thus, the vision of Thomas Jefferson contains the origins of the transcontinental claim of 1819.[82]

The Lewis and Clark expedition was but one of a series of American military-commercial incursions into the Louisiana territory under the guise of scientific exploration. In two expeditions in 1805-6, Zebulon Pike explored the Missouri, Arkansas, and Red Rivers, discovering the Colorado peak that bears his name. In addition, the Dunbar-Hunter, Sibley, and Freeman expeditions explored "Louisiana" as far west as Santa Fe, alarming Spanish authorities throughout the region. The United States appeared to be moving toward asserting control over an expanse of territory bound only by the limits of the American imagination.[83]

Yet in the end, Jeffersonian diplomacy failed to resolve the dispute with Spain over the boundaries of the Louisiana Purchase, in part because of French opposition but primarily because of Jefferson's reluctance to use force to assert the American claim. Though he pushed the Mobile Act through Congress, he proved unwilling to risk war by implementing it. The numerous westward expeditions had the effect of provoking Spain but by themselves did little to extend American control of the region. That Spain's ministers knew Jefferson would not resort to force made it easy for them to ignore the bluster of Pinckney.[84] Jefferson's unwillingness to use military power as an instrument of policy stands in sharp contrast to the course that James Monroe and John Quincy Adams would follow in eventually bringing Spain to terms.

Monroe's departure from Madrid in July 1805 marked the end of the first phase of negotiations over the disputed lands. Direct negotiations did not resume until after the fall of Napoleon. The United

States refused to negotiate with either the puppet government of the Napoleonic era or the Spanish government in exile known as the regency. Diplomatic relations with Spain, broken off in 1809, were not reestablished until 1816.

Yet suspension of direct talks did not still American yearnings for the Floridas. On the contrary, as time passed, the region gained in strategic and economic importance. Few Americans doubted that the Floridas in the hands of another power posed a serious security risk for the United States along its southern frontier. The geographical contours of Florida led some to compare it to a pistol whose barrel pointed directly at New Orleans. In time of war it would be an impregnable base from which to invade the United States. Moreover, south Florida controlled the sea lanes leading into the Gulf of Mexico. Ownership of Louisiana required that body of water to be an American "lake." Finally, Americans alleged that the Floridas in Spanish hands functioned as a refuge for "marauding Indians" and runaway slaves, who periodically launched cross-border raids on local U.S. settlements. Although of lesser substance than the first two concerns, this last reason worried Americans, especially southerners, the most.

Beyond posing a threat to American security, Spanish control of the Floridas acted to stunt the economic growth of the lower South by limiting access to the Gulf of Mexico. Livingston's original instructions called for the purchase not of Louisiana but of New Orleans and West Florida, for an effective regional transportation system depended on access not just to the Mississippi but also to the rivers flowing through West Florida to the Gulf, such as the Mobile and the Apalachicola. Having failed as Livingston's assistant to gain uncontested control of West Florida in the Louisiana Purchase, James Monroe—first as secretary of state and then as president—labored hard to appease the South by acquiring all of Florida. As secretary of state under James Madison, he adopted a bold policy aimed at doing so. He had believed during the talks in Madrid in 1804-5 that a more resolute military stance was necessary and now pushed for the adoption of such a position. In the end, however, Monroe and Madison, like Jefferson before them, could not accept the consequences of taking by force what could not be obtained by negotiation.[85]

The "No Transfer Resolution" marked the first phase of this bolder policy. Passed by Congress in January 1811, the resolution stated that in view of its overriding interest in the territories along its southern border, the United States could not, "without serious inquietude, see any part of the said territory pass into the hands of any foreign power." It authorized the president to seize East Florida (West Florida being already considered part of the United States) in the event that "any foreign power" attempted to occupy it or any "existing local authority" proved ready to cede it. The No Transfer Resolution came to be of lasting importance, not only in the case of the Floridas but in the development of a hemispheric U.S. foreign policy. Its injunction against the transfer of territory to "any foreign power" prefigured the Monroe Doctrine's noncolonization clause.[86]

In 1811, however, the purpose of the No Transfer Resolution was to prevent Great Britain from seizing the Floridas from Spain. Gaining control of West Florida was made easier by the presence of a large number of American settlers in the province. In September 1810 a contingent of these settlers, aided by Americans from across the border, had successfully declared their independence from Spain and petitioned the United States government for annexation. The Madison administration, fearing potentially troublesome claims of the insurgents, in October 1810 ordered troops to take control of West Florida to the Perdido River. By mid-1811 the province was in the control of the United States except for the city and fortifications at Mobile.[87] Spain's tenuous grasp on the Florida peninsula appeared to be slipping as well, and fears arose that Great Britain would move to fill the vacuum created by the collapse of Spanish authority. The No Transfer Resolution demonstrated congressional resolve that the United States would not stand idly by and let this happen.

Having warned Great Britain to keep hands off, the Madison administration began efforts to acquire East Florida from the "existing local authority." But the East Florida officials were unwilling to hand over the province; unlike those in West Florida, most of East Florida's inhabitants were satisfied to remain under Spanish rule, if for no other reason than the laxness of that nation's authority.[88]

Thus rebuffed, American negotiator General George Mathews intrigued to foment a rebellion in East Florida by promises of rewards for those taking part. In effect, he attempted by bribery to stir up a revolution where no discontent existed. American naval forces moved to support this effort. On 18 March 1812 Mathews landed at Amelia Island, off the Georgia-Florida border, to accept the cession of East Florida from the "patriot" forces (comprising primarily American citizens) who had declared the territory independent the day before. Mathews then led American ground and naval forces in the capture of St. Augustine, the capital of East Florida. The whole sordid affair had been orchestrated to comply with the requirements of the No Transfer Resolution; Mathews thought he had won a great victory for his country.[89]

The Madison administration was not prepared for the lengths to which Mathews had gone or for the domestic and international outcry that followed. Though Mathews had departed with implied orders to take East Florida by force if necessary, and though the fact that his communications to Washington during his months of preparation had gone unanswered indicated tacit approval, when word arrived as to the full extent of his actions, Monroe promptly disavowed them and relieved the general of his command. Strong public protest apparently forced this about-face. A well-publicized case of a British agent's attempts to intrigue with American citizens had surfaced only a short time earlier; now the administration faced the embarrassment of being caught in a similar act. Its solution was to repudiate Mathews while retaining the fruits of his exploits.[90] Accordingly, Monroe, through an intermediary, disavowed Mathews's actions to the unrecognized Spanish representative to the United States, Don Luis de Onís.

But the Madison administration refused to withdraw the occupying forces unless the Spanish government promised no reprisals against the "patriots" who had taken part in the rebellion. In the meantime, Governor D.B. Mitchell of Georgia took command of the American troops in East Florida and awaited war with Spain. Lacking the military strength needed to reply to this provocation, Spain agreed to the demand of the United States not to prosecute its rebellious subjects.[91] Yet Onís rejected an offer made through the British minister in July 1812 to cede East Florida and give up the claim to West Florida in exchange for the United States government's dropping of the spoliation claims. Congress also frustrated the plans of the Madison administration in July 1812 by rejecting a measure authorizing the seizure of East Florida. United States forces finally withdrew from East Florida in May 1813; West Florida (to the Perdido River) remained under American control.[92]

In 1815, the return of peace and the reinstatement of Ferdinand VII on the Spanish throne led to the resumption of formal negotiations over the question of the limits of Louisiana. The long diplomatic hiatus had worked no substantive changes in the positions of the two nations. Spanish Minister Onís offered to cede all Spanish lands east of the Mississippi River in exchange for a western boundary at the Mississippi. And because matters were further complicated by the support of American citizens for Spain's rebelling colonies in South America, Onís called also for the suppression of the recruitment and arming of patriot expeditions taking place in Philadelphia, Charleston, and other cities. He further demanded that the South

American rebels be excluded from American ports and prevented from getting supplies from the United States.[93] The question of U.S. aid to the South American revolutionaries worsened an already intractable diplomatic controversy. The issue grew in importance as the negotiations progressed.

Monroe countered Onís's offer with a proposal drawing the western boundary at the Colorado River of Texas, include all American territory to the tributaries of the Mississippi River. But in instructions to George Erving, United States minister to Spain (the negotiations having been transferred there in early 1816), Monroe wrote that "if indispensably necessary" President Madison would agree to a western limit as far east as the Sabine River, with the remainder of the boundary to be determined by joint commission. Monroe stipulated, however, that "any adjustment" by commission must not affect the American claim to the Columbia River.[94] Though Erving did not propose the Sabine boundary to Spain in 1816, Monroe's instructions are significant because they foreshadow what would later be called the "sellout" of the claim to Texas as well as the extension of a transcontinental boundary in 1819. Moreover, it is significant that when the Madison administration submitted Erving's instructions for congressional inspection, it omitted that part offering to retreat to the Sabine, no doubt because of the outrage it would have provoked among westerners and southerners.[95]

The reopened negotiations with Spain quickly reestablished the stalemate of 1805. The talks were transferred several times from Madrid to Washington and back, as both sides stalled, awaiting a shift in circumstances that would strengthen their negotiating position. The Spanish government thought that the United States, weakened by the recent war, would be in no position to dictate terms. Moreover, the ministers of Ferdinand VII were confident in 1816 and 1817 that Great Britain, as the chief defender of monarchical interest, would support their position. The Madison administration, on the other hand, recognized the impossibility of retreating too far on the boundaries of Louisiana; the Senate would approve no treaty placing its western limits at the Mississippi. In 1817 the dispute remained unresolved and seemingly intractable.

Aggravating the conflict with Spain were a number of problems with Great Britain. The Treaty of Ghent had merely halted the war with Great Britain; it did not resolve most of the issues that had caused the conflict. Lingering strife with the British restricted the options open to James Monroe (elected president in 1816) in bringing Spain to terms, for the Spanish government knew that so long as important issues divided Great Britain and the United States, it could rely on at least tacit British support for its negotiating position. In this way the U.S. dispute with Spain was linked to relations with Great Britain. A favorable settlement with Spain depended upon resolving the problems with Great Britain.

Much as in the controversy with Spain, an issue involving national boundaries divided the United States and Great Britain. It too had origins some years in the past, in this case the Treaty of Paris of 1783. The treaty stipulated that the Canadian-American boundary be defined by a line drawn due west from the northernmost point of the Lake of the Woods (which extends north from present-day Minnesota into Ontario and Manitoba) until it reached the Mississippi River. Geographers of the eighteenth century, however, did not know that the northernmost point of the Lake of the Woods was more than 150 miles north of the source of the Mississippi. Several attempts to resolve this discrepancy had failed.[96]

The discoveries of Lewis and Clark and the developing interest each nation had in the northwestern fur trade extended the boundary dispute across the Rocky Mountains to the coast, where the United States and Great Britain vied for control of a region in which Spain and Russia also had an interest. John Jacob Astor's Pacific Fur Trading Company complicated the issue in 1811 by founding a settlement named Astoria at the mouth of the Columbia. Astor envisaged this post as the hub of a fur trading empire from which he could reach the markets of the Orient. But the War of 1812 foiled his plans. Fearing attack, Astor's agents at Astoria sold the post in 1813 to British subjects, who renamed it Fort George. In British hands it remained, despite an article in the Treaty of Ghent calling for the restoration of all territories taken during the war. The burgeoning, lucrative fur trade had upped the ante; the British Northwest Company urged London not to abandon the post to the Americans. Here matters stood in 1817.

Fishing rights off the coasts of British North America formed a second major area of disagreement between the United States and Great Britain, one of more immediate concern to Americans (especially New Englanders) than the boundary question. The Treaty of Paris of 1783 guaranteed the "liberty" of Americans to fish in the waters of British North America, including the Grand Banks, the most bountiful fishery in the world. But disagreement arose over the word "liberty." The British understood the word to mean a privilege that could be revoked; to the Americans the word implied an inalienable right.

At Ghent the British negotiators argued that the "liberty" to fish in their colonial waters, suspended during the war, could be reinstated only in exchange for American concessions. Over Henry Clay's heated objection the American commissioners offered Britain the right to navigate the Mississippi in exchange for renewed access to the fisheries. This was, in principle, an enormous concession and indicates the importance of the fisheries to the United States. Yet the British, knowing that the right to navigate a river that did not extend into Canada was of limited value, rejected this offer.

It is difficult to overstate the importance of the fisheries to the economy of New England. They constituted the source of the region's single most important industry; the Adamses had long championed their defense. John Adams had been responsible for the insertion of the word "liberty" in the treaty of 1783, and John Quincy proved no less committed to ensuring New Englanders continued access to such an important source of wealth. As minister to Great Britain, Adams had hinted that the issue might lead again to war—an unauthorized threat, but one indicating the extent of his commitment to the interest of New England.

A third major dispute between the United States and Great Britain concerned the terms of their mutual trade. The Commercial Convention of July 1815 had merely restored reciprocity in the direct trade between the two nations. Great Britain still prohibited U.S. vessels from entering its colonial ports in the West Indies. The problem especially concerned the shipowning and merchant interests of the Northeast, who stood to make immense profits if the West Indian trade could be opened. Exclusion from this trade placed shipowners at a competitive disadvantage, for they could not benefit from the "triangular trade" that allowed British vessels to unload their cargoes in the United States, take on American goods, and then make a profitable stopover in the West Indies before returning home. American ships often made the voyage from Britain empty, at enormous cost to their owners. As minister to Great Britain, John Quincy Adams had lobbied hard but to no avail for modification of colonial trade restrictions. Despite major changes in other areas of British society, colonial trade monopolies were still sacrosanct.[97]

In sum, major stumbling blocks stood in the way of Anglo-American harmony in the fall of 1817. Although the harsh rhetoric of war had abated, no substantive issues (with the exception of the Rush-Bagot Agreement, demilitarizing the Great Lakes) had been

resolved. For the United States, circumstances demanded reconciliation: only by eliminating the threat of British naval intervention in
the Western Hemisphere could a strong and independent foreign
policy be pursued. That goal remained distant in 1817.[98]

Although problems with Spain and Great Britain dominated the
concerns of the Monroe administration, the domestic scene was far
from tranquil. The aftermath of the second war with Great Britain led
to what economic historians term a "readjustment" period for the
American economy.[99] The general though by no means uniform
prosperity of 1815-18 masked an underlying weakness that led to a
depression beginning in mid-1818. By the latter part of 1817 the
outlines of this crisis were clear.

At the heart of the nation's economic problems lay a crippled
currency. The War of 1812 had left a legacy of debt; devalued paper
currency from dozens of state banks flooded the land. Secretary of the
Treasury Albert Gallatin estimated that by 1816, $68 million worth
of state banknotes were in circulation.[100] State banks had stopped
specie payments amid wartime uncertainty in August 1814; financial
chaos ensued as state banks refused to accept other currencies except
at a discount. The federal government was forced to take its revenues
in these depreciated state currencies, which could be spent only in
the areas of issue. The rapid inflation that resulted during 1815-18
helped both to fuel the economic expansion and to create the conditions for economic collapse.

Congress created the Second Bank of the United States in 1816 to
restore confidence in the nation's currency. The bank was to resume
specie payments, thereby setting an example for the state banks to
follow, yet it began operation with only $6 million in specie reserves,
hardly sufficient to engender confidence in the dollar. Moreover, the
bank faced a short-term mercantile debt to Europe of $64 million,
incurred in 1816.[101] These factors, combined with mismanagement
and fraud by the bank's officers, made the task of stabilizing the
currency impossible.[102]

Only an adequate supply of specie could restore faith in the nation's currencies by providing hard money backing. But the supply of
hard currency was shrinking in 1817, largely because of a steady
outflow to the Orient.[103] In 1817 alone, Americans exported $4.5
million in specie primarily in exchange for the highly valued goods of
China. The export of specie by a nation possessing (at that time) no
silver or gold mines angered many Americans.[104] Writers of the
period assailed the effects on the nation's economic health. The
discontent took on a sectional aspect: because nearly all the mer-

chants engaged in the China trade were located in New England or
New York, it seemed to many that a selfish monied elite was under-
mining the interests of the nation. Adding to the resentment, New
Englanders controlled most of the specie reserves in the United
States.[105]

Anger over the export of specie by northeastern mercantile interests formed but one aspect of the larger economic struggle usually
known as "sectionalism." In many respects the trans-Appalachian
West and the South functioned as colonies of the Northeast. Southerners shipped their cotton north to be exported on the vessels of
northeastern mercantile interests, in exchange for manufactured
goods and banking and commercial services. Northeasterners sent
manufactured goods to the West, usually in exchange for agricultural
produce and specie. The West in turn shipped foodstuffs and livestock
to the South in return for plantation products such as molasses and
sugar.[106] Geography and technology reinforced this relation: an extensive river system created, in the days before the steamboat, a one-
way route from the West to the South, while a bustling coastwise
trade connected the South and the Northeast. High mountains made
land access to the West difficult and expensive, hindering that region's development. The result was to center financial power in the
Northeast, reinforcing a predominance dating from the time of independence.[107]

In 1817, however, the sectional balance of power seemed to be
shifting. Spurred by abundant agricultural production, the West and
the South were experiencing prosperity in the years following the war
with Great Britain, while the Northeast was approaching economic
stagnation. Its re-export trade of foreign goods, upon which so many
fortunes had been built, steadily declined. Shipping of all sorts faced
increased competition from European nations now at peace. No new
source of wealth stood ready to fill the gap; the development of large-
scale manufacturing was still a few years away. Nevertheless, the
merchants of the Northeast could call upon powerful resources in
order to maintain their region's supremacy—not least, a newly
elected president favorable to their interests.

Beneath the boundary questions, currency problems, and sectional
disputes lay the intractable question of slavery. Hopes that the slave
institution would wither away had been shattered by the invention of
the cotton gin. The opening of vast new lands in the Southeast,
combined with the potentially unlimited British demand for cotton,
promised decades of profitability for a slave-based mode of agriculture. Indeed, any fair-minded observer recognized that the export

of cotton and the slavery that produced it were essential to American economic prosperity.

Yet slavery made a mockery of pretensions to national unity. Its persistence revealed that the founding fathers had produced not one American dream but two, and that those two dreams were in conflict. The attitude of John Quincy Adams captures this conflict. In his youth Adams had been taught by his mother to despise slavery. A staunch defender of the rights of free blacks, Abigail even fought for the integration of the Quincy school.[108] As in so many other areas, John Quincy's outlook on race was shaped by his mother. While he did not view blacks as fully equal to whites, he saw no grounds to justify their enslavement. More important, he believed that slavery degraded the moral fiber of the slaveowner. He wrote in his diary that slavery "taints the very sources of moral principle" by giving Christian sanction to human bondage and encouraging disdain for labor. Union with the "slave scourging republicans" of the South called into question the very legitimacy of the nation that presumed to be the source of human freedom. As Henry Adams later wrote, "Slavery drove the whole Puritan community back on its Puritanism." [109]

For years, however, Adams kept his doubts about slavery confined to his diary. Like other politicians of the day he knew that to voice them publicly would end his hopes for the presidency. In 1804 he opposed efforts to bar slavery and the importation of slaves in the Louisiana Territory. As a diplomat, he fought hard to extract indemnities from Great Britain for slaves taken during the War of 1812. He assisted owners in their efforts to recover slaves who had fled to Canada. Now, as secretary of state, he would have to labor to bring Florida, yet another slave-holding state, into the Union.[110]

Adams rationalized his proslavery actions as legal or diplomatic necessity, but his conscience gnawed at him nonetheless. It had always been an article of faith with him that the role of the "man of the whole nation" did not necessitate compromises of personal integrity, that national leadership required no compromise of moral values. Yet the slavery question and the other problems facing the United States in 1817 seemed to demand compromises not just of the parties involved but of Adams's conscience as well. And now, occupying a seat of real power, he could no longer evade responsibility for the course of public policy. Returning home after years of faithful service abroad, his hopes for the presidency depended on the favorable resolution of these problems.

That seemed an insurmountable task. He wrote in his diary on 21 September 1817, his first day in office as secretary of state, that "the path before me is beset with thorns, and it becomes more doubtful than ever whether I shall be able to continue long in it. At two distinct periods of my life heretofore my position has been perilous and full of anxious forecasts, but never so critical and precarious as at this time."[111]

TWO

Developing a Strategy

John Quincy Adams arrived in New York on 6 August 1817, ending a nine-year absence from his native land. The tempestuous fifty-day voyage from Great Britain (Adams wrote that his wife "thought herself dying" from seasickness) had not helped still his own anxieties about his new job. He confided in his diary that "so keen indeed was the emotion of contemplating the probabilities of the future time that nothing but a firm reliance upon Him who has ever been my preserver and the dispenser of every blessing supported me from despondency."[1]

The elite of New York enthusiastically welcomed the new secretary of state. Adams had been removed from the broils of domestic politics for nine years and as such had neither the friends nor the enemies that political involvement entails. Some of the most powerful individuals in America gathered to welcome him, including John Jacob Astor (the richest man in the country), Governor DeWitt Clinton, and Archibald Gracie. For several days Adams was the toast of New York. He was escorted on a tour of the city's museums, was made the guest of honor at a formal banquet given by the mayor, and even sat for a portrait.[2] A formal banquet at Tammany Hall on 11 August 1817 highlighted his stay. With Astor as his escort, he was feted by two hundred gentlemen described by the local papers as being "of the greatest respectability."[3] Given Adams's impatience with social chitchat, one can be sure that the nation's foreign policy was a prominent topic of discussion at these gatherings.

From New York, Adams and his family—wife Louisa Catherine and sons George (age sixteen), John (age fourteen,) and Charles Francis (age ten)—journeyed to Quincy, Massachusetts, for the long-awaited reunion with Abigail and John. When John Quincy departed for Russia in 1809, his parents had feared it was a final farewell; his return sparked a rebirth in both of them. For Abigail, it was the happiest day of her elderly years; she had lived to see her prized son accede to his destined place in the highest councils of the land.[4]

Adams stayed in Quincy for nearly a month, renewing old friendships, visiting old haunts, and basking in the adulation of his parents.

It must have been a time of deep satisfaction and introspection for him, an opportunity to savor his considerable achievements. Yet the demands of his new job did not allow for very much time off. He had committed himself to being in Washington on 20 September, in time to welcome President Monroe back from his tour of the nation. In an age of slow and undependable transportation, he was not a day late.

Adams felt some trepidation before his meeting with the new president. In a diary reflection written the day he arrived in Washington, he wrote: "Whether my appointment was for my own good or for that of the country is known only to God. As yet I have more reason to lament than to rejoice at the event." He had not always been an admirer of Monroe. He knew that he had been selected to head the Department of State at least in part because of his New England background. Adams also knew that the president thought his long absence and lack of political following would tend to work against any ambitions he might have about succeeding Monroe in the White House. Adams feared that his fractious and combative nature might get the better of him amid the intrigues of cabinet politics. He wrote his mother that "my place is subordinate. . . . my duty will be to support and not to . . . oppose the President's Administration. . . . If I can't, my duty is to withdraw from public service."[5]

While it is fair to say that he respected Monroe's judgment, Adams was often critical of what he perceived to be the president's indecisiveness. The two men never became close friends but nonetheless developed a solid working relationship. Monroe heeded Adams's opinions on policy matters more than those of any other adviser. From the outset, they met daily to discuss matters of state.[6] The new secretary not only knew much more about the actual state of international affairs than did the president but could control the information Monroe received on certain issues such as the negotiations with Spain. These factors, combined with Adams's impressive powers of argumentation, explain his dominant influence in foreign affairs.[7] Although Adams did not formulate the broad goals of administration policy, he was given wide latitude to implement them. It is safe to say that without his astute management of affairs, the Monroe administration would not have would not have enjoyed its impressive number of foreign policy successes. Adams was exaggerating only slightly when he later wrote: "Of the public history of Mr. Monroe's administration, all that will be worth telling to posterity hitherto has been transacted through the department of state."[8]

James Monroe, though but nine years older than Adams, had been a Revolutionary War hero, while Adams watched the hostilities with his mother. Along with Supreme Court Justice John Marshall, Monroe represented the last politically active link to the founding fathers. He had paid his dues. Like Adams, Monroe had built his life around public service. He had served as secretary of war and of state under Madison and in a number of diplomatic posts under Jefferson. He also had been governor of Virginia and a member of Congress from that state.[9] Shaped in the ideological image of Madison and Jefferson, he was the natural successor to the presidency in 1816.

Monroe's intellectual prowess certainly did not win him the presidency. A contemporary described his mind as "neither rich nor brilliant, but capable of the most laborious analysis."[10] George Dangerfield calls him "the third of the Virginia Dynasty, in the order of intelligence no less than in that of succession."[11] Lacking the broad conceptions and visions of Jefferson and Madison, he was nonetheless the ideal candidate to carry on the traditions of his illustrious Virginian predecessors. He maintained a regular correspondence with both men during his presidency, keeping them well informed of affairs of state and remaining anxiously attentive to their advice.[12]

Monroe was a committed republican revolutionary, and like Adams, he identified the preservation and growth of the United States with the success of the republican cause globally.[13] His task as president, in his view, was to fulfill a modified Jeffersonian vision of a nation of independent farmers and merchants based on a balance of agriculture, manufacture, and commerce. In this vision, the individual would be free to choose where to live and what to do, unbeholden to any person or government. While changing times had forced the modification of Jefferson's pure agrarian vision, the "mission" of America had not changed—that of a nation destined to set an example of human freedom and republican government to the world.[14] Monroe was convinced that he had a special role to play in bringing about this global transformation.

James Monroe's view of the political realm, like that of John Quincy Adams, was largely defined by the myths of classical republicanism. Monroe clung to the Revolutionary-era notion that a common purpose united all Americans. He feared political parties and the factionalism they represented. Though a strong supporter of the War of 1812, he knew that it had created divisions in American society nearly fatal to the republican experiment, and as president he strove to restore a national unity of purpose.[15]

In one sense, Monroe was correct in assuming a national unity of purpose. Citizens from all segments of society believed that the United States had a responsibility to spread its values and institutions to a world dominated by monarchy and desperately in need of republican-style enlightenment. Few doubted either the superiority of American ideals or the flow of the tide of history in the direction of their universal application. Few questioned the fundamental premises or uniqueness of American society and government, nor would many have disputed the legitimacy of spreading their values and institutions to the farthest reaches of the globe.

Yet changing historical conditions in the late eighteenth and early nineteenth centuries made the Jeffersonian vision of America anachronistic even as its realization came within reach. The classic Jeffersonian vision saw a nation of independent farmers and small-scale manufacturers producing for the domestic market, insulated from the struggles of Europe. Americans, however, possessed of seemingly limitless natural resources, and their rapidly improving technology soon demonstrated an awesome capacity to produce. From the South came cotton, tobacco, and rice; from the middle states, flour, meat, tar, and turpentine; and from New England, pot and pearl ash, lumber, the products of whaling, and fish.[16] Americans produced far more than the home market (consisting of less than 10 million people in 1817) could consume. This fact made foreign trade the linchpin of domestic prosperity and drew the United States unavoidably into world affairs. The abundance of natural resources that made possible the Jeffersonian image of America as an agrarian paradise ironically prevented the purest realization of that image by requiring Americans to produce for a world, not just a domestic, market.[17]

This "problem" of abundance had tangible manifestations. The War of 1812 had been caused in part by the hardships created when Americans could not freely export their agricultural surplus.[18] The war made clear what Republicans had long sensed but never fully incorporated into their ideology—that foreign trade, rather than being antithetical to republicanism, was essential to its survival.[19] After the Treaty of Ghent the search for new markets became the explicit aim of American foreign policy.

Accordingly, President James Monroe adopted as his primary goal the expansion of foreign trade. In order for America to serve as an example to an oppressed world, domestic prosperity had to be ensured by finding markets for the nation's produce.[20] A contemporary writer described foreign trade as "the very lungs of liberty," the means not only of ensuring stability at home but also of spreading American values, institutions, and ideals abroad. The traditional ambivalence about foreign trade was replaced by the conviction that not only was foreign trade essential to the quest for a good society but that it would also have a missionizing effect on the rest of the world.[21]

Yet the consensus that existed in the abstract for the spread of American institutions and ideals broke down when the extension of commerce became a prime means for their propagation. It was clear that, depending on the direction of American commercial expansion, certain groups and regions stood to gain more than others and that not all avenues of expansion could be pursued simultaneously. Unity of purpose did not imply commonality of method. Disagreement over the direction of commercial expansion would prove a basic point of political contention during Monroe's presidency.

Three principles guided the Monroe administration in its efforts to expand American foreign trade: first, the negotiation of reciprocity treaties with foreign states when possible and the enactment of commercial retaliation when necessary; second, good relations with Great Britain; third, a strengthening of the military, with special emphasis on an enlarged, more powerful navy. These three goals provided a framework for the administration's foreign policy.

A commercial policy based on the principle of reciprocity had evolved out of the traditional American advocacy of free trade between nations, one of the founding ideals of American independence.[22] Popularly known through the work of Adam Smith and David Ricardo, free trade had been a radical idea in the late eighteenth and early nineteenth centuries. It meant an end to the navigation acts, colonial monopolies, and other kinds of commercial restrictions that formed the basis of the European colonial system. Both Benjamin Franklin and John Adams had been advocates of free trade. Adams had incorporated the principle into the Model Treaty Plan of 1776.[23] John Quincy Adams carried on this tradition in his own career, elevating free trade to the status of a moral duty between nations.[24]

The advocacy of the principle of free trade was another aspect of the American global challenge to the monarchic-mercantile status quo. To the American mind, free trade represented a decisive break with the past and a forward step for humanity. Yet it would be a mistake to view this American drive too idealistically. As a nation excluded from most colonial markets, the United States by necessity advocated free trade. The looming problem of overproduction demanded the easing of commercial restrictions. Free trade would allow Americans to exploit their substantial comparative advantage in foreign shipping rates. In the direct trade with Europe and to other areas of the world, American shippers could undercut the prices of their competitors. Indeed, freight rates for American shippers to the

Far East averaged half that of their foreign rivals.[25] Under such conditions "free trade" would assure American dominance in international commerce. A historian of American commercial policy Vernon Setser puts the matter into perspective: "If economists had not already developed the principles of economic liberalism, American statesmen would have been under the necessity of inventing them."[26]

In theory committed to a doctrine of perfectly free trade, American statesmen found this goal unattainable in practice. From the time of independence the nations of Europe, particularly Great Britain, worked to limit American access to their colonial markets.[27] Europeans resisted efforts to overthrow mercantilism, ignoring the self-serving American argument that free trade would serve their best interests in the long run. Opposition to free trade necessitated a strategy, first developed by James Madison in 1789, of commercial discrimination in the form of tariff and tonnage duties against nations that refused to sign reciprocity treaties with the United States.[28] This strategy was aimed at compelling the Europeans to allow at least a system of equality of duties as a form of reciprocity if they would not agree to a totally free trade.

The combination of negotiating reciprocity treaties when possible and enacting commercial retaliation when necessary became a guiding principle of the Monroe administration. A prominent example of this policy was the determined effort to reopen the British West India trade, closed to Americans since independence. Between 1815 and 1829 there were no less than five major pieces of legislation, five diplomatic negotiations, and two presidential proclamations devoted to securing access to a trade of marginal importance to national prosperity. The Monroe and Adams presidencies marked the period of open warfare against what remained of the European mercantile system.[29]

At first, reciprocity and commercial discrimination were intended as tools to be used to bring about a totally free trade. But these tactics became ends in themselves in the years following the Treaty of Ghent. Changing economic conditions had inspired a new vision of American empire based not on free trade but on protection of certain sectors of the economy. The shortages caused by embargo and war had led to the growth of an extensive manufacturing sector in the United States and a sizable constituency that wanted it protected from foreign competition, once peace was restored. Accordingly, in 1816 Congress passed, with Madison's support, a tariff protecting a broad array of American manufactured goods. Although the tariff of

1816 was only moderately protective, it was but the first of several pieces of protective legislation to be enacted.[30]

The support of a protective tariff by a Republican president represented a dramatic break with the past. Jeffersonian philosophy traditionally had feared the growth of a large manufacturing sector as corrosive to the morals of an agrarian society. After the War of 1812, however, it was clear that this belief ill suited the current circumstances. In order to thrive, America needed a strong manufacturing sector, if only to assure national security and independence.[31] Indeed, by 1820 the economist Mathew Carey would argue that free trade caused economic depression and therefore endangered national survival. The American Society of the Encouragement of American Manufactures was established to fight for a protective tariff. Its members included Jefferson, Madison, and John Adams.[32]

In short, starting from the moral principle of free trade, American commercial policy by 1817 had evolved into a neomercantilist doctrine intended to expand American agriculture and raw material exports while protecting domestic manufactures. Reciprocity offered Americans a natural advantage in foreign trade as surely as navigation laws guaranteed European trade monopolies.[33] The ideal of "free trade" provided a universalistic basis for a commercial policy essentially nationalistic in its aims.

This evolution of principles and policies regarding trade represented a significant departure from revolutionary ideals in the name of defending the Republican "experiment." Most Americans implicitly believed that prosperity at home contained the seeds for universal human progress. Monroe and Adams faced a world fundamentally hostile to the American nation. The Congress of Vienna symbolized the effort to stop the spread of republicanism, as did the vigorous reimposition of colonial navigation laws and other commercial restrictions in the years after 1815.[34] The neomercantilist policy of expanding raw material and agricultural exports while protecting manufactures was a pragmatic strategy for solidifying republicanism in the United States by increasing the nation's wealth and power. Though the policy compromised the revolutionary ideal of a truly free world commerce, Republican leaders would have argued that with hostile powers threatening the nation's existence, only building up the United States could ensure that republican ideals would survive.[35] In effect, neomercantilism was a nationalist policy with an idealistic rationale, a policy designed to advance human progress by serving American self-interest. At some future time a world order might exist favorable to free trade, but for the moment necessity dictated a compromise of revolutionary ideals.

Reconciliation with Great Britain, the second guiding principle of the Monroe administration in its efforts to expand American foreign trade, represented a major foreign policy shift. For nearly forty years the United States and its former enemy had alternated between open conflict and uneasy peace. The strife bred bitter feelings on both sides. British journalists and publicists viewed their one-time colonials with arrogant contempt. American writers responded with indignant attacks on monarchy and colonialism which to some extent served to define the nation's identity. This "warfare of the mind," as John Quincy Adams termed the verbal hostilities, did not bode well for better relations between the two nations. Indeed, to anyone reading British and American newspapers and periodicals in the aftermath of the war, the prospects for reconciliation would have seemed remote.[36] Yet in spite of the acrimony, powerful forces were drawing the United States and Great Britain together.

Historically, the Republican party had opposed close ties to Great Britain. This constituted one of the party's major differences with the Federalists over the years. But the near-catastrophic consequences of the War of 1812 led to a reevaluation of traditional Republican policy. Many Republicans, including Jefferson, came to realize the importance of Anglo-American cooperation for the prosperity and security of the United States. Jefferson wrote to John Adams in 1816 that he now believed the British to be the "natural brethren and friends" of the Americans. He observed that the national interest required that Great Britain remain the dominant power in Europe so as to counterbalance Continental alliances potentially threatening to the Western Hemisphere. To James Monroe, Jefferson wrote, "Is it not probable that the circumstances of the war and her own [Great Britain's] circumstances may have brought her wise men to begin to view us with . . . kindred eyes?" To the Briton Sir John Sinclair, Jefferson urged that both nations "throw aside all personal feelings" and "look only to their interests."[37]

The most important of these interests was the large volume of trade between the United States and Great Britain. Each nation was the other's largest trading partner. More than 40 percent of American agricultural exports went to Great Britain during the period 1815-26. Cotton accounted for nearly half of those exports. The era of "King Cotton" had begun; for forty years southern cotton cultivated by the sweat of black slaves kept British textile mills humming. The British, in turn, satisfied the American demand for manufactured goods, the tariff of 1816 being inadequate to offset Great Britain's comparative advantage in this sector. The transatlantic trade proved vital to the economic health of both nations, as the erstwhile belligerents re-established an important commercial relationship.[38]

This burgeoning trade drew the United States tightly into the economic orbit of Great Britain. For a quarter-century after 1815, fluctuations in the British economy directly effected American pros-perity. The United States was a primary producer of agricultural goods and raw materials for British industry.[39] The Anglo-American trade cycle worked like this: during periods of economic expansion a rising demand for American produce, especially cotton, led to the increased import of British manufactured goods into the United States. As British exports to the United States tended to exceed American exports to Great Britain, a trade deficit was created. During the expansion phase, this deficit was financed by promises of future shipments of American produce. As business expansion slowed in Great Britain, so did the demand for American goods, thereby wors-ening the trade deficit. Americans then had to pay for British goods with specie, as British merchants in a time of slack demand became reluctant to accept as payment promises of future shipments of American produce. The export of specie drained the reserves of the large banks of the eastern seaboard, which as a result were forced to initiate a nationwide credit contraction. Such was the sequence of events leading to the depression of 1819. American prosperity hinged on a strong demand for its agricultural products, particularly cotton, and Great Britain exercised by far the greatest influence over that demand.[40]

A second factor drawing the United States and Great Britain to-gether in the years after the War of 1812 was the personality and policies of the British foreign secretary, Lord Castlereagh. Given wide latitude by Lord Liverpool to conduct foreign policy, Castlereagh cultivated relations with the United States on the basis of economic self-interest, not emotion or ideology. Like Monroe and Adams, Cas-tlereagh ignored that segment of public opinion demanding reprisals against the former foe. He was not deaf to such appeals; he too viewed the American declaration of war in 1812 as an unpardonable act, coming as it did at one of the most perilous moments of the struggle against Napoleon. Yet Castlereagh knew that the final defeat of Napoleon had left Great Britain dangerously weakened. A massive war debt undermined the economy and threatened social stability. John Quincy Adams, as minister to Great Britain, observed these problems at first hand. In early 1817 he wrote to Monroe that "the load of taxation to pay the interest on the national debt is greater than the [British] nation can bear." Social chaos appeared imminent: "The very elements of the political system seem to be breaking up. . . . The people are in great distress, looking on every side for relief." [41]

Under such conditions, national interest demanded reconciliation with the United States; Great Britain could no longer afford to be the enemy of its largest trading partner. Moreover, William Huskisson and Thomas Wallace, influential members of the Board of Trade, began to advocate the loosening of mercantile restrictions.[42] Influenced by the work of Smith and Ricardo, they too had become convinced of the advantages of a freer world trade. Castlereagh agreed. Thus, Great Britain moved in the direction of a more liberal commercial order (albeit one based on the self-interest of comparative advantage) at the same time that Monroe and Adams worked for a similar end.[43]

Castlereagh hoped to conciliate not only the United States but Europe as well. Great Britain required peace in order to recover from the devastation of the struggle with Napoleon. Castlereagh wrote to the British minister in Washington, Charles Bagot, that "the avowed and true policy of Great Britain . . . is to appease controversy, and to secure, if possible, for all states a long interval of repose." [44] American policymakers echoed these lines. John Quincy Adams wrote to his father in 1816, "My specialty at present is to preach peace," convinced as he was that peace was necessary for the "interests and happiness of both nations." [45]

Reconciliation of the former foes had begun almost immediately after the end of the war with an agreement in July 1815 reestablishing commercial ties. The Rush-Bagot Agreement of April 1817, demilitarizing the Great Lakes, gave tangible evidence of lessened tensions. By the fall of 1817, although major issues still divided the two powers, reconciliation with Great Britain had become a guiding, if publicly unrecognized, principle of American foreign policy. It would prove decisive in resolving the dispute with Spain.

The third guiding principle of the Monroe administration in its effort to expand American foreign trade concerned the construction and maintenance of a formidable military force. Republicans traditionally had mistrusted large military establishments as subversive of republican institutions. Yet once again, the War of 1812 led to a reevaluation of a basic tenet of the Republican faith. John Quincy Adams wrote: "The most painful, perhaps the most profitable, lesson of the war was the primary duty of the nation to place itself in a state of permanent preparation for self-defense." [46] The buildup had begun during the Madison administration. One of Monroe's last acts as secretary of war had been to draft a report for the Senate Committee on Military Affairs recommending a 20,000-man army, a force four times its prewar size.[47] Madison began the military buildup almost immediately following the end of the war. He called for establishing a regular army, increasing the size of the navy, improving the system of coastal defenses, and better disciplining the militia.[48] To do so, Madison had to overcome a congressional desire to shrink the military back to its prewar size. In April 1816, however, Congress passed a mammoth naval appropriations bill providing funds for the construction of nine 74-gun ships of the line, twelve 44-gun frigates, and three steam batteries for coastal defense. The "74s" would be the equal of any ships afloat. The prospect of a fleet of such warships caused considerable concern to the British government, for the Americans had proved themselves formidable naval antagonists in the war.[49] Still, a policy of cooperation promised the two nations a virtual monopoly of the seas.

James Monroe's inaugural address made clear why the nation needed a military buildup. He called for the rigorous defense of the commercial and navigation interests upon which all Americans depended for prosperity. Citing the experiences of the war with Great Britain, he drew the following conclusions: "We must support our rights or lose our character, and with it, perhaps, our liberties. A people who fail to do so can scarcely be said to hold a place among independent nations. National honor is national property of the highest value. The sentiment in the mind of every citizen is national strength. It ought therefore to be cherished."[50] Accordingly, Monroe recommended further strengthening coastal defenses, the army, and the navy so as to ensure the rights of American commercial shipping worldwide. In this respect Monroe's views presaged the theories of Alfred Thayer Mahan, who later in the nineteenth century wrote of the necessity of a navy sufficiently powerful to defend American interests around the globe.[51]

Taken together, the three guiding principles of the Monroe administration's foreign policy—reciprocity treaties and commercial retaliation, reconciliation with Great Britain, and a strengthened military—constituted a blueprint for global expansion. The principles had been formulated during the last two years of the Madison administration and represented the major lessons of the near-catastrophic war with Great Britain. Along with support for a national bank, they stood as a dramatic break with the traditional philosophy of the Republican party. The vision of a decentralized, inward looking agrarian republic had been replaced by an imperial vision which reflected many of the basic tenets of the disgraced Federalist party. The irony is that the final collapse of the Federalist party as a national force saw the substantive triumph of its principles in the policies of James Monroe.[52]

To reconcile the divisions caused by the War of 1812, James Monroe made an extended tour of the Middle Atlantic states, New England, and the upper West in the summer of 1817. Ostensibly undertaken to inspect the nation's military fortifications, Monroe's tour had the unstated purpose of gaining support from both Federalists and Republicans for his new administration. The first incumbent president since George Washington to take such a tour, Monroe aimed to reestablish the national consensus fundamental to the republican vision, a consensus that had been shattered by the War of 1812. Traveling as a private citizen and at first without official escort, Monroe evoked the symbols of republican simplicity even as he articulated a program that rejected it.[53]

Leaving Washington in June 1817, he made his way up the Atlantic seaboard, stopping in most of the major cities along the way. At Trenton he visited the battlefield where he had been wounded, reviving memories of the Revolutionary era and his own ties to it. In New York City, Monroe was welcomed by a committee of notables including Governor DeWitt Clinton, John Jacob Astor, and Senator Rufus King, the Federalist whom Monroe had defeated in the 1816 election. The president stayed in New York for a week (as Adams would do in August), visiting West Point and addressing the New York Society for the Encouragement of Manufactures, to whom he advocated protective tariffs for the "glutted markets" of the United States.[54]

Monroe's meeting with his recent opponent, Rufus King, symbolized his efforts to achieve national reconciliation. King had represented the remnants of a shattered political party in 1816, a party tarred with allegations of treason. Now Monroe extended forgiveness, and King became a prominent ally of the administration in the Senate. He received frequent confidential briefings from Adams on affairs of state. King knew that Monroe as yet lacked a well-defined base of support, and he did all he could to have his constituency (primarily the New York mercantile establishment) heard by the administration. King's ardent attempts to reopen the British West India trade perhaps explain why the administration took such an active interest in this issue. When King wrote to Monroe in 1817 regarding the scarcity of silver coin in New York, Monroe responded, "Your suggestions on this, or any other subject, will always be received with attention and pleasure."[55]

Monroe also had a long and complicated relationship with John Jacob Astor. A German immigrant who never mastered his adopted tongue, Astor cultivated the friendship of many influential politicians and, in doing so, was able to exert a significant influence on American foreign policy, if only by his proximity to power. Historian James Ronda writes: "Few other businessmen in the early republic had so thoroughly mastered the art of personal politics as had John Jacob Astor. His politics were not so much a matter of party and ideology as friendship and influence."[56]

Astor played a prominent role in the nation's finances in the early part of the nineteenth century. Along with merchant David Parish and financier Stephen Girard, he had saved the federal government from bankruptcy in 1814 by investing large sums in government securities. Consequently, Astor became an advocate of the establishment of the Second Bank of the United States as a means to stabilize the nation's currency and ensure that the financial obligation represented by the securities would be paid in full. He wrote to a business associate about his desire for a new national bank, "which we must have or we are all gone."[57] Subsequently, Astor purchased a large block of national bank stock, served on the bank's board of directors, and was briefly president of the New York branch.[58]

Astor had made his fortune in the fur trade. Since 1807 he had been attempting to wrest control of the trans-Mississippi fur trade from Canadian competitors. In this endeavor he was assisted and encouraged by the United States government, which viewed his efforts as an unofficial yet effective way of extending national power. Astor planned to establish a chain of trading posts along the route blazed by Lewis and Clark from which the pelts of the interior could be shipped to Astoria (founded by Astor's employees in 1811) at the mouth of the Columbia River. From there the furs would be shipped to Canton in exchange for the teas, spices, and nankeens of China. Furs played a vital role in developing the China trade, for they were one of the few American commodities besides specie that the Chinese were interested in acquiring. Jefferson, who thought Astor "a most excellent man," wrote to the fur magnate: "Your name will be handed down with that of Columbus and Raleigh, as the father of the establishment and founder of such an empire which will arise from commerce."[59]

Not formally aligned with any political party, Astor nonetheless was able to secure government action whenever his interests were threatened. Perhaps the best example of the influence at Astor's disposal was the "Punqua Wingchong" affair. In 1808, in violation of the embargo, Jefferson allowed Astor's ship *Beaver* to embark for Canton. On board was a supposed eminent Chinese mandarin, Punqua Wingchong, stranded in the United States by the embargo, who wished to return to his homeland. Jefferson rationalized that to allow the mandarin's return would be a fine way to curry favor with the Chinese. Madison and Albert Gallatin also helped to obtain the special dispensation, although Gallatin doubted the veracity of the story. Astor's outraged competitors in the China trade, landlocked by the embargo, noted that eminent Chinese mandarins did not leave China to visit other lands. They alleged that Punqua Wingchong was a petty shopkeeper and that the whole affair was a ruse to allow Astor to make a killing at the height of the embargo-caused shortage of goods. Whatever the supposed mandarin's true identity, Astor's ship returned from Canton carrying goods worth $200,000 more than it had taken to China. "Punqua Wingchong" disappeared into the streets of Canton, never to be heard from again.[60]

Astor's biographer, Kenneth Wiggins Porter, describes Madison's relation to the fur magnate as "undoubtedly something more than a formal friendship." Yet Astor formed his closest official ties with James Monroe. In May 1814 Monroe helped him obtain special permission to send a ship to Mackinac Island, which had been captured by the British, to retrieve goods belonging to Astor and worth a considerable sum of money. The timing of this grant of permission is suspicious, considering that Astor only one month earlier had suggested his plan to finance the war by purchasing government securities.[61] In 1817 Astor advised Monroe on the dispensing of patronage in the port of New York—positions of special interest to a large importer. Astor wrote to Monroe with complete frankness whenever government policy seemed likely to endanger the interests of his American Fur Company.[62]

Further solidifying the relationship of the two men was Monroe's personal debt to Astor of $5,000. Astor had offered the loan during the war when he heard that Monroe was experiencing financial difficulty. The fur magnate showed great forbearance in collecting the debt, as Monroe's shaky personal finances made it impossible for him to repay his obligation while president. It was Astor's good fortune to have a man in the White House who was literally in his debt during the period 1817-25, a critical time for the American Fur Company. This is not to imply overt corruption on Monroe's part; it merely demonstrates how well-placed special interests can influence national policy. Kenneth Wiggins Porter describes the Monroe-Astor relationship best: "I do not suggest for a minute that Monroe would, against his better judgement, allow Astor favors which would be injurious to the country, but it does seem altogether natural that whenever Monroe received an application for some consideration of a nature to which the president could accede without undue strain on his conscience he would be much more likely to give a favorable response to Astor than to someone to whom he did not feel the same sense of obligation. . . . But what would be the repercussions should a similar situation be made public today?"[63]

Astor's American Fur Company and the United States government maintained a symbiotic relationship in the early nineteenth century. Astor relied on federal support of his interests when necessary. The government, in turn, viewed his development of the fur trade as the first stage of the settlement of the West.[64] In this way the special interests of an individual operating beyond the nation's boundaries became identified with the national interest. Astor and others like him bore the responsibility of spreading American civilization and values into new areas, defining by their enterprises the "national interest."[65] The irony is that public-spirited men such as Jefferson, Madison, Monroe, Adams, and Gallatin pursued their patriotic goals by working so closely with Astor, a man described by a sympathetic biographer as "putting his private interests before everything else, and never pausing to consider the public consequences of his action."[66]

Although President Monroe spent much of his time in private consultation with wealthy and powerful individuals such as Astor, his trip was definitely a public affair. The high point of the tour was his arrival in Boston on 2 July 1817. A crowd of 40,000 filled the streets as he proceeded to the Boston Common to be met by a bipartisan commission of notables including Governor John Brooks, General Henry Dearborn, and Thomas H. Perkins, a prominent merchant with a large interest in the China trade.[67] For five days Monroe toured the fortifications, monuments, and churches of Boston, often in the company of influential Federalists who had vehemently opposed the wartime policies of Madison but now supported a Republican president who advocated so many of their views. So much political harmony in what had been the hotbed of Federalism made party strife seem a thing of the past. Monroe stressed the themes incorporated in his inaugural address: that "discord does not belong to our system"; that the American people "constitute one great

family with a common interest"; that the promotion of "true harmony" was the object of his "constant and zealous exertions"; and
that if the United States would persevere "in the path . . . already
traced," it would not fail, "under the high favors of a gracious providence, to attain the high destiny" awaiting it.[68]

Monroe's visit to the Northeast in the summer of 1817 reinforced
the connections of the administration to the nation's mercantile-
financial elite. That a Virginian would visit the region evoked a
favorable response from many who had been wary of yet another
president from that southern state. Monroe, in turn, was pleased by
the welcome he received. Former Senator Jeremiah Mason, a Federalist from New Hampshire, wrote to Rufus King that Monroe was
"much satisfied" with the reception given him "especially in New
England, where he had never been before and which exceeded his
expectations in all respects." Mason added that Monroe seemed
"inclined to conciliate the federalists and gain their support." He
concluded that "the federalists this way have been tickled and at this
moment feel better disposed towards him [Monroe] than formerly."[69]
Another former Federalist senator, Christopher Gore (whom Monroe
had visited at his estate in Waltham, Massachusetts), was even more
candid in a letter he wrote to King: "It is perfectly well understood
that Monroe intends, so soon as his hands are a little stronger, to
follow his instincts and name the distinguished Federalists of New
England to office."[70] The Boston merchant Henry Lee (who also had
a substantial interest in the China trade) summarized the effect of
Monroe's "goodwill tour": "We are now all Republicans, even the
Essex Junto."[71]

The exaltation created by the president's visit prompted one
Boston newspaper to proclaim "the era of good feelings" in American
politics.[72] Certainly the old Federalist-Republican schism no longer
seemed so great, especially now that a Republican president was
advocating a national bank and a protective tariff. Yet even as the old
conflicts were ending, new divisions appeared in American politics,
this time within the Republican party itself. Western and southern
members of the party had interests very different from those of the
Middle Atlantic and New England states. Not all westerners and
southerners looked favorably on the president's intimacy with the
northeastern economic elite. To speak, as Monroe did, of eliminating
"discord" and "party spirit" is to forget the diversity of interests
within the nation which creates discord and party spirit. A nation's
foreign and domestic policies cannot benefit all factions equally. In
the end, the course chosen reflects those forces exercising real con-

trol. Monroe's tour in 1817 gave definite indication as to what interests his administration would serve first in its efforts to serve all. It is therefore not surprising that William Crawford of Georgia, Monroe's secretary of the treasury, wrote to Albert Gallatin: "Seriously, I think that the president has lost as much as he has gained by this tour, at least in popularity."[73]

John Quincy Adams returned from Great Britain to find the broad goals and principles of the Monroe administration's foreign policy in place. They represented a continuation of the directions charted during the last two years of the Madison presidency, which in turn reflected the the collective wisdom of the Republican party. But it was Adams who solved the riddle of how to handle the dispute with Spain.

John Quincy Adams agreed with James Monroe's plan to defend the republican experiment by expanding American foreign trade. As minister to Great Britain, Adams had worked for better relations with that nation, for the principle of reciprocity, and for a strengthened military. The program represented the pragmatic pursuit of American self-interest championed by Adams. Yet the success or failure of a nation's foreign policy depends on the consistency with which it is pursued. Dissenting factions, both within Congress and in the administration, can sabotage the application of a policy. Equally important, specific diplomatic problems (such as the recognition of South American countries' independence) may have solutions which per se seem reasonable but which contradict larger foreign policy goals. Adams's genius as a statesman was that in dealing with specific crises he never lost sight of how their solutions affected what he conceived to be the nation's overall interest. In this way, Adams exercised a decisive effect on Monroe, who at times failed to see the interrelationship of seemingly discrete diplomatic problems. Adams approached each diplomatic challenge with cool-headed detachment, making recommendations based not necessarily on the merits of each case but on how they fit into the larger foreign policy picture.

Thus, Adams approached the negotiations with Spain within a broader foreign policy framework. Successful resolution of the dispute with Spain depended less on face-to-face talks with Onís then on the progress of United States foreign policy generally, especially in regard to Great Britain. The terms of any treaty reflect the objective power relationships existing between the contending nations. In the fall of 1817, in the atmosphere of reaction engendered by the Congress of Vienna and with the continued existence of Anglo-American hostility, that power relationship still seemed to favor Spain.

Accordingly, Adams crafted a foreign policy aimed at tilting the balance of power between the two nations in the direction of the United States. His twofold strategy involved, first, isolating Spain from the other European powers (especially Great Britain), and second, applying steadily increasing military pressure on the poorly defended Spanish North American possessions. The intent was to place Spain in a position in which the United States could dictate the terms of a treaty, safe in the knowledge that no power stood ready to aid Spain if the United States chose to assert its claim by force. This strategy applied two of the guiding principles of administration foreign policy, reconciliation with Great Britain and a stronger military, to a specific diplomatic problem. The "two-track" approach of diplomatic and military pressure unfolded bit by bit in 1817-18.

Taking office six months after Monroe's inauguration, Adams moved quickly to make his presence felt. Because he faced opposition to his policies and his personality in both the Congress and the administration, his success as secretary of state depended as much on outmaneuvering domestic opponents as on dealing with foreign governments. He immediately began to demonstrate his mastery of bureaucratic intrigue.

His first chance to do so came during the preparations for the departure of the "South American Commission." In May, Monroe had authorized plans for three commissioners to journey to South America to gain information on the nature of the revolutionary struggles occurring there. The United States had not yet formally recognized any of the rebellious colonies, although private citizens sympathetic to the patriot cause had provided substantial support. Influential members in the Congress and the cabinet, including Speaker of the House Henry Clay and Treasury Secretary William Crawford, pushed for immediate recognition.[74] Monroe, although ideologically sympathetic to the patriot cause, was reluctant to take so important a step as recognition without more knowledge about the rebels' prospects for success.

Complications delayed the South American Commission's departure, originally scheduled for July 1817: first, problems in finding commissioners acceptable to all interested parties, then the illness of the son of one of those chosen.[75] When Adams arrived in New York in early August, he was briefed on the situation by one of the commissioners, John Graham, chief clerk of the state department and a loyal supporter of James Monroe.[76]

John Quincy Adams opposed the recognition of the South American insurgent governments. Though he sympathized in principle with their struggle, Adams doubted that the Latin Americans could achieve either civil liberty or self-government of the North American variety.[77] He also opposed recognition as needlessly antagonistic toward Spain. For the United States to aid the rebels by the act of recognition would worsen the deadlock with Spain; to Adams, the potential damage to American national interest far outweighed idealistic notions about aiding "our republican brethren to the south." Monroe came to agree with this view. An unstated purpose of the South American Commission was to allow him to delay making a final decision on recognition.[78]

Adams, anticipating that Henry Clay would begin a campaign to force the administration into recognition, moved to delay further the departure of the commissioners until he could be certain that the coming session of Congress would be over by the time they returned with their findings. He did so in a way that made clear his own (and Monroe's) priorities. The commissioners were scheduled to sail to South America aboard the USS *Ontario*, commanded by Captain James Biddle. In late September, however, Adams issued Biddle new orders, directing him instead to sail to the Northwest coast and take possession of Astoria at the mouth of the Columbia. The Treaty of Ghent stipulated that all territories captured during the war be returned "without delay," yet Astoria remained in British hands. Now Adams instructed Biddle, assisted by John Prevost, to depart as soon as possible for Astoria "to assert there the claim of sovereignty in the name . . . of the United States, by some symbolical or other appropriate mode of setting up a claim to national authority and dominion." Adams stressed that "no force is to be employed" in taking the territory; he intended only that symbolic control be asserted over the Northwest coast. The expedition represented the first step toward a transcontinental boundary.[79]

It is significant that Monroe made arrangements to have John Jacob Astor informed of these plans.[80] Astor stood to gain more than anyone from the recovery of the post, and he had agitated for its reoccupation since the end of the war, at one point offering to send one of his own ships to accomplish the task. Exactly what precipitated (after two years of inaction) the decision to retake Astoria in the fall of 1817 is unclear, but the fact that Astor and other private citizens with an interest in the northwest coast had recently conferred with both Monroe and Adams suggests that national honor was not the only reason.[81]

Compared to the interminable delays associated with the South American Commission, the expedition to the Northwest departed with amazing speed. Even though the decision to undertake the mission appears to have been made only in late September, Biddle and Prevost had set out by 10 October for the northwest coast.[82] Meanwhile, the South American Commission remained stalled until a new vessel and supplies could be procured. The commissioners did not sail for South America until 4 December 1817. The numerous delays had caused Clay and Crawford much consternation; to Adams, however, things had gone exactly as planned.

Meanwhile, Adams's next opportunity to assert his influence came at the first meeting on 30 October of Monroe's still incomplete cabinet: Secretary of War John C. Calhoun of South Carolina and Attorney General William Wirt of Maryland had yet to assume their posts. Nevertheless, several crucial issues relating to Latin America and Spain were taken up at the meeting, and the decisions set the tone for the conduct of administration foreign policy. Monroe posed a series of questions to his advisers which, taken together, reveal the interconnection of the Latin American and Spanish problems:

1. Has the president the power to acknowledge the independence of the South American insurgent governments?
2. Is recognition a justifiable cause of war for Spain, or any other power?
3. Is it "expedient" for the United States now to recognize the independence of Buenos Aires?
4. What should United States policy be toward Spain?
5. Is it "expedient" to take military action against the insurgent strongholds at Amelia Island, Florida, and Galveston Island, Texas?
6. Is it still advisable to send the South American Commission on its long-delayed mission? [83]

The pressure on the administration to recognize the insurgent governments increased with the arrival in Washington of Buenos Aires envoy Hermenegildo Aguirre. Aguirre had cultivated influential friends in the United States, among them Henry Clay, and had pleaded his country's case to Adams only days before.[84] Monroe now needed to ascertain the limits of presidential power regarding recognition so as to prepare for Clay's challenge to his authority. At this early stage in the history of the republic it was still unclear where the power of recognition lay, although precedent pointed in the direction of the executive rather than the Congress. Clay's challenge would prove a decisive test case of this issue. Monroe knew that recognition of the insurgents would poison relations with Spain. The Spanish government, struggling to preserve a decaying empire, had made it clear that recognition of the rebels would spell the end of the negotiations with the United States. This alone prevented Monroe from acting on recognition. Yet the rising tide of public opinion in favor of recognition necessitated finding a constitutional argument to justify what was in essence a tactical decision to withhold extending diplomatic ties to the revolutionary governments of South America.

A related issue was the occupation of Amelia and Galveston islands by forces allied to the South American revolutionary cause— only part of a broad pattern of guerrilla activity in the name of South American independence which was occurring all along the Spanish borderlands. The groups harassed Spanish shipping and, when possible, set up outposts in the name of the insurgent governments. Though these expeditions included unsavory elements, the revolutionary credentials of most of their leaders were indisputable.[85] Motivated by patriotic ardor and dreams of glory, the South American revolutionaries roamed the Gulf Coast region in defiance of the meager Spanish forces stationed there.

Yet the activities of the seagoing guerrillas threatened United States interests in two ways. First, some of the privateers, contrary to orders, had seized American ships in the Gulf. Though few in number and committed by renegade elements, the seizures outraged American shipowners, who appealed to the government for protection.[86] Second, and more important, in the name of South American independence the revolutionaries liberated Spanish territory in Texas and in Florida which the United States coveted for itself. Their presence complicated resolution of the territorial issues with Spain. The question was, should the United States remove the South American patriot elements from Amelia and Galveston Islands by force?

John Quincy Adams argued for the use of military force. In his diary he wrote of the cabinet discussion: "It appeared to me that all the gentlemen were backward upon giving their opinions. . . . I finally gave mine explicitly that the marauding parties at Amelia Island and Galveston ought to be broken up immediately." Adams also supported going ahead with the South American Commission so that the commissioners could justify to the insurgent governments the American attacks on forces aligning themselves with the revolution. On these two points Monroe agreed with Adams, as he did with the secretary of state's recommendation to await the next dispatch from minister George Erving in Madrid before forming a new policy toward Spain.[87]

As frequently would be the case, it was Adams's insights and forthright arguments that convinced Monroe. The decision to attack Amelia and Galveston represented another step along the two-track policy of putting military *and* diplomatic pressure on Spain. It is significant that Adams labeled the forces already on the two islands as "marauding parties." Though he was not entirely without justification in using the term (some American shipping had been seized by the patriots), the bulk of the evidence indicates that the Amelia party, at least, was operating under a commission granted by the Venezuelan revolutionary government.[88] Yet Adams referred to the post as a "piratical establishment" that United States security interests demanded be overthrown. Ultimately, the true nature of the of the forces occupying Amelia and Galveston islands was irrelevant to Adams and Monroe. The liberation of the islands from Spanish control was not appealing to men attempting to wrest those areas from Spain. Whatever the character of the forces there, circumstances demanded that they be labeled pirates in order to justify their removal. The administration could then retain the seized territory (as it did Amelia Island) on the grounds that Spain was unable to control them. Thus, under a reasonable pretext a clear message could be sent to the Spanish government that failure to negotiate would lead to the outright seizure of disputed territories.

John Quincy Adams had established himself as a force to be reckoned with less than six weeks after assuming the office of secretary of state. The diversion of the *Ontario* to the northwest coast and the consequent delay of the South American Commission made clear his priorities. The decisions made at the October 30 cabinet meeting reflected his geopolitical approach to foreign policy and his Machiavellian strategic sense. The two incidents set the stage for diplomatic triumphs to come.

His auspicious start as secretary of state did little to quell Adams's nagging sense of self-doubt. Anticipating the difficult road ahead, he suffered from sleepless nights and painfully drowsy days.[89] In a palsied hand he wrote to his father that his new post was "as burdensome as I had expected, and how I shall be able to get through the winter is yet a problem for solution. The moral difficulties have not yet begun to present themselves." To his mother, John Quincy was even franker: "I am endeavoring gradually to establish a regular order in the course of business, for my own observance; but the session of Congress is at hand which shall quickly increase the load of business, and until I shall have gone through that trial it will be impossible for me to ascertain whether my strength will be equal to my task, or will sink under it."[90]

THREE

First Moves

John Quincy Adams did not exaggerate the immensity of his work load. Only a man who lived to work could have stood the pace. In a very real sense, Adams *was* the Department of State. The department, which at the time included no more than a dozen employees, was without an assistant secretary, which meant that Adams was solely responsible for all departmental decisions as well as the drafting of instructions to the American ministers abroad. Moreover, he was in charge of overseeing the census of 1820, arranging for the publication of legislation, consulting with the president on pardons, and running the patent office.[1] Routine duties ranged from meeting with foreign dignitaries and advising the president to supervising the daily operation and reorganization of the Department of State. His tasks were not made easier by either the confused condition of the department's files or the incompetence of its chief clerk, Daniel Brent. But Adams, a first-rate administrator, devised a departmental filing system that remained in use until 1915.[2]

In addition to his other work, Adams was commissioned by Congress to prepare a report on the various systems of weights and measures in use throughout the country and the prospects for the establishment of uniform standards. Adams had for some time been personally interested in the subject of weights and measures and seized upon the task with gusto. He somehow found the time to research and write a landmark treatise that recommended the adoption of the metric system by the United States. Written between 1817 and 1821, Adams's *Report on Weights and Measures* is an American classic on the subject. The report is the product of voluminous research as well as philosophical, historical, and sociological insight. John Adams described it as a "mass of historical, philosophical, chemical, metaphysical, and political knowledge."[3] Yet John Quincy Adams did the project in his spare moments, arising earlier in the morning or taking time during his vacations to write or to do research.[4]

Besides the drafting of scientific treatises and state papers, Adams wrote at length in his diary. Beginning in 1785, he had kept a remarkably inclusive record of his daily affairs and emotions, a practice continued until his death in 1848. The diary provided Adams with a private forum in which to vent his frustrations and anxieties; Samuel Flagg Bemis described it as "a secret tuning fork for his pent-up emotions."[5] Adams went to great lengths to find time to write in his diary, occasionally fearing that it intruded on his other duties. It is unclear whether or not he intended his diary to be published, as portions of it were some years after his death. The self-conscious tone of many of the entries indicates that he thought someone was looking over his shoulder, even if it was only his own conscience.[6] Nonetheless, the worth of the diary as a historical source is inestimable. Whatever tendency Adams had consciously to distort the record he was compiling, its sheer mass suggests that it provides a remarkably candid view of Adams himself. The diary's frank observations, comprehensiveness, hostility, self-loathing, and personal, political, and historical reflections make it an unparalleled narrative of the early republic.[7]

The crush of business required Adams to rise each day between five and six in the morning and even earlier during the longer days of summer. After spending his mornings reading scripture and writing (or working on his report on weights and measures), he would go to his office at the Department of State around noon, rarely returning home before five. His evenings were normally spent preparing for the following day's tasks.[8] Despite this Herculean self-discipline, Adams berated himself for laxness in the performance of his duties. The specter of inadequacy loomed over him, warded off only by constant exertion. He feared the loss of his talents: " My most earnest prayer to God is that if my powers of usefulness and active industry are taken from me I may be reasonably sensible and humbly resigned to my condition and removed from the earthly scene before the effects of my incapacity have been felt in the counsels and affairs of my country."[9]

John Quincy Adams extended the principle of rigid self-discipline to the upbringing of his three sons. He was a stern father with great expectations of his children. Indeed, his love for them was conditioned on their achievements. Like his father before him, Adams raised his three sons to be leaders. The imperatives of the "Adams family myth" were visited upon his children, with the added burden of a second generation of greatness for them to live up to.

Adams could be devastating in correcting perceived breeches of good conduct. Soon after becoming secretary of state he wrote a blistering letter to John Adams, Jr., who was then staying with his uncle in Massachusetts: "You conclude by saying that you hope I will forgive anything rash in my son, but I shall do no such thing. If my son be rash he must take the consequences. . . . You boast of studying hard, and pray, for whose benefit do you study? Is it for me or for your Uncle's? —Or are you so much of a baby that you must be coaxed to spell your letters by sugar plums, or are you such an independent gentlemen that you can brook no constraint, and must have everything you ask for? If so, I advise you not to write for anything from me." [10]

These were strong words from any parent, but particularly so from one whose duties had kept him separated from his children for years at a time. While their father was in Russia, George and John endured six years of separation from their parents, left in the care of their grandparents Abigail and John. Such long separations meant that like his father before him, John Quincy Adams exercised much of his influence over his sons via letter. Yet the trials of separation made him no less stern a taskmaster, nor did they prevent him from conditioning his love for his children on their right conduct and achievement. Adams clearly felt disappointed by what he perceived to be the underachievement of his sons. He lamented that they did not love literature and learning as much as he had as a youth. He judged them to be unruly and lacking the seriousness of purpose necessary for greatness. In a letter to his mother in 1816 he described them as "average" children, adding, "I certainly can imagine something more flattering. . . . But I am aware that no amount of labor will turn a pebble into a diamond." Adams gradually resigned himself to the fact that his sons suffered from what he termed the "blast of mediocrity." [11]

All three of John Quincy Adams's sons became lawyers. George Washington Adams, a sensitive and intelligent young man, suffered most from his father's expectations. His love of poetry and romance, his proclivity toward "wasting time," even the burdens imposed by his name made him feel always inadequate to the life set before him. He could do nothing to fulfill his father's expectations. Even winning Harvard's Boylston's Prize over a group of competitors that included Ralph Waldo Emerson failed to quench his father's disappointment. George suffered from a recurrent nightmare in which his wooing of a college sweetheart was interrupted by the image of father advising him, "Remember, George, who you are and what you are doing." [12] George's early promise disintegrated into a life of drinking, gambling, and indebtedness. The only true love of his life was a chambermaid, Eliza Dolph, who bore him a child but whose social station made her unacceptable as a wife. In April 1829, his parents summoned George to Washington to assist in their return to Quincy. Facing certain chastisement for his dissolute living and mortified by the prospect that his parents would learn of his paternity, George Washington Adams slipped from the deck of the steamship *Benjamin Franklin* to his death in the waters of Long Island Sound.[13]

, John Adams, Jr., did little better than his older brother in withstanding the crushing burdens of the Adams family myth. Possessed of a fiery temperament, in 1823 John led a student rebellion at Harvard that resulted in his expulsion for riotous behavior. His failure at managing his father's ill-considered investment in the Columbian Mills, a grain distribution business in Washington, presaged his slide into alcoholism and oblivion. He died in Washington in 1834.[14]

Only the youngest, Charles Francis, fulfilled his father's expectations. Rather than being intimidated, Charles thrived on his father's influence. Perhaps owing to the security afforded by a childhood in the company of his parents, he fought off the bouts of depression suffered by all the Adams children. Like his older brothers, he was given to drinking and carousing; in his late teens he even kept a mistress. Yet his instinct for survival guided him to a marriage with the socially prominent Abigail Brooks. Taking up the Adams mantle of greatness for the third generation, Charles in the 1840s became a leader in the cause of antislavery. Ironically, his greatest achievement—preserving British neutrality during the Civil War as American minister to Great Britain—occurred after his father's death.[15]

As always in the life of John Quincy Adams, familial concerns took a back seat to public duties as he and Monroe began to implement their foreign policy. The president, in his first annual message to Congress on 2 December 1817, announced plans to seize Amelia and Galveston islands from the South American "pirates" who had occupied them.[16] Monroe introduced three reasons to justify the planned assault. First, he claimed that the patriot force had violated American neutrality laws by recruiting United States citizens for their ranks. Second, Monroe doubted that the patriot operation had been authorized by any insurgent governments, "as it would be difficult to reconcile it with the friendly relations existing between the United States and the colonies." Finally, the president claimed that the Amelia establishment "had assumed a more marked character of unfriendliness to us," becoming "a channel for the illicit introduction of slaves into the United States, an asylum for fugitive slaves from neighboring states, and a port of smuggling of every kind."[17]

The plans to occupy Amelia and Galveston inflamed those supportive of the South American independence movement. Henry Clay of Kentucky led the opposition. He sponsored a resolution calling for the "just observance" of neutrality in the South American independence struggles, arguing that American policy in practice hindered that cause. He called for the revision of the neutrality laws to correct their perceived partiality towards Spain.[18] To Clay, the imminent actions against Amelia and Galveston were but the most recent evidence that American policy worked against the cause of South American independence.

Despite his strong protests, Clay in early December stopped short of the outright condemnation of the Amelia and Galveston seizures. Others were not so reticent in expressing their views. William Duane, the pugnacious publisher of the *Philadelphia Aurora*, pulled no punches in criticizing the administration on this and other topics. An ardent advocate of the patriot cause, Duane claimed that the Amelia establishment had been authorized by two of the insurgent governments and that it was "essentially conducive to the promotion of their independence."[19] On 9 December, Congressman John Rhea of Tennessee sponsored a resolution asking that the president lay before the House "any information he may possess and think proper to communicate" regarding the character of the Amelia and Galveston "pirates" and that he restate his reasons for suppressing their activities.[20]

John Forsyth of Georgia, who would prove a loyal ally of the administration in the House, objected to that part of Rhea's resolution requiring the president to restate the reasons for his actions. Forsyth claimed that to do so would imply dissatisfaction with the reasons given in the president's message a week earlier. After some debate the House adopted Rhea's resolution with Forsyth's amendment, in effect asking the administration to report on its actions rather than justify them. In so doing, the House sent a clear signal that it would do little to challenge the executive in foreign policy matters, preferring instead to act in an advisory role.

To John Quincy Adams fell the task of assembling the documents Monroe thought "proper to communicate" regarding the forces at Amelia and Galveston. It was but the first of many occasions in which Adams would be called upon to report to the Congress on foreign policy questions. In doing so, he usually demonstrated a talent for marshaling evidence to support administration positions, but in this case his report was embarrassingly lacking in documentary evidence to uphold the president's contentions regarding the forces at Amelia. The documents submitted to the House on 10 January 1818 comprise mainly the allegations of Beverly Chew, customs collector of New Orleans, that members of the Jean Lafitte gang had occupied Galveston Island and were using it as a base to launch attacks against shipping in the Gulf of Mexico. Chew also charged that the pirates were engaged in smuggling slaves into the United States.[21] Reports of attacks on American shipping in the Gulf had been arriving periodically for most of 1817.[22] These reports also warned of patriot preparations for an attack on Pensacola.[23] Yet Luis Aury, the patriot commander, had abandoned Galveston in April 1817, moving first to Matagorda along the Texas Gulf Coast and then to Amelia Island, where he assumed command of forces formerly under the control of the Scottish adventurer Gregor MacGregor. Only after Aury departed from Galveston did Lafitte's gang move in. At this point the establishment at Galveston became indisputably piratical in nature, and most of the documents Adams submitted to Congress refer to it. Yet Monroe repeatedly suspended the orders to seize Galveston.[24]

United States land and naval forces did capture Amelia Island on 23 December, but Adams's report contains only one document pertaining to the nature of the establishment at Amelia. It is a letter from John McIntosh, a Georgia planter, to Crawford, dated 30 October 1817, alleging that Aury commanded a group of "about one hundred and thirty brigand negroes—a set of desperate and bloody dogs." McIntosh claimed that "Aury's blacks . . . make this neighborhood extremely dangerous to a population like ours," and he feared the possibility that their presence would incite a slave revolt.[25] Beyond this one piece of speculation, Adams's report contains nothing to substantiate the charges of slave trading and piracy by Aury and his men. Ironically, the administration tolerated the presence of Lafitte's gang because it was in fact composed of pirates who preyed on Spanish shipping and who could be removed when necessary—as they were in March 1821. The very legitimacy of Aury's nascent patriot government at Amelia Island was what constituted the threat to the United States, by creating another obstacle to the acquisition of the Floridas.

Adams's report was little more than an attempt to defuse criticism of the president's actions by creating an illusion of House participation in the making of foreign policy. Further evidence that the administration had no intention of being completely frank with the Congress is found in Adams's diary, which reveals that one portion of the documents "implicat[ed] the British government in such a manner that the president has thought it proper to omit certain passages of the letter in his communications to the House." Yet Monroe authorized a complete copy of the letter in question to be given to Bagot for transmission to his government.[26] In short, Monroe and Adams were more candid with the British government than with the House of Representatives.

When news of the seizure of Amelia Island arrived in early January 1818, the administration faced the question of what to do next. Monroe, leaning toward restoring the island to Spain, convened his cabinet on 6 January to discuss the matter. He presented for consideration a draft message announcing the intention to withdraw from Amelia. Adams and Calhoun argued strongly for keeping possession of the island. Crawford, supported by Wirt and Secretary of the Navy Benjamin Crowninshield, favored its return. They feared that to retain Amelia would risk war with Spain.[27] Adams put little stock in Crawford's opinions— "Crawford's point d'honneur is to differ from me, and to find no weight in any reason assigned by me" —and dismissed Wirt and Crowninshield as sycophants who would always agree with Monroe. Only Calhoun (who frequently agreed with Adams's positions) found favor with the secretary of state: "Calhoun thinks for himself, independent of all the rest, and with good judgment, quick discriminations, and keen observation. He supports his opinions with powerful eloquence."[28] The meeting of 6 January ended without having reached a final decision.

Adams continued his efforts to persuade the president to retain Amelia during a second cabinet meeting on the matter on 9 January. "I repeated the arguments of the former day, and new ones as they occurred to me now." He contended that under the No Transfer Resolution of 1811 the president had no right to abandon the island without congressional approval. The division in his cabinet disturbed Monroe, who still did not make a final decision. The infighting made a strong impression on Adams: "The cabinet councils open upon me a new scene of the political world. There is a play of passions, opinions, and characters different in many respects from those in which I have been accustomed. . . . There is slowness, want of decision, and a spirit of procrastination in the president; which perhaps arises more from his situation than his personal character."[29]

Adams's intense lobbying efforts paid off. On 12 January, Monroe announced his intention to retain possession of Amelia Island "for the present." Once again the president's first instincts had been overridden by the powerful arguments of his secretary of state. Yet Monroe doubted the wisdom of his decision when an unconfirmed newspaper report arrived on 19 January that as many as two hundred American merchant ships had been seized in Havana as retaliation for the capture of Amelia Island. Adams wrote in his diary of Monroe's "alarm" at the report and of his fears that the incident might provoke a war with Spain, backed by other European powers. Adams glumly noted that "this incident is, in truth, an untoward one, and therefore most likely to be well founded." [30] By 21 January, Monroe and Adams had found that the report was false, but the president's panicked response to the rumor of seized American ships reveals the risk he perceived in Adams's aggressive border diplomacy.

Having decided to keep Amelia, the administration moved to head off further criticism of its actions. Monroe formally announced the capture of the island in a 13 January address to Congress, notable as much for what it did not say as for what it did. Avoiding explicit reference to the plans to retain Amelia, the message stressed that the action had been necessary to protect United States security along its borders. Monroe repeated his claim that the "foreign adventurers" on the island had acted without the authorization of any South American insurgent government.

The president also introduced a new reason to justify the seizure, one not contained in his first message of 2 December. He announced that the "law of 1811" [the No Transfer Resolution] "was considered applicable to the case" from the very beginning. Only now, Monroe said, was the "law of 1811" considered proper to mention, having been kept secret until this time. The "law of 1811" (actually a series of resolutions by the Congress) was premised on the idea that "the United States . . . cannot without serious inquietude" see any part of the Floridas pass into the hands of another foreign power; it empowered the president to occupy temporarily any threatened territories in the province. It had been the basis for the occupation of West Florida and had also been used to justify the abortive Mathews mission of 1812. Now Monroe invoked it to defend the suppression of a force he characterized as "unauthorized by and unknown to the colonial governments." [31]

The No Transfer Resolution had first been used to defend the Amelia operation in a report to Congress by Henry Middleton, chairman of the Committee on Foreign Relations, on 10 January 1818. The report was intended to preface the documents submitted to the committee by the administration, but the contents of the report bear the stamp of John Quincy Adams.

Middleton, a close administration ally, prepared the report under Adams's supervision. At the secretary's prompting, Middleton emphasized the illegal introduction of slaves into the United States as the major reason for seizing the island.[32] Moreover, Adams revealed to Middleton the "secret laws" of 1811. His diary entry on the subject shows Adams to be a proponent of a powerful executive branch: "I gave him [Middleton] all the additional information that I possessed concerning it—I showed him the *secret laws*, those singular anomalies of our system which have grown out of the error in our Constitution which confers upon the legislature the power of declaring war; which in the theory of government according to Montesquieu and Rousseau is strictly an executive act. Whenever secrecy is necessary for an operation of the executive involving the question of peace and war, Congress must help pass a secret law to give the President the power—now secrecy is contrary to one of the first principles of legislation; but this absurdity comes unavoidably from that of being given to Congress instead of the executive the power of declaring war."[33]

Adams's critique of the congressional warmaking power was characteristic of his view regarding executive authority. He was perhaps the staunchest advocate of his time of a strong executive branch, particularly for the conduct of foreign policy. He believed that the secrecy and need for flexibility (including the use of force) associated with an effective foreign policy required that the president be given wide latitude to conduct affairs without interference from Congress. He argued that the constitutional powers of the executive were more general, and hence subject to broader interpretation, than those of the Congress, which were enumerated.[34] His mistrust of the wisdom of "the people" is demonstrated by his ridicule of the idea that an assertive legislature was needed to protect against runaway executive power. Indeed, for most of his life Adams was more concerned about the encroachment of the Congress on the powers of the executive.[35]

The new defense of the Amelia action articulated in Middleton's report provoked widespread criticism in the nation's press. Both the questionable documentary evidence and the use of the No Transfer Resolution drew fire. The Kentucky *Reporter*, noting that Amelia Island was "beyond our territorial jurisdiction," asserted: "We cannot . . . discern the right of the Executive to make a hostile attack upon it. We cannot perceive in the documents published sufficient grounds to justify the course." The paper termed the seizure of the island "premature and unconstitutional."[36] The *Argus of Western America* attacked the president's hypocritical use of the No Transfer Resolution, commenting, "We do not like the two sided vindication of our government. . . . Aury [the leader of the Amelia force] could not have been a pirate and a lawful commander at the same time."[37] The *New York Evening Post* described the president's conduct as "a daring military usurpation of the most alarming nature," undertaken "without authority, and diametrically in the face of the Constitution."[38] The *City of Washington Gazette*, though sympathetic to Monroe's actions, blasted Middleton's report: "Confident that we are that the administration stands upon pretty solid ground, we are sorry to see its credit impaired by so futile a document."[39]

The most scathing and comprehensive critique appeared in the *Philadelphia Aurora*. In a series of articles, the paper systematically refuted the administration's arguments justifying the seizure of Amelia, denouncing the "shameless and futile documents presented as a pretext." The *Aurora* described the documents in the Middleton report as "evidence of the infirmity of the human mind." It accused the administration of "bad faith and public deception," as well as of causing "articles to be written in the public offices" for publication in pro-administration newspapers such as the *Washington National Intelligencer*, the *Boston Patriot*, and the *Richmond Enquirer*. "By means of these *machines* the people are *managed*—an impulse is then given to the class of sycophants . . . who in every populous place, return the service of slaves for the emoluments or promises of petty offices."[40]

The *Aurora* perhaps went too far in asserting the existence of "machines" to "manage" public opinion. However, it was no exaggeration to say that some of the nation's newspapers were little more than mouthpieces for the Monroe administration. One such journal was the *Washington National Intelligencer*. Its publishers, Joseph Gales and William Seaton, were Washington "insiders" whose editorial loyalty was rewarded by regular access to those in power. Their paper served as a public forum in which the administration could publish the documents necessary to marshall public support for its initiatives.[41] The *National Intelligencer* supported the Amelia action, as it did nearly all the administration's policies, and in late January rebutted the *Aurora*'s attacks, declaring that its arguments had "no real bearing on the question."[42]

Despite the inconsistencies in the president's defense of the seizure of Amelia, Congress did nothing to end the occupation—for two reasons. First, few congressmen wished to challenge the role of the executive in conducting foreign policy; as long as even the illusion of consultation, in the form of the submission of selected documents, was maintained, most were content to give the president a free hand. Second, they knew that the occupation of Amelia related directly to the stalled negotiations with Spain; even though they recognized the contradictions and questionable constitutionality of Monroe's actions, the majority would not risk undercutting the president's bargaining position by challenging his authority to act militarily.

One would have supposed that direct aggression against Spanish possessions would cause a serious setback in Spanish-American relations. The negotiations had been stalled since January, when Monroe had informed Onís of the futility of continued talks.[43] A draft project of a treaty proposed by Spanish Foreign Secretary Cevallos the previous August had been rejected by American minister Erving on the grounds that he was not empowered to negotiate.[44] In short, virtually no progress had been made in the talks since their resumption in 1816. This stalemate would not seem to have been helped by the invasion of Amelia Island.

The plans to seize Spanish territory announced in the president's message of 2 December provoked only a mild protest from Onís, however. In a note to Adams of 6 December, he avoided direct condemnation of the invasion plans, focusing instead on the failure of the United States government to prevent the patriot forces from recruiting and outfitting their expeditions in American ports. In the face of a direct violation of Spanish territory, Onís refrained from making a strong protest. Instead, he ended his note with the plaintive observation that "there was not the slightest motive" for the president's plans, requesting only "a precise and satisfactory explanation" for them.[45] In fact, on 10 December, in the wake of the announcement to occupy Amelia Island, Onís wrote to Adams of new instructions he had just received from Madrid and inquired as to when the negotiations could be resumed.[46] The Spanish minister's proposal to resume the talks while a portion of his nation's possessions were under siege reinforced Adams's belief that the only way to resolve the dispute with Spain was by the selective application of military force. The two men met for preliminary talks on 19 December.

Onís's willingness to return to the bargaining table despite U.S. aggression is explained by the generalized crisis facing the Spanish empire in the early nineteenth century. With the exception of Cuba, all of Spain's Western Hemisphere colonies were in revolt. Initially, the Spanish forces in the New World had been able to quell the often poorly organized and ill-supported rebellions. But by 1817, Buenos Aires and Chile had firmly established their independence, and the success of numerous other struggles appeared imminent.[47] Unlike others in the Spanish ruling class, Onís recognized that the empire stood on the verge of collapse and that the dispute with the United States was but a part of this larger problem.

The chaotic state of Spain's government during the post-Napoleonic restoration prevented the adoption of a coherent, workable policy to deal with the crisis of empire. Ferdinand VII, "the desired one," had regained his throne amid great rejoicing by the Spanish people, yet he proved to be one of the worst kings in Spanish history. Ignored by his father, Charles IV, and abused by his mother, Maria Luisa, and her infamous consort Godoy, Ferdinand lacked the self-confidence and good judgment necessary to be a wise ruler. Suspicious of the Spanish governmental bureaucracy (for good reason), he relied for his advice on an inner circle of favorites known as the *camarilla*. This "government within a government" of self-seeking sycophants played upon the king's pride and fears to prevent the formulation of a realistic colonial policy. The inescapable facts were that Spain was too poor economically and too weak militarily to maintain an empire in the manner and on the scale that had previously existed. However, the *camarilla*, comprising primarily aristocrats and courtiers, encouraged Ferdinand to believe that the colonial rebellions and the dispute with the United States could be resolved by the firm application of military force and by enlisting the support of the European powers, especially Great Britain. Their prescriptions ignored both the decrepit state of the Spanish military and the reluctance of the European powers to become involved in Western Hemisphere affairs.[48]

While the *camarilla* connived to maintain its control over the king, the cabinet of ministers that was nominally in charge attempted to implement a realistic policy for resolving Spain's problems. This proved an impossible task, although not for lack of ministerial talent: besides Onís, men such as Don Pedro Cevallos, Don Jose Pizarro (foreign ministers), and Martin Garay (minister of finance), among others, had solid credentials and long experience in governmental affairs. Yet their efforts to bring Spanish policy into line with reality failed, both because the precarious terms of their employment (between 1814 and 1820 government ministers stayed at their posts an average of six months), and because of the fact that the Consejo de Estado, the ruling council of ministers, held little real power, being often preempted by the machinations of the *camarilla*.[49]

Nothing illustrates this last point better than the Russian ship deal of 1817-18. The dream of the military reconquest of South America had fascinated elements of the Spanish ruling class from the time of the outbreak of the colonial rebellions. Members of the *camarilla* envisioned a powerful force invading the New World and reestablishing the wealth and glory of bygone centuries. But Spain lacked the vessels to transport and defend such a force. Ferdinand turned to his friend and fellow monarch Alexander I of Russia for help. With the assistance of Russian Minister Dmitri Tatishchev (an intimate of the Ferdinand) and unbeknown to Foreign Minister Pizarro, an agreement was reached to purchase from the Russian navy eight ships that were to be the core of an invasion armada. Unfortunately, Ferdinand did not have his agents check the condition of the ships before making the deal. Wormeaten and obsolete, six of the eight vessels nearly sank on the voyage from Russia to Spain and had to be scrapped. Of the two that did depart for South America, one began taking on water at the Azores and had to turn back, and the sole remaining vessel of this pathetic would-be flotilla suffered the ignominy of capture by a Chilean frigate before firing a shot.[50] The huge scandal created by the incident ironically led to the downfall of the Pizarro ministry in 1818, in spite of the fact that Pizarro did not learn of the ship deal until six months after it had been made. The affair typifies the inadequacies of the Spanish government in the years following the restoration of Ferdinand VII.

Though lacking an effective government, Spain was not bereft of able diplomats. One of its most talented was Don Luis de Onís. From a distinguished Salamancan family, Onís represented the cream of the Spanish diplomatic corps. Having received a classical education with an emphasis in the law, Onís spoke four foreign languages and even achieved some proficiency as a doctor.[51] He had served in numerous positions both at home and abroad since beginning his diplomatic career in 1780, earning a reputation for competence and resourcefulness. Eminently loyal to the Spanish ruling family, he cast his lot with the Regency government-in-exile during the Bonapartist interlude. In 1809 he was appointed minister to the United States.[52]

Onís met with a cold reception in Washington. The Madison administration, uncertain as to the outcome of the power struggle in Spain and unwilling to antagonize either side, refused to recognize Onís's diplomatic credentials. Nonetheless, Onís stayed in the United States as the unofficial representative of the Regency, taking up residence in Philadelphia. From there he lobbied the United States government and the public at large for the cause of Spain. He decried the use of American ports for the fitting-out of privateers to aid the South American insurgents. He protested the fomenting of revolution by American agents in East and West Florida. And he made Spain's case to the public in a series of pamphlets published under the pseudonym "Verus" in 1810, 1812, and 1817.[53]

Onís's formal recognition as minister in 1815 did not improve his opinion of the United States or its leaders. He distrusted Madison and Monroe and considered the United States to be bent on territorial aggrandizement. He wrote in his *Memoria*: "The Americans believe themselves superior to all the nations of Europe, and see their destiny to extend their dominion to the isthmus of Panama, and in the future to all of the New World." His opinion of the United States was not helped by acts of vandalism committed against his Washington residence, including the hanging of a dead fowl on his bell rope.[54]

Onís's greatest attribute as a diplomat was his ability to make realistic policy recommendations based on a clear assessment of the state of affairs. The best example of this is his efforts in 1817-18 to convince the Spanish government that compromise with the South American insurgents offered the only hope of maintaining even a semblance of the empire. In several letters to Pizarro (with whom he had a close personal relationship), Onís advocated a policy granting essentially commonwealth status to the colonies, allowing them to trade and manufacture goods without restriction.[55] Pizarro, himself an advocate of moderation in dealing with the colonial rebellions, agreed that innovative measures had to be pursued. Yet Onís's suggestions were never formally considered by the Consejo de Estado, thanks to the opposition of influential members of the *camarilla*.[56] Free trade within the empire was a revolutionary idea, and even if the *camarilla* had favored its adoption, it is not certain that the king would have agreed, certainly not in 1817. Ferdinand had no desire to preside over the restructuring of the Spanish empire, even when faced with the possibility of its outright loss. But that the Consejo de Estado refused even to consider such measures is indicative of the dogmatism and rigidity characteristic of the Spanish ruling class at the time.

Thus, Onís was the envoy of a foreign office only nominally in control of foreign affairs. His great handicap as a negotiator was that his instructions lacked the flexibility necessary to reach an agreement with the Americans. Certain members of the *camarilla* feared that if the foreign minister were given full powers to negotiate, he might make concessions detrimental to the "honor" of the king. Hence, Onís's instructions left him little latitude to make the sort of compromises that might salvage a treaty which, if not ideal in all respects, would at least represent the best terms possible under the circumstances. Trapped between the inadequacy of his instructions and the mounting military pressure of the United States, Onís struggled valiantly to reach an agreement that would ensure the security of the Spanish "borderlands" of the Southwest. This would prove to be his primary goal in the negotiation.

Onís outlined the Spanish position in three notes to Adams, dated 29 December 1817, and 5 and 8 January 1818. In them, he repeated the argument that West Florida formed no part of Louisiana and that Spain had acquired both Floridas from Great Britain in the Treaty of 1783. He also claimed that the long history of Spanish exploration along the Gulf Coast from Mexico to Florida made that area Spanish territory. He contended that French explorers such as La Salle were interlopers who had never successfully challenged Spanish dominion over the region. Onís concluded that French Louisiana was restricted to the territory not controlled by Spain: that is, the lands north and east of the juncture of the Mississippi and Missouri Rivers.[57] Thus, the Spaniard showed, to his satisfaction at least, the historical limits of French Louisiana.

Despite his historical argument, Onís offered a settlement based on the *uti possidetis*, or state of possession, as it existed between Spain and France in 1764. Such terms provided for a western boundary beginning at the Mermento River and extending north to the Missouri River along a line to be determined by joint commission.[58] This offer, though it rebutted American claims to a western boundary at the Rio Bravo, represented one of the first cracks in the Spanish negotiating position. Formerly adamant about placing the boundary of Louisiana at the Mississippi River, Onís, by offering to draw the western boundary even a few miles to the west at the Mermento, opened the door to further concessions.

Adams made a curt and concise counteroffer on 16 January. Observing that Onís's notes had merely restated points first made ten years earlier during the initial negotiations on the matter between the two nations, Adams wrote that the president "consider[ed] that it would be an unprofitable waste of time" to discuss them further. Instead, Adams listed the American terms: Spain to cede all territory east of the Mississippi and a western boundary running along the Colorado River of Texas to its source, thence north along the front range of the Rockies. Adams proposed that the claims of Americans against Spain be settled according to the unratified Convention of 1802.[59] These terms were nearly identical to those offered by Monroe and Pinkney in 1805. Adams now restated them vigorously.

Onís responded with equal vigor in a note dated 24 January. Commenting that "truth is of all times; and reason and justice are founded on immutable principles," he blasted Adams's dismissal of the Spanish position: "There is not a single fact . . . that can affect the certainty or decisive force" of the claims of his nation. He decried an offer that called on Spain "to cede provinces and territories of the highest importance without proposing an equivalent or compensation." [60] Finally, Onís questioned which Colorado River was being proposed as the western boundary, presuming incorrectly that Adams meant the Colorado River of Natchitoches rather then another river of the same name located several hundred miles west in Texas. In short, the two negotiators had not only failed to resolve their differences; they could not even communicate their geographic references clearly.

Despite his outrage, however, Onís made two more concessions in his note of 24 January. First, he offered a western boundary running north from the Gulf along the Arroyo Hondo (formerly a neutral zone between the Spanish and French outposts at Los Adaes and Natchitoches, respectively). This would move the western boundary a little farther west, between the Mermento and Calcasieu Rivers (see Map 2). Second, Onís agreed to the cession of the Floridas. This was the first formal offer (Pizarro's unanswered project of August 1817 excepted) to cede the Floridas to the United States. It represented a unilateral concession, perhaps wrung from the Spanish diplomat by the invasion of Amelia and Adams's unyielding position as outlined in his 16 January missive. Onís added only one new, meekly worded demand: that the United States take "effectual measures" to suppress the South American privateers operating out of American ports. [61]

These concessions must have brought a smile of satisfaction to Adams's normally hard-boiled countenance. Having labored intensely to prevent Congress from undercutting the attempt to bring pressure on Spain by the takeover at Amelia, Adams now had the first tangible evidence of the success of this stratagem. But he did not indulge in too much self-congratulation; although the offer to cede the Floridas was a promising start, there was still much he wanted from his Spanish counterpart. Sensing that he had Onís backpedaling, Adams made no immediate reply to the offer of 24 January.

After waiting for two and a half weeks for a response, Onís again wrote to Adams on 10 February. He began by speculating that "the multiplicity of business . . . which engages you" must have prevented a reply to his note of 24 January. This was nonsense. Adams had no more pressing business than the negotiation with Spain. His delay in answering Onís was calculated to rattle the Spaniard, to create the impression that time now favored the Americans. The tactic of delay, so effectively used by Spain earlier in the long negotiation between the two nations, was now employed by the United States to cultivate the impression that if Spain did not settle matters quickly, the Floridas might no longer be Spain's to cede. Onís, at the limit of his

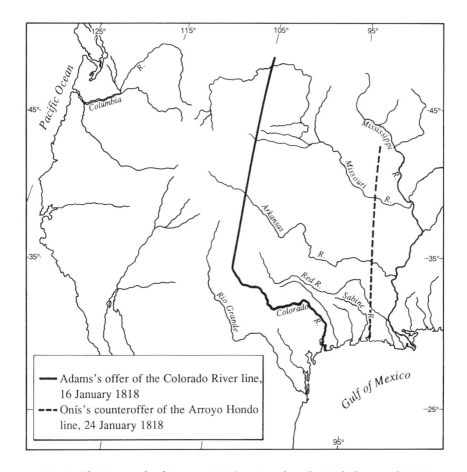

Map 2. The Proposals of January 1818 (projected on the Melish map of 1818)

instructions, requested Adams's patience so that he could "immediately dispatch a courier to Madrid, to inform the government of the demands of [Adams], and request more ample powers adopted to them."[62]

Meanwhile, John Quincy Adams was hard at work preparing a detailed refutation of the historical claims outlined in Onís's notes of 29 December, 5 January, and 8 January. The document, dated 12 March, combined historical argument with rhetorical assertion in a manner rarely matched by American diplomatists. Adams began with a scathing rejoinder to the strong language of Onís's previous note: "The observation that truth is of all times, and that reason and justice are founded upon immutable principles, has never been contested by the United States; but neither truth, reason, nor justice consists in the stubbornness of assertion, nor in the multiplied repetition of error." The United States could not reply to Onís's arguments, or even "continue at all a discussion sullied by such unworthy and groundless imputations."[63]

Adams then outlined a detailed, labyrinthine historical argument designed to prove that the Mississippi River had been discovered by the French, that La Salle had laid claim to the Texas Gulf Coast region as far west as the Rio Bravo, and that this boundary was formalized as Louisiana through the granting of a charter in 1712 by Louis XIV to a French nobleman named Crozat.[64] He introduced a long list of historical documents to support his assertions, simultaneously accusing Onís of having "in vain ransacked the records of the Spanish monarchy" to support *his* claims. The imperious, hectoring tone and vituperative language of Adams's note are remarkably similar to those of his letters chastising his sons for inferior academic performance. Indeed, it is difficult to determine whether Adams addressed his sons in the manner in which he addressed foreign diplomats or addressed foreign diplomats as he addressed his sons.

Determining the validity of Adams's historical argument as to the ownership and limits of Louisiana would require extensive investigation. In the bewildering morass of claims and counterclaims made by the Spanish and the French, the "truth" of the matter is elusive and probably unknowable. Ultimately, it was also irrelevant to the negotiation between Spain and the United States. Onís and Adams were both attempting to cloak nationalistic pretensions in the garb of historical fact. One can be sure that had their positions been reversed, each man would have adopted with ease the arguments of the other. Such is the life of a diplomat. Their sparring in early 1818 merely represented the opening blows of a contest that both men knew was a long way from finished.

In the years after the Congress of Vienna, elements of the Spanish ruling class relied on the assistance of Great Britain in resolving the territorial dispute with the United States. The Spanish government was convinced that Great Britain would not allow East Florida to pass into American hands because of the threat that would pose to British possessions in the West Indies. Also, Spanish officials judged that the British would not stand idly by and watch the Americans usurp the territory of a fellow monarchy.[65] In 1817, Pizarro dispatched two notes to the British minister in Madrid, Henry Wellesley, reminding him of his nation's interest in the matter and urging British action.[66]

Spain had also attempted to enlist British support in quashing its colonial rebellions. In 1812 efforts had been made to employ Great Britain to mediate the disputes by offering the British special commercial privileges as incentive to do so. These efforts failed, for Castlereagh did not want to incite the jealousy of the other European nations by acquiring special trading privileges for Great Britain. Instead, he drafted four preconditions for mediation: Spanish abolition of the slave trade, a general amnesty for all South American rebels, legal equality of South Americans with Spaniards, and an open trade between the South American colonies and the nations of the world with Spain allowed "a fair preference." And Castlereagh added a fifth stipulation: no force was to be used in the mediation.[67] These "preconditions" for mediation were a prescription for the radical restructuring of the empire along the lines proposed by Onís and rejected by the *camarilla*.

Despite the monarchical sympathies of the British crown, British policy showed no signs of intervening in the South American rebellions on terms acceptable to Spain. One might think this would have discouraged the Spanish government from expecting British help in resolving the dispute with the United States, yet throughout 1816 and 1817 Spain attempted to persuade Great Britain to mediate the dispute with the United States. Castlereagh had no enthusiasm for this plan. He wrote to Wellesley in April 1817 that he saw no reason to "entangle ourselves . . . with a new and complicated mediation with the United States in favor of Spain." Castlereagh distrusted the Spanish government, terming it "perverse and . . . shortsighted." He was reluctant to endanger British relations with the United States by engaging in a mediation that offered Great Britain no real benefits.[68] That the Spanish government remained confident of British assistance in the matter is further indication of the diplomatic myopia prevalent at the Court of Madrid.

With no intention of actually taking part in a mediation with the United States, Minister Wellesley in Madrid urged Castlereagh to make it appear that Great Britain was willing to do so. Such a gesture would mollify Spain and enhance Britain's image as a good ally. The plan was to offer to mediate if the United States would also invite such efforts.[69] The British knew that the Americans did not want their involvement in the dispute and so had little fear of U.S. agreement to such a proposal. Charles Bagot made the offer to Adams on 27 January 1818.

Monroe's cabinet, meeting on 31 January 1818, unanimously opposed the mediation proposal. There was no reason to involve a third party in the dispute with Spain now that events were moving in the favor of the United States. British participation could only lead to a close examination of the more unsavory aspects of American policy, such as the Amelia expedition and the U.S. privateers who were aiding the South American insurgents. More could be obtained by isolating Spain diplomatically; a third party might propose a settlement giving the United States less than it could get on its own. Calhoun even feared that the mediation proposal was a trick whereby Spain would declare war and then use the mediation process to secure objectives unwinnable on the battlefield. Only Adams questioned the advisability of flatly rejecting the mediation offer. Fearing that the Spanish dispute ultimately could not be settled without European interference, he hesitated to foreclose that option completely.[70] But in the end, Adams too went along with the decision to reject the British offer.

The administration gave two different explanations for its rejection of the mediation offer. Adams informed Bagot that mediation might "excite ill-will and irritation in the minds of the people" against Great Britain, particularly if that nation were seen as stifling the aspirations of the United States.[71] To Onís, Adams wrote in his note of 12 March that the United States wished to remain free of "the labyrinth of European politics."[72] Of course, these explanations merely served as excuses for the real reason—that the United States stood to gain more on its own from Spain than through a mediator.

The rejection of the mediation offer met with no surprise in Great Britain. Bagot wrote to Castlereagh that "exactly as your Lordship foresaw," the United States had turned down the offer. Castlereagh's gambit had worked to perfection: he had posed as a good ally to Spain by offering to mediate, yet had risked nothing, safe in the knowledge that the United States would refuse. Bagot added in his letter to Castlereagh that Monroe had "assured me distinctly" that the United States would not go to war over the dispute with Spain. Significantly, Bagot described the administration as "really indifferent" regarding the western boundary, "being persuaded that it is not with old Spain that they shall finally have to settle that question."[73]

British mediation in the Spanish question could only have harmed the promising yet still fragile reconciliation between the United States and Great Britain. The problems of fisheries, neutral rights, commercial relations, and national boundaries would be difficult enough to resolve without British involvement in the dispute with Spain. Moreover, by late 1817 another factor was making reconciliation between Great Britain and the United States a necessity—a growing mutual fear of Russia.

American fears of Russia stemmed from that nation's growing presence on the northwest coast. Although agents of the tsar had been active in the region for two hundred years, the Bostonians who began arriving there in 1790 saw the presence of the Russians as a threat to American interests. At stake was control of a key corner of the transoceanic trade with the islands of the South Pacific (particularly Hawaii) and China. Of course, Great Britain and Spain also had interests in the region. Spain claimed territory along the coast extending to 61 degrees north latitude. In 1790 the Spanish seizure of several British vessels at Nootka Sound nearly caused a war between the two nations. But Spain's claim was strictly nominal; that nation had no settlements north of San Francisco.[74] During the last part of the eighteenth century and the early part of the nineteenth, however, Russia had been extending its influence by establishing permanent settlements: at Kodiak Island in 1783, Sitka in 1799, and Fort Ross (just north of San Franciso) in 1812. The settlements were part of a Russian plan to build a vast fur trading network that would include China, Hawaii, and California.[75] The partial realization of this plan disturbed both the British and the Americans, who naturally coveted the wealth of the northwest coast for themselves.

American mercantile interests there dated from Captain Robert Gray's voyage to the Columbia River in 1787; from this expedition stemmed all subsequent United States claims to the region. The lucrative trade in furs from the Northwest to Canton was dominated by Boston firms, with the exception of John Jacob Astor, whose interests in the area have already been noted. Americans had clashed with Russians along the coast as early as 1805. In that year an emissary of the tsar wrote to St. Petersburg that the region "would be an inexhaustible source of wealth . . . were it not for the Bostonians who undermine our trade with China in furs, of which they obtain huge numbers on our coasts."[76] In the years that followed, the Russians attempted unsuccessfully to dislodge the Americans from the northwest coast. In 1809 the first accredited Russian diplomatic representative to the United States, Andre Dashkov, failed in his efforts to persuade Washington to restrain Americans from trading guns to the native peoples of the region.[77] In 1810 John Quincy Adams, then minister to Russia, rejected Russian proposals to delimit a boundary between the claims of the two nations in the Northwest. This refusal was in keeping with the American policy of refusing formal recognition of Russian control of any part of the area.[78]

American interest in the northwest coast, interrupted by the War of 1812, rekindled after 1815. Between 1815 and 1820, 106 American trading ships from firms such as Bryant and Sturgis, James and Thomas H. Perkins, and Astor's American Fur Company sailed to the area then known as Russian-America.[79] As the American economic stake in the region grew, so did concerns over the burgeoning Russian presence. These concerns were made known to the administration through the agency of Nicholas Biddle, a Philadelphia aristocrat with close ties both to the mercantile elite and to James Monroe.[80] In a letter to the president dated 12 November 1817, Biddle wrote of "a matter about which I should wish to speak with you. It concerns the approach of the Russians down our [*sic*] Pacific Coast. It is not enough to enjoy a great part of Europe and Asia, not enough to possess the Northwest Coast down as low as Norfolk Sound and the 47th degree, but they must cross the Columbia and encroach at Bodega within 30 miles of the Spanish settlements in California. These movements offer a wide field for reflection—but it would be vain to write about it, and I must therefore defer it . . . until I have the pleasure of seeing you."[81]

Further evidence of the growing concern about Russian expansionism is a presidential memorandum headed "The Political Picture of Europe, 1817." Although decrying the fact that Great Britain was ambitious, the document asserted "that the government of Saint Petersburg is not less so." It warned that "the colossal power of Russia has been wholly increased . . . in a word, Russia has gained further to the South." Russia, the paper claimed, was now the second leading power in Europe, and the supreme land power on the Continent: "Her policy is not very difficult to ascertain—she seeks to aggrandize herself."[82] The reports of William Pinkney, then American minister to Russia, fueled suspicions of the tsar's intentions. In August 1817 Pinkney warned that "the activity of this government in exploring, and colonizing, and consolidating its power . . . seems rather to increase than to diminish."[83]

The tsarist government reacted with alarm to the rapid American penetration of the northwest coast in the years after 1815. In 1817 the governing board of the Russian-American company submitted a report detailing the activities of Americans engaged in trading guns to the native peoples in exchange for furs. The report also lamented the fact that supplies for the Russian settlements were obtained primarily from Americans, at premium prices.[84] Responding to these concerns, Captain Vasilli Golovnin sailed to the northwest coast to examine conditions for the tsar at first hand. His findings, released in 1819, stressed the need for "decisive steps" to defend the territory from foreign encroachment. He recommended that naval patrols be established along coastal areas claimed by the tsar, and that in the future the colony be supplied by shipments from Russia.[85] Russian anxiety about the Americans climaxed in 1821 with the promulgation of the tsar's ukase closing the Russian territorial waters (which extended for a hundred miles offshore) to all foreign vessels.[86]

Anglo-Russian relations deteriorated simultaneously with the increasing tensions between Washington and St. Petersburg. The major difference was that while the Americans clashed with the Russians only in the matter of the northwest coast, the British disagreed with their erstwhile ally on a range of issues, the most important of which concerned the very nature of the postwar alliance. Castlereagh intended that the concert of Europe act only to maintain the balance of power in Europe. He opposed employing the Quadruple Alliance for any purpose other than defending monarchy on the Continent.[87] Conversely, Tsar Alexander I, in the grip of a messianic religious fanaticism, favored the use of the alliance to defend the interests of monarchy wherever it was threatened. To do this, he created the Holy Alliance, composed of Russia, Austria, Prussia, and France. Castlereagh, contemptuous of the tsar's crusading zeal, referred to this organization as "a piece of sublime mysticism and nonsense."[88] The fundamental disagreement between the two dominant powers of the post-Napoleonic world split the European alliance from the beginning.[89]

But this was not the only point at issue between the two dominant powers. In France, the two nations vied for the favor of Louis XVIII. In Italy and Germany, Great Britain supported Austria in its efforts to forestall the growth of Russian influence over the principalities in those two regions. In Spain, the tsar's support for the reconquest of the colonies and the tangible manifestation of this support represented by the ship deal caused as much consternation in London as it did in Washington. In the East, Russian and British interests clashed at Constantinople and in Persia. Finally, the two nations locked horns on the northwest coast of North America as the drift southward of Russian settlements collided with British claims to the region. The final defeat of Napoleon saw the rise of Russia as the preeminent challenger to British global supremacy.[90]

Charged with sorting out this tangled skein of diplomatic and political problems, John Quincy Adams closed out his diary in 1817 with a brief prayer "that I may know and faithfully discharge the duties of my station, and that my heart and mind be prepared for every disputation of the divine wisdom and goodness."[91] Certainly, no one would have accused Adams of laxness in the performance of his duties. By the spring of 1818 he had already wrung more concessions out of the Spanish than his predecessors had in a decade. Yet he paid a price for his accomplishments. His problems with insomnia were compounded by a chronic case of rheumatism.[92] Fixated on his work, Adams had time for little else. Still, his efforts dissatisfied him. He complained in his diary that "everything is hurried, and of course, scarcely anything is done well."[93]

His wife Louisa Catherine suffered too, hovering on the edge of a nervous breakdown. In February Adams wrote that she was beset by "extreme agitation and fatigue beyond the power of her constitution to bear."[94] The demands of the cabinet post strained further a marriage already lacking in intimacy. A cold formality marked their relationship. In his diary, Adams referred to her only as "my wife." Mrs. Adams, left to her own devices by her husband's busy schedule, spent many evenings dining at the home of the French minister Hyde de Neuville—that is, when her frequent illnesses did not confine her to bed.

The former Louisa Catherine Johnson had trod a difficult road as the wife of John Quincy Adams. They had met in 1796 in London, where Louisa's father was serving as the American consul. Naturally shy and given to social awkwardness, she had to endure the jealous spitefulness of her sisters once it became clear that the son of John Adams was interested in her. But the courtship of Louisa and John Quincy (like their marriage) lacked passion and romance. Indeed, Adams chose Louisa as his mate at least in part because his pragmatic judgment told him that it was time to take a wife, and the daughter of a prominent Maryland family seemed a socially appropriate choice for the ambitious young diplomat. He proposed to her before he returned to his post at The Hague; despite Louisa's pleadings, however, he refused to marry her before leaving on the grounds that his duties and paltry salary would not allow him to attend to a wife. He admonished her to work on improving her intellect until his return "which might be in one year or in seven."[95]

The two-year separation before their marriage erased whatever spontaneity or joy the union might have contained. Courtship by mail proved difficult for Louisa. She worried that letters could not convey her feelings and that John Quincy would look askance at them for their imperfections in grammar and expression. Moreover, the long engagement left her in an unbearably awkward social position. Yet Adams embraced their separation as an important test of their relationship. He wrote that she should "consider untoward events as a test of character, and that a large portion of all human events consists of suffering with dignity and composure, without weakness or unavailing regret."[96] Such words did little to ease Louisa's misery. She fretted that her suffering would make her unattractive when she and Adams were finally reunited: "I am so miserably dull, stupid and wan that I have gained the appellation of the Nun."[97]

The brief moment of bliss experienced by the couple in the wake of their wedding in London in 1797 was shattered only two weeks later by the news of the financial ruin of Louisa's father. Nearly penniless, the Johnsons were forced to depart England quickly, leaving their new son-in-law to assist in settling the family's affairs.[98] A more inauspicious start to the marriage could hardly be imagined. Adams, always worried about the precarious state of his own finances, now had the added concern of his new in-laws' financial setbacks. Louisa believed that she never fully recovered the confidence of her husband afterward.[99]

Lousia did not meet Abigail and John until 1801. Both of Adams's parents had opposed their son's engagement, but the distance between them, as well as John Quincy's age (thirty at the time of his marriage) prevented a strong protest. Nonetheless, Abigail had inquired before the wedding whether he had gotten over "Maria" (Mary Frazier); she also lamented the fact that Louisa's mother was English and that she had been raised in Europe. That the interests of Mary Frazier should elicit Abigail's concern is ironic, considering her veto of that relationship a few years earlier. In any case, Louisa's introduction to the Adams clan in 1801 precipitated further suffering. Her sense of inadequacy was accentuated amid the bustling and opinionated Adams women, who informed her of John Quincy's love for the beautiful and talented Mary Frazier. And Abigail's coolness to the wife of her prized son was immediately apparent. Louisa's reaction to all this was to seek refuge in illness: "It was lucky for me I was so depressed, and so ill, or I should certainly have give mortal offense."[100]

John Quincy Adams's constant criticism of Louisa's management of family affairs and of her limited intellectual achievements did not help her already poor self-image. She always felt inferior to Abigail, well known as one of the best-read women in the United States. Uncomfortable with the social events of European court life, she experienced acute feelings of loneliness and isolation; and as the wife of the nation's most widely traveled diplomat, she endured continual changes of address and years of life away from friends and family.[101]

Her husband's official absences and grueling work schedule meant that she was often left to raise the boys (notoriously unmanageable) alone. The long separations, the lack of intimacy between herself and her husband, and the pain and sacrifice that a public career required made Louisa doubt whether John Quincy's strivings were worth it: "I was not patriotic enough to endure such heavy personal trials for the political welfare of the nation whose honor was dearly bought at the expense of all domestic happiness." [102]

John Quincy Adams's relationship to his wife was yet another way in which his personal experience mirrored that of the nation. The spirit of sharing and cooperation that was central to John and Abigail seems to have been almost entirely absent between John Quincy and Louisa. Lousia was neither the emotional soulmate nor the practical helpmate to John Quincy that Abigail was to John. Rather than a partner in marriage, Louisa functioned as John Quincy's subordinate, in charge of maintaining a happy and well-run home but largely excluded from a meaningful role herself. It is clear that she chafed at her position; she wrote to a friend of the unhappiness of living with a man who considered himself "utterly superior to myself." [103] In this respect, Louisa's marriage as compared with Abigail's reflected the evolution of the status of American women from the comparative equality of the Revolutionary era to their more restricted role as guardians of the hearth in the nineteenth century. [104]

Yet one should keep John Quincy Adams's insensitive—indeed, despotic—treatment of his wife in perspective. He had warned her of the suffering and sacrifice that marriage to a man of national destiny would entail. [105] Moreover, it is fair to say that her suffering merely matched his own. His career as a public servant was neither financially nor emotionally rewarding. The position of secretary of state, like his previous public posts, offered Adams little personal or familial happiness. The tranquil life of a man of letters for which he yearned seemed more distant than ever, given parental expectations, his sense of duty to God, and the demands of a nation's destiny.

In the spring of 1818 John Quincy Adams prepared to meet yet another challenge, this time from opponents of the president's South American policy. Their aims threatened to shatter Adams's fragile diplomatic structure.

FOUR

"The South American Question"

The South American struggles for independence complicated the efforts of Monroe and Adams to expand the power and influence of the United States. There is no doubt that most North Americans, in a demonstration of reflexive ideological affinity, exulted at the prospect of republicanism triumphant in the Western Hemisphere; they equated Spanish rule with colonialism, Catholicism, and corruption. Despite this popular ideological sympathy, geopolitical considerations prevented Monroe and Adams from taking any substantive action to aid the South American insurgents. Spanish officials made it clear that to do so would result in the breaking off of negotiations and possibly war. Great Britain, too, nervously watched the development of U.S. relations with the rebel governments. Castlereagh feared that the United States might exploit its ideological and hemispheric ties to the South Americans as a means of gaining commercial supremacy in what promised to be a lucrative market. Unilateral steps by the United States in favor of the South American insurgents would severely set back the process of reconciliation with Great Britain which was integral to the success of Monroe and Adams's foreign policy. Consequently, in 1817 and 1818 the Monroe administration adopted a policy of what it termed "an impartial neutrality" toward the South American struggles.

This policy displeased a sizable number of politically active Americans, primarily from the trans-Allegheny West, whose interests in the South American cause went beyond mere ideological sympathy. They called for active U.S. support of the South American insurgent governments. Motivated by a combination of ideological, altruistic, and self-interested considerations, their efforts to influence South American policy posed a direct challenge to the foreign policy of Monroe and Adams. Indeed, the success of their foreign policy hinged on successfully meeting that challenge.

James Monroe's "impartial neutrality" toward the South American insurgent governments, like so many of his other policies, followed the course charted by James Madison. South America had become a serious issue only after 1815. Until that time, preoccupation with the war with Great Britain and the rebels' dubious prospects for success prevented the formulation of a clear policy toward the South American insurgents.[1] Their struggles for independence presented a new problem for North American decisionmakers in that the neutrality statutes of the 1790s applied to wars only between independent states, not between mother country and colony. Although Madison did not extend direct aid to the rebels, he did interpret the neutrality statutes in such a way as to allow rebel vessels into American ports, in effect recognizing their belligerency; without extending diplomatic recognition to the insurgent governments, he permitted United States citizens to trade with the rebels in direct violation of the Spanish colonial monopoly. Onís, who considered the insurgent vessels piratical, protested this policy to no avail.[2]

When Monroe took office in April 1817, there was mounting evidence that the patriots would soon be victorious. In July 1816 the United Provinces of the Rio de la Plata (present-day Argentina) had declared their independence. The following February the victory of José de San Martin's forces at Chacabuco brought Chilean independence a giant step closer. In the spring of 1817 popular interest in and enthusiasm for the patriots escalated, partly because of their successes and partly as a result of the agitation of public figures such as Henry Clay, who mustered all his oratorical skill on their behalf.[3]

American public support of the revolutionary movements went beyond mere rhetoric. A thriving underground trade network, centered in Philadelphia and Baltimore, supplied the rebel movements with arms, supplies, and, in some cases, mercenary forces. Privateers, outfitted in and operating out of American ports, enjoyed the lucrative spoils of plundered Spanish shipping. Neither repeated protests to the American government by Don Luis de Onís nor the passage of further neutrality statutes in March 1817 and April 1818 were effective in suppressing this popularly supported and profitable activity. So extensive was the de facto aid to the revolutionary cause that Monroe privately suggested that formal recognition would do little to increase the material support the rebels were already receiving.[4]

Responding to the increasing public and congressional pressure to act, Monroe agreed in late April 1817 to send a commission to tour South America, ostensibly for the purpose of gathering information on the revolutionists and assessing their prospects for success (see Chapter 2). Yet the commission's real purpose was to provide an excuse for the administration not to act, for Monroe at that time had no intention of aiding the South American insurgents, whatever their condition.[5] There were three reasons.

First and most obvious, Spain would not tolerate direct U.S. aid to the insurgents, either diplomatic, economic, or military. The widespread and illegal outfitting of privateers and recruitment of mercenaries occurring in American ports outraged the Spanish but could be rationalized by them as beyond the control of the federal government. Formal executive action in favor of the South American insurgents, however, would force the Spanish government, for reasons of pride and international prestige, at the very least to break off negotiations with the United States. The Monroe administration was well aware of Spain's attitude on this question. In August 1817 Minister Erving in Madrid wrote to Adams that while the Spanish-American dispute was "full of difficulties," the "greatest arises out of the misconception of this government with regard to our obligations as a neutral between her and her colonies." [6] Indeed, preventing the United States from recognizing the insurgent governments was a primary Spanish aim in the negotiations. Pizarro wrote to Onís that the way to head off recognition by the Americans would be to "stuff their mouths with the negotiation." [7]

A second and more important factor restraining the United States from recognizing the South American insurgent governments was the fear of antagonizing Great Britain. Monroe and Adams's entire foreign policy hinged on cultivating good relations with that nation (see Chapter 2). Recognition or other forms of direct aid to the South American rebels would have provoked a severe response—although not one due to British concern over the integrity of the Spanish empire. Ambiguity marked British policy toward South America in the years after the final defeat of Napoleon. The European powers looked to Great Britain, the presumed archdefender of monarchy, to champion the restoration of monarchical influence in South America. Yet the British had engaged in a prosperous, growing, and illegal trade with the Spanish colonies throughout most of the eighteenth century.[8] Necessitated by the shortages of the Napoleonic wars, this trade proved vital to the British economy, particularly during Jefferson's embargo. In short, while restorationist ideology pushed Great Britain toward the restoration of Spanish rule in South America, commercial self-interest pulled in favor of the colonies' independence.[9]

Accordingly, Castlereagh crafted a policy that appeared to support the restoration of Spanish rule but only under such conditions as to ensure their commercial independence. In principle, he was willing to mediate the South American conflicts; in practice, his preconditions (including commercial freedom for the South American nations) such a mediation ensured that Spain would reject his offer.[10]

Thus, Great Britain, though taking no substantive measures, maintained its status as a loyal ally to Spain, thereby restraining precipitate action by other members of the alliance, especially Russia. Moreover, this ambiguous policy kept the United States guessing as to British intentions in South America.[11]

In fact, the actions of the United States played a major role in shaping Britain's South American policy. During the first decade of the nineteenth century the United States became Britain's major competitor for the burgeoning South American trade.[12] After the war the North American presence remained substantial in such areas as Cuba and Chile.[13] Castlereagh was obsessed by the fear that the United States might use its ideological and hemispheric ties to the South Americans to preempt British commercial interests.[14] Diplomatic recognition of the insurgent governments by the United States therefore represented a major threat to Great Britain, and Bagot was alarmed by the efforts of Clay and others to force such a move.

Hence, Castlereagh made clear to the U.S. government the possible consequences of recognition. Adams warned Monroe in 1816 that Great Britain would side with Spain in a conflict arising from diplomatic recognition of the rebels.[15] Although Adams gradually began to perceive the true nature of British South American policy, in early 1818 he still feared the consequences of recognition on Anglo-American relations. From 1815 to at least 1818, Castlereagh walked a diplomatic tightrope that simultaneously created a fear in Washington of European intervention in the New World and avoided committing Great Britain to any definite course of action.[16] It was an adroit act of statesmanshp during a period often termed "the golden age of diplomacy."

Significantly, Great Britain exercised greater influence over U.S. South American policy in 1817-18 than did Spain. Had Castlereagh been willing to join or at least acquiesce in the diplomatic recognition of the colonies, the United States would have had little to fear from the reaction of Spain or the other European powers. Conversely, without the support of British sea power, the military reconquest of South America was idle speculation.[17]

The third factor restraining Monroe and Adams from active support of the South American insurgents, one whose relative weight is difficult to judge but whose importance is indisputable, was the opposition of the northeastern mercantile establishment to direct aid for the South American patriots. These merchant capitalists, whose influence on the Monroe administration has already been noted, strongly supported the president's policy of "impartial neutrality" because they feared the consequences to their direct trade with the loyal Spanish colonies should the United States antagonize Spain by aiding the rebels. In 1817-18, North American trade with the loyal Spanish colonies far exceeded that with the rebellious provinces.[18] Cuba in particular provided a valuable market, annually importing approximately 100,000 barrels of American flour.[19] In return, the "Pearl of the Antilles" supplied the United States with sugar, coffee, and molasses. Finally, Cuba proved an indispensable source of specie at a time when U.S. reserves of the precious metals were inadequate to maintain the stability of the dollar. John C. Calhoun alluded to this last point when he observed that a cutoff of the Cuban trade "would greatly increase the embarrassments of our circulating medium."[20] In 1820 Calhoun wrote to Andrew Jackson that Cuba "is in my opinion, not only the first commercial and political position in the world, but is the key stone of our Union. No American statesmen ought to ever withdraw his eye from it; and the greatest calamity ought to be endured by us, rather than it should pass into the hands of England."[21]

In 1818, approximately fifty American vessels arrived in Havana each month, the great majority of which belonged to New York and New England shipowners. Their interest in the Cuban trade dated from the last years of the eighteenth century. After a period of decline, the Cuban trade had rebounded vigorously with the resumption of peace in 1815.[22] To threaten this lucrative trade by aiding the patriots, whatever the moral or political arguments, would court economic disaster for this particular group of Americans. It is therefore not surprising that in December 1817 Nicholas Biddle wrote to Monroe urging continued neutrality in South American affairs "for our own security."[23]

The concerns of the northeastern mercantile establishment were articulated in a slim yet influential volume know as "Yard's Pamphlet," after its author James Yard. Published in early 1818, the work predicted that direct aid to the insurgents would lead to war with Spain and in grave terms described the consequences of such a conflict to American commerce. Yard speculated that in the event of war, Great Britain would seize both Cuba and Puerto Rico. He rejected arguments that a free South America would be a commercial boon to the United States, commenting that "the intercourse we now have with the single island of Cuba, is of more value to the United States, in one year, than that with Mexico would be in ten!"[24] He feared that South American agricultural products would compete with those of the United States on the world market, and that Great Britain ultimately stood to gain the most from a free South American trade.[25] Biddle, in another letter to Monroe, described "Yard's Pamphlet" as "a very able argument," adding that "the hopes of great commercial advantage from the emancipation [of South America] are completely illusory."[26]

In sum, geopolitical considerations and the domestic special interests that had informed those considerations prevented Monroe and Adams from actively supporting the South American revolutionary cause in 1817-18. Yet divisions within the Republican party leadership as to the nature and viability of the new governments to the south also worked to prevent American aid to the rebels.

On the one hand, Madison and Monroe were solidly behind the insurgents and did not doubt their capacity for self-government. Madison called on Monroe to support the revolutionaries "whatever may be the consequences" and in 1823 suggested a joint proclamation with Great Britain in favor of South American independence. Madison idealistically viewed the conflicts as part of "the great struggle of the epoch between liberty and despotism."[27] Monroe, too, had no doubt that the interest of human progress lay in the emancipation of the Spanish colonies. The foreign policy considerations that retrained him from recognizing the insurgent governments did not diminish his sympathy for their struggles.[28]

Conversely, Thomas Jefferson and John Quincy Adams both seriously doubted the capacity of the South Americans for self-government. In May 1817, Jefferson wrote to Lafayette that although the independence of South America was "no longer in question," the prospects for republicanism were considerably less bright. "Ignorance and bigotry, like other insanities, are incapable of self-government," wrote the Sage of Monticello. To Baron Alexander von Humboldt, Jefferson commented: "Whether the blinds of bigotry and the shackles of the priesthood, and the fascinating glare of rank and wealth, give fair play to the common sense of the mass of people, so far as to qualify them for self-government, is what we don't know." Jefferson feared that postrevolutionary chaos in the colonies could give rise to a South American Bonaparte.[29]

John Quincy Adams held even deeper suspicions regarding the South Americans. His inveterate Hispanophobia was not confined to Old Spain. Adams rejected as "superficial" the perceived similarities between the South American insurgencies and the American Revolution: "Ours was a war of freemen for political independence—This is a war of slaves against their masters." He viewed the American Revolution as a two-stage struggle for both political and civil rights, whereas in the South American conflicts, "civil rights, if not entirely out of the question, appear to have been equally disregarded or trampled upon by all parties." Adams asserted (without evidence) that "there is no more liberty of the press at Buenos Aires than at Madrid." To him, the upheavals in South America more closely resembled the French Revolution than the American War of Independence. Beyond his ideological mistrust of the independence movements, Adams doubted that the South American market would be of great value to the United States: "Do what we can, the commerce with South America will be more important and useful to Great Britain than to us, and Great Britain will be vastly more important to them than we, for the simple reason that she has the power of supplying their wants by her manufactures. We have few such supplies to furnish them."[30]

In light of these suspicions and considering his role as the chief architect of American foreign policy, it is not surprising that of all the cabinet members, John Quincy Adams pushed hardest for remaining neutral toward the South American revolutionary movements. Monroe, though aware of the larger goals of American diplomacy, might have been swayed by public and congressional pressure to take action on behalf of the new republics had Adams not constantly reminded him of the stakes involved. Adams knew that the administration's South American policy was the trump card in the negotiations with Spain. The spring of 1818 was not yet the time to play it.

Opposition to the administration's neutrality policy centered in the trans-Allegheny West. To many politicians and journalists of the "New West," neutrality in a struggle between republicanism and monarchy was an abnegation of the American mission to foster republicanism. Few were as ambivalent as Adams and Jefferson regarding the capacity of the South Americans for self-government; a widespread belief was that though they might be oppressed and degraded, the sheer power of republican institutions and ideals would uplift them. Henry Clay captured this sentiment: "Whenever I think of Spanish America, the image irresistibly forces itself upon my mind of an elder brother, whose education has been neglected, whose person has been abused, and who has been disinherited by the unkindness of an unnatural parent."[31] Clay's sympathetic yet paternal tone illustrates well the dominant outlook of westerners towards the South American independence movements.

Certain that the South American struggle was just, westerners were equally sure that its ultimate success depended on support from the United States. The Congress of Vienna symbolized the global

reaction against republicanism; to stand by while the Europeans
snuffed out the growth of liberty in South America was to court its
extinction in the United States as well.[32] A state of mind developed
that the United States could not remain neutral in a struggle in which
its interests were so integrally, if indirectly, involved.

Many westerners, including Clay, little feared the possible consequences of diplomatic or military involvement in the South American struggles. Toward Spain, the politicians and newspapermen of
the region held an almost uniform contempt. A contentious editorial
on the recognition question in the *Nashville Clarion* reflects this
sentiment: "What then, have we to apprehend? Perhaps—yes! perhaps—a quarrel with Old Spain. Let it come. If Old Spain wishes to
draw the sword because we will not acknowledge the sway of the
Pope, Ferdinand, and the Inquisition, in contradistinction to a rational system of republican government, let her come on."[33] Toward
Great Britain, the westerners evinced similar disdain. The near-
catastrophe of the War of 1812 did little to temper the jingoistic
enthusiasms of men who remembered the triumphs of Jackson and
Perry while forgetting the burning of Washington and the Essex Junto.
Westerners either did not understand or did not appreciate the intimate connection between South American policy and the relations of
the United States to the European powers. From this perspective,
Western agitation for aid to the insurgent governments appears ill-
considered and detrimental to the interests of the nation as a whole.

But the debate over South American policy highlights the fundamental differences between the interests of the trans-Allegheny West
and those of the Northeast and the South. The prosperity of both the
Northeast and the South hinged on expanding trading ties with Great
Britain and avoiding war with Spain, an occurrence that would be
disastrous for American commerce. Northeastern commercial and
southern agricultural interests had little to gain from aiding the
South Americans and everything to lose if such a policy disrupted
relations with Great Britain and Spain. In contrast, westerners shared
indirectly, if at all, in the transatlantic and Cuban trades and therefore
had substantially less concern that they not be interrupted. To the
"Men of the Western Waters," America's commercial future lay in
the potentially great market of South America. In short, beneath the
political debate over South American policy lay a very real clash of
sectional commercial interests.

Geography played a major role in defining these sectional interests. The Allegheny Mountains formed an imposing barrier to trade
and travel; the few roads that linked the West to the coast were poorly

maintained and often impassable. So difficult was travel in the days before the railroad that in 1817 the journey from Cincinnati to New York took at least fifty days. (In contrast, packets on the westward run from Liverpool to New York averaged less than forty days to complete their voyage.)[34] Such remoteness had a profound effect on western economic development. High freight rates made manufactured goods brought from the coast prohibitively expensive.[35] Moreover, western agricultural products, thanks to their bulk, could not profitably be transported to the coasts; thus westerners were deprived of a substantial portion of the home market.[36] Representative Henry St. George Tucker of Virginia commented on this situation in 1818: "Even in the country where I reside, not 80 miles from Tidewater, it takes the farmer one bushel of wheat to pay the expense of carrying two to a seaport town."[37]

The effects of peacetime foreign competition further hindered western economic development. The shortages created by the disruptions of the Napoleonic era had spawned a small yet significant manufacturing sector in the West; cities such as Pittsburgh, Lexington, and Cincinnati flourished as manufacturing centers during the early years of the nineteenth century.[38] After 1815, however, western manufacturers faced severe competition from cheap British goods, which in the years after the War of 1812 were exported to the United States and sold below cost.[39]

Compounding the problems of high freight rates and foreign competition, westerners faced a severe shortage of hard currency after the War of 1812. The traditional shortages caused by the flow of specie eastward to pay for manufactured goods and defray freight rates had been worsened by a serious balance-of-payments deficit in the years 1816-18. This deficit drained the nation of a substantial portion of its hard currency reserves, and as an outlying region the West felt the contraction most acutely.[40] A flood of paper money distributed by the dozens of state banks created after the war made the situation worse.

In sum, the trans-Allegheny West remained in quasi-colonial relation to the coastal regions in the years following the War of 1812. Despite the West's growing economic and political power, the region's future depended on the policies of an administration whose chief constituency was the old-line mercantile interests of the Northeast. The West's advocacy of aid to the South American patriots was but one aspect of this larger sectional struggle.

Henry Clay devised a comprehensive plan to alleviate the problems of the West. To protect infant manufactures of the region, he proposed a tariff. To solve the problem of inadequate transportation, he advocated a federal role in internal improvements. And to provide credit for all who desired it, he supported the establishment of the Second Bank of the United States. Together, these three elements were known as the "American System" and would become a major part of Clay's legacy to American political development. By 1818 he had already established its legitimacy by adroit legislative alliance building. Solidly backed by the trans-Allegheny West on all three issues, he engineered alliances in the Fifteenth Congress first with the South and West on the National Bank question, then with the Northeast and West on the tariff. On the question of federal subsidies for internal improvements Clay gained the clear support of the West, while the Northeast and the South split on the issue.[41] Thus, Henry Clay pushed through the House a program that met the needs of his region. Whatever his political ambitions, he spoke for his constituency as surely as Monroe and Adams did for theirs. In Clay, they faced an articulate and energetic politician whose support for the South American revolutions was merely the foreign policy side of a popular domestic agenda.

Westerners envisioned double benefits from a free South America: the end of Spanish rule would open the region to the merchants of the Ohio and Mississippi River valleys, with New Orleans as the natural gateway to the southern markets; in return for their goods, westerners would receive the fabled gold and silver of Spanish America, which would finance noninflationary economic growth and free them of dependency on the U.S. coastal regions. Clay alluded to this prospect when he said to the House: "We may safely trust to the daring enterprise of our merchants. . . . The precious metals are in South America and they would command the articles wanted in South America. . . . Our navigation would be benefited by the transportation and our country will realize the mercantile profits."[42]

Diplomatic recognition would be but the first step in capturing the South American market. Ultimately, aggressive American action would ensure not only the elimination from the region not only of Spain but of Great Britain as well. Americans would reap the full political and economic benefits of republicanism triumphant in the Western Hemisphere. A popular maxim of the day captures the essence of this plan: "U.S. textiles plus rational liberty equals the exclusion of European influence from Latin America."[43]

Competing neomercantilist visions of American empire, then, underlay the debate over South American policy which took place in 1817 and 1818. The Northeast and the South opposed a policy that might disrupt the Anglo-Asiatic trade nexus critical to their prosperity. The trans-Allegheny West, fueled by republican ideology and visions of commercial dominion in a free South America, favored a more active role in the independence struggles. The "South American question" is a prominent example in the history of the early republic of a sectionally based foreign policy conflict.

John Quincy Adams did not see it that way. Opponents of the administration's neutrality policy he judged guilty of a misguided idealism. He equated those who wished to aid the South American cause with the Francophiles of the 1790s. Adams believed that both groups were willing to jeopardize the interests of the United States (and hence the interests of the republican cause) by committing the nation to a struggle of dubious legitimacy. He wrote to his father in December 1817: "And now, as at the early stages of the French Revolution, we have ardent spirits who are for rushing into the conflict, without looking to the consequences."[44]

Adams took an even harsher view of Henry Clay's championing of the South American cause. His suspicions of the Kentuckian dated at least from the time they had served together as negotiators at Ghent. There, Clay's whiskey drinking and all-night card parties had offended the puritan sensibilities of Adams, who believed that frivolity had no place in such important business as peace negotiations. Clay's advocacy of the South American rebellions Adams now interpreted as a vindictive attempt to destroy both himself and the administration, motivated by Clay's anger over not having been named secretary of state. At the opening of the Fifteenth Congress in December 1817, Adams noted in his diary that "Mr. Clay has already mounted his South American great horse . . . Clay's project is that in which John Randolph failed, to control or overthrow the executive, by swaying the House of Representatives."[45] He was convinced that by "violent, systematic opposition" to the administration, Clay intended to pave the way to the presidency.[46] These comments typify Adams's tendency to personalize every political issue and to attribute selfish motives to those who opposed him.

John Quincy Adams considered himself above such petty political machinations. He feigned a lack of interest in the presidency—the end to which his efforts were ultimately directed. He replied "very explicitly in the negative" when asked by his friend Alexander H. Everett why he did not "expose" Clay's motives publicly: "I told him I should do absolutely nothing . . . my business was to serve the public to the best of my abilities, in the station assigned to me, and not to intrigue for further advancement—I never by the most distant hint to anyone ever expressed a wish for any public office, and I should not now begin to ask, for that [the presidency] which of all the others ought to be most freely and spontaneously bestowed."[47]

These words are vintage Adams. They both capture his reflexive tendency to deny his desire for public office and reveal what was to him the only acceptable way to fulfill his inexpressible yet undeniable ambition. Adams's refusal to woo the electorate was rooted in his basic suspicion of popular democracy. This suspicion, like so many of his other beliefs, derived from his parents and what he perceived to be the lessons of classical republicanism. From them he had come to distrust the complete sovereignty of the people via the ballot box as potentially disruptive, given his perception of the public's impulse to be swayed by its passion and enthusiasms. Adams believed in a political leadership drawn from a natural aristocracy possessed of the moral and spiritual values needed to ensure the survival of the republic. The task of political leaders was to lead, not follow, the masses by articulating the true interests of the nation.[48]

Adams was by nature and upbringing incapable of actively campaigning for election. Making promises to interest groups, kissing babies, playing to the crowd were unthinkable to him, violations both of the "Adams family myth" and of the vision of the Founders. Only once in his life did he spontaneously and naturally mix with a political crowd.[49] His belief that achievement, not politicking, was the path to high office was augmented by the perception of his destiny to lead. In this respect, it is not surprising that Adams viewed his political opponents as motivated by either naked ambition or a desire to damage him personally. He had, after all, been raised to believe in his unique role in the maintenance of the republican "experiment" in free government. His professional career, oriented as it was to the assumption of the identity of the nation's interests with his own, naturally led him to characterize opponents as motivated by selfish, unpatriotic concerns.

These attitudes made Adams contemptuous of Clay, who, like many politicians of the day, wore his ambitions on his sleeve. Indeed, Adams's reference to the presidency as the office "which of all others ought to be freely and spontaneously bestowed" reveals that he mentally inhabited a world that no longer existed (if it ever had), a republic in which leaders were chosen on the basis of merit and service rather than political wheeling and dealing. In Adams's idealized republic, no legitimate diversity of interests could exist. Raised to believe that virtue and achievement would be rewarded, he was learning that in post–War of 1812 American politics, how one played the game was irrelevant to one's chances for success. Self-interest, not selfless service, was the prime vehicle for political advancement. It was a fact that Adams found impossible to acknowledge fully.[50]

Confronted with Clay's opposition to the administration's foreign policy and to his own presidential ambitions, Adams attempted to sway public and congressional opinion on the South American question. He first did so in a series of letters published in the *National Intelligencer* under the pseudonym "Phocion."[51] Appearing in December 1817, the Phocion letters articulated the case for continued neutrality in South American affairs even as they distorted the issues involved. They asserted that their "only object" was "to produce such a discussion as may serve to enlighten the public mind," and that "the establishment of truth should be the object of all parties." From there, Adams proceeded to misrepresent not only the South American cause but the purposes of administration foreign policy. Warning that Americans were not "propagandists . . . making it our business to send missionaries through the world to preach the true political faith," he observed that "the ferment of the Spanish colonies, not having been founded on principles, but having merely grown out of circumstances, has nearly subsided . . . and has been put down in great measure by the dissensions of the colonists and the misconduct of their leaders." In other words, Phocion doubted the influence of republicanism in the South American revolutions, denied any connection to the North American independence struggle, and minimized the prospects for victory. He claimed that the South American revolutionary leaders had been "limited to an endeavor to obtain a place of refuge . . . in the pestilential soil of Guayaquil."[52]

Nothing could have been further from the truth. By December 1817 the United Provinces of the Rio de la Plata had maintained their independence for four years. San Martin's victory at Chacabuco in February 1817 proved decisive in winning Chilean independence. In the north, Bolivar's daring maneuvers culminated in the liberation of Bogotá in 1819. The South American independence movement was flourishing by late 1817, and although Adams correctly pointed out its differences in some respects from the North American struggle, to dismiss the patriot efforts entirely was a distortion of the truth.

Phocion's distortion of the movement as a whole led him to question the nature of the forces at Amelia and Galveston Islands. These he characterized as an "association of adventurers, renegades, and desperadoes, from the four corners of the earth," whose sole aim was the indiscriminate plunder of commercial shipping. He asserted the right of the United States "to constitute itself the protector of its own seas" and "protect the renewal of the scenes of horror" such as "when Lafitte held Barataria."[53] This defense of the seizure of Amelia was made ironic by the reference to Lafitte, who remained undisturbed in his stronghold at Galveston until 1821.

The Phocion letters next questioned the interests of Great Britain in the South American struggles. The British, he observed, would like nothing better than that the United States play "the cats-paw" in expediting South American independence. Desiring a free South America yet unwilling to say so openly, the British wanted the United States to act as "abettors of rebellion," "causing us to be viewed with distrust and suspicion by all those powers (the nations of Europe) who are our natural allies." Phocion claimed that while the British knew the United States would gain little commercially from a free South America, Great Britain "must gain immensely." "It is apparent we should certainly be no great gainers by doing the dirty work of Great Britain."[54]

This utterly distorted the actual state of affairs. Castlereagh aimed to prevent, not to encourage, the United States from aiding the South Americans. Adams knew, however, that the American public, still smarting from the recent war, would never accept a neutrality policy motivated in part by desire not to offend Great Britain. Therefore, he constructed an argument calculated to be well received by the public rather than the one that comported with the facts.

In a second Phocion letter, Adams addressed the role of blacks in the South American revolutions. Knowing that the votes of southern congressmen would be decisive in defeating Clay, he crafted an argument designed to play on their greatest fears. Commenting that "this is no time to engage the scruples of a false delicacy, in the discussion of dangers, which, being understood, may possibly be averted by a wise policy," Adams described "the preponderating weight" that blacks were playing in the revolutionary struggles and the threat they posed to the hemisphere. He argued that black emancipation should be gradual, "proportioned to the moral improvement that may be visible among them." He raised the specter of more Santo Domingos, of a mass of freed slaves spreading throughout the Western Hemisphere, endangering the American South. Nothing could have been better calculated to frighten southerners into withholding support for South American independence. That Phocion greatly exaggerated both the influence of blacks in the independence struggles (black participation being minimal in most of the conflicts) is secondary to the fears his predictions must have engendered in the minds of many Americans.[55]

That the Phocion letters systematically distorted the truth in discussing the South American revolutions is worsened by the attitude Adams adopted in writing them. Claiming that "the establishment of truth should be the object of all parties," he propagated falsehoods on a crucially important issue about which most Americans had little knowledge.[56] Adams avoided discussion of the administration's geopolitical strategy, in which South America was merely a pawn, because of the public outcry it would cause. Instead, he supported administration policy with arguments which he knew to be false but which were calculated to be effective in making his case.

Adams's choice of a pseudonym—Phocion was an Athenian leader of the fifth century B.C. known for his selfless service to Athens, austere life-style, and fear of democratic "extremism"—is revealing. Adams, like his Athenian predecessor, apparently was sufficiently fearful of popular debate that he deemed it necessary to mislead the public, presumably so that it would not pursue actions against its own interests. The duplicitous nature of the Phocion letters reveals that Adams's continual affirmations of the importance of virtuous conduct did not preclude his own manipulation of public opinion. The letters highlight the contradictions inherent in Adams's attempt to maintain an impeccable record of personal integrity while acting in the public realm of politics.

Adams also acted to thwart the efforts of Don Manuel Hermenigildo de Aguirre to pressure the administration into recognizing the United Provinces. Aguirre had been sent as an agent of the Buenos Airean and Chilean insurgent governments to obtain both diplomatic recognition and military aid for San Martin's struggle to liberate Peru.[57] Arriving in July 1817, Aguirre had no success convincing Acting Secretary of State Richard Rush to alter the neutrality policy. Several meetings with Adams in late October proved equally futile. But Clay's campaign in favor of recognition rejuvenated Aguirre's mission. Feted by Washington society as the representative of a legitimate South American government, Aguirre attempted to use his popularity to increase the pressure on the administration. In early December he sent a note to Adams "demanding" recognition of the United Provinces—a note that Adams conveniently misplaced.[58] In any case, Adams rejected Aguirre's plea for recognition on the grounds that his credentials did not empower him to make such a request.[59] After several more fruitless meetings, Aguirre asked whether he should go to Baltimore or Philadelphia (where sympathies for the South American patriots ran high) to make his case directly to the people. Adams, refusing to be intimidated, replied that his de-

mands were "under consideration" by the president and that if
Aguirre's presence should needed in Washington, he could immediately be "given notice."[60] Frustrated by such evasiveness, Aguirre
threatened the closure of Buenos Aires to the commerce of the
United States. Adams now had the South American where he wanted
him; he rejoined that if the port of Buenos Aires was to be closed to
American shipping, he wanted to see it in writing so that the United
States could prepare an appropriate response.[61] Embittered, Aguirre
left the country in early 1818, writing to his superiors: "I believe that
if they [the United States] do anything in our favor even indirectly,
it will be for the purpose of enriching their merchants."[62]

In early 1818 another South American emissary, Don Vicente
Pazos, arrived in Washington to protest the seizure of Amelia Island.
Pazos had been instrumental in drafting a constitution for the abortive "Republic of Florida" and had been elected a member of its short-
lived representative assembly.[63] Now he tried to obtain reparations
from the United States for property seized during the occupation. His
credentials to do so were enhanced by the support of Lino de Clemente, agent of the insurgent government of Venezuela, who called
on Pazos to protest the Amelia Island attack as a violation of the
rights of the South American republics.[64]

Once in the United States, Pazos gained the support of William
Thornton, commissioner of patents and an ardent advocate of the
patriot cause. Through Thornton, Pazos met many influential Americans: Clay, the journalist Baptis Irvine, and Commodore David Porter, among others. With the assistance of Irvine and Porter, Pazos
began work on a pamphlet detailing his grievances. In early February
he presented his "Exposition, Remonstrance, and Protest" to
Adams.[65] The work argued that while international law prohibited
the United States from seizing Amelia, the South American republics, as recognized belligerents of war, could legally capture the island
from Spain. Moreover, Pazos brought to Washington sworn deposi-
tions from Americans living in St. Marys, Georgia (across the sound
from Amelia) that no runaway slaves had been harbored by Aury's
force, and that goods captured on the high seas had been deposited at
the St. Marys custom house, not smuggled into the United States as
Monroe had charged.[66]

Pazos's pamphlet received much publicity in the press and the
enthusiastic support of Clay, who saw it as a sure way to embarrass
the administration. Pazos met several times with Adams and Monroe
during February without receiving any firm reply to his pleas for
reparations. In early March with Monroe's approval, Adams informed

Pazos that the president saw "no reason for revoking any of the measures which have been [taken] . . . and nothing that requires any other answer to your representations."[67] Rebuffed, Pazos took his case directly to the Congress. On 6 March he prepared a memorial outlining his grievances and requesting reparations. Clay presented the memorial to the House on 11 March, touching off a three-hour debate over whether it should be formally received.

The Pazos Memorial debate exposed the sectional cleavages in the House. Administration supporters, led by John Forsyth of Georgia (soon to replace Erving as minister to Spain), argued that Pazos, as an agent of a foreign power, was acting improperly in appealing to the Congress for redress. Supporters of Pazos pointed to the legitimacy of his grievances and the failure of the administration to respond to them.[68] Eventually, by a vote of 124 to 28, the House passed Forsyth's resolution to refuse the memorial. Nearly every opponent of Forsyth's measure came from the trans-Allegheny West.[69]

The House's refusal to accept the Pazos Memorial was a major congressional victory for the administration. It signaled that Clay might not be able to marshal the same support on foreign policy questions that he could command on domestic issues. Adams savored the triumph. He naturally saw Pazos and Clemente, as well as Aguirre, as "tools against the administration," whose actions were "in concert with and dictated by Clay."[70]

Despite overcoming the efforts of Aguirre and Pazos, John Quincy Adams could not rest easy regarding "the South American question." Clay had yet to raise the issue on the floor of the House, as he had threatened to do since December; his wine-induced pledge "I'll beat you, by———!" still rang in Adams's ears.[71] Now, as Congress neared the end of session, his Kentucky nemesis prepared to act. The only question was what form Clay's challenge would take. In order to shore up congressional support for the administration, Monroe directed Adams to collect documents in the government's possession relating to South American independence and the negotiations with Spain. The aim, as with the Amelia documents, was to create the illusion of consulting with the Congress on foreign affairs. Congress had requested the documents in December; now Adams concentrated on completing the task of assembling them in order to provide a counterweight to the arguments of Clay.

Neither the documents relating to the independence of South America nor those concerning the negotiations with Spain revealed much substantive information. Those on South America were chosen to prove Adams's contention that Aguirre was not empowered to request the recognition of the United States.[72] Nothing in the collection (comprising primarily Aguirre's letters to Adams) helped Congress to understand either the nature of or the prospects for success of the South American independence struggles. Similarly, the documents relating to the negotiations with Spain failed even to hint at the role of Great Britain in bringing Spain to terms. Adams merely assembled the notes exchanged between himself and Onís, ending with his own vitriolic missive of 12 March (see Chapter 3). The net effect was to cast Adams in the role of a stern and unyielding defender of American national interests, an impression spread far and wide by the publication of the letters in a special supplement to the *National Intelligencer* of 24 March 1818.[73]

Adams also assembled a third set of documents, relating to the Amelia Island affair. The controversy over the incident refused to die. House critics, dissatisfied with the administration's defense of its actions, on 20 March requested all documents not previously released that related to the occupation of the island "if not inconsistent with the public interest." [74] Monroe prefaced these documents by claiming that no patriot government had sanctioned Aury's actions, and that the "Republic of Florida" had been created solely to prevent the cession of East Florida to the United States.[75] The documents themselves supported neither of Monroe's claims. Most concerned Onís's complaints to Adams over the operations of privateers out of American ports, a long-standing and illegal practice (and one the federal government had done little to halt) but one that had no direct link to the patriot actions at Amelia.[76] Indeed, the few documents even mentioning Amelia Island concerned allegations that some members of the patriot force had been recruited in New York—a serious charge, but hardly proof of Monroe and Adams's contention that Aury's force was sheerly piratical.[77]

Adams finished compiling the documents not a day too soon. Monroe submitted them to the House on 25 March, the same day on which Clay formally raised "the South American question." The timing was more than coincidental, for on 24 March, Congressman Hugh Nelson of Virginia (a loyal administration ally) warned Adams that Clay's challenge was imminent.[78] The first full-scale congressional debate on South American policy in United States history began on this note.[79]

Clay refrained from a direct assault on Monroe's South American policy, recognizing that control of foreign affairs traditionally rested with the executive. Instead, he introduced a resolution calling for $18,000 to be added to the annual appropriations bill currently under consideration. The funds would pay the salary and expenses for a minister to the United Provinces, to be sent "whenever the president shall deem it expedient to do so."[80] The resolution would allow House members to express their support for recognition (symbolized by the appointment of a minister to an insurgent government) while not obligating Monroe to take action. Even though such a measure would effect no immediate substantive change in policy, its passage would be a major political victory for Clay: if Monroe yielded and recognized the United Provinces, American neutrality in the independence struggles would effectively be ended; if the president still refused to act, Clay could claim that he was ignoring both public and congressional opinion. In either case, Clay would emerge stronger politically.

Clay opened the debate with a three-hour oration that wrapped a profusion of idealistic rhetoric around a cold assessment of what the United States stood to gain from South American independence. He stressed the commercial benefits to the United States. He pointed out the advantages of the "direct distribution" to the United States of the region's precious metals, which probably would result in "the entire command of the India trade." Moreover, he minimized the danger that Spain might react violently to recognition, observing that the Spanish monarchy did not have the financial resources to declare war. He argued that Great Britain "is more concerned than even this country in the success of the cause of independence in Spanish America."[81] Though he coyly noted that his measure merely recommended a course of action to the president, Clay also defended the involvement of the House in the making of foreign policy: "nowhere" did the Constitution imply "that the executive act of sending a minister to a foreign country should precede the legislative act which shall provide payment of salary." Foreign policy, he said, should be made jointly by the executive and legislative branches.[82]

Clay's speech voiced the opinions of many congressmen from the trans-Allegheny West, thereby setting the tone for the remainder of the debate. Opponents of the resolution minimized the commercial advantages of a free South America, feared that recognition would lead to war with Spain, and denied the constitutionality of allowing the House to share directly in the making of foreign policy.[83] Furthermore, the fact that the South American Commission had yet to return with its findings (thanks to Adams's machinations) influenced some House members to vote against the measure.[84] Contrasting commercial interests within the House also influenced the outcome of the debate. At one point Clay accused Samuel Smith of Maryland of opposing recognition because it might jeopardize Smith's own special trading privileges with the loyal Spanish colonies.[85] Smith answered this charge by noting that the trade of Spain and its loyal colonies with the United States exceeded that of any other nation except for Great Britain and France.[86] "Yard's Pamphlet" too persuaded some House members that the United States stood to gain little commercially from a free South America.[87] Clay acknowledged Yard's influence when he said "permit me to express a distrust of all pamphlets of this kind."[88]

After four days of debate, the House rejected, by a vote of 45 to 115, Clay's resolution to provide monies for a minister to South America. The Kentuckian's strategy of winning the western vote while gaining at least a split in the coastal regions, so successful in domestic questions, failed when applied to foreign affairs. The vote again reflected sectional divisions, but this time Clay won only a small majority of the trans-Alleghency West vote, while the Northeast and the South overwhelmingly rejected his measure.[89] A potentially devastating blow to administration foreign policy had been thwarted.

Adams smugly noted in his diary the defeat of Clay's resolution: "The present session [of Congress] will stand remarkable in the annals of the Union for showing how a legislature can keep itself employed when having nothing to do. . . . The proposed appropriation for a minister to Buenos Ayres has gone the way of other things lost upon earth, like the purchase of oil for lighthouses in the western country."[90] The defeat of Clay's measure, along with the rejection of Pazos's and Aguirre's pleas, meant that for the moment Adams was free to pursue his two-track diplomatic and military strategy to bring Spain to terms.

Adams had played a major role in defeating Clay; indeed, William Duane thought the secretary had overstepped his bounds. He wrote in the *Aurora* that "the department of state [that is, Adams] did shamelessly interfere to influence a vote in Congress. . . . when the question concerning South America was about to be brought forward in Congress by Mr. Clay, the whole weight, influence, and activity of the executive was brought to bear upon the members of Congress . . . the sole end and purpose in view was to prostrate Mr. Clay and arrest his popularity."[91]

Adams ignored such charges as the soured grapes of the opposition. All that mattered to him was that he fended off a major challenge to administration foreign policy. Circumstances, however, would not allow Adams any respite from his duties. Even as he savored the defeat of Clay, a new crisis was brewing in the swamps of East Florida.

FIVE

Jackson's Invasion of Florida

John Quincy Adams was not the only one satisfied by Clay's defeat. The initial widespread support for South American recognition steadily eroded as the public realized its implications for the United States. Madison astutely observed in a letter to Monroe that "the nation will . . . disapprove any measure unnecessarily involving it in the danger of war." [1] Even the *Richmond Enquirer*, a critic of the administration's neutrality policy, welcomed the defeat of Clay's resolution: "The proposition of Mr. Clay is wrong. . . . It is a proposition against the established order. . . . What has the House of Representatives to do with foreign embassies? We believe the president to be a warm and sincere friend of the patriot cause. . . . We believe he might recognize the independence of La Plata [Buenos Aires]—but he wishes to make up his mind with the utmost deliberation and await the return of the commissioners; why not allow him time? " [2]

Of course, it was neither the possibility of war with Spain nor the failure of the South American commissioners to make their report that had influenced Monroe to refuse to recognize the South American republics. These factors had served merely as public rationales for administration policy. Yet they were very effective in controlling the activities of the House, which had for the moment assured executive control of foreign affairs. At this point, Monroe and Adams's biggest problem in the House concerned the misguided efforts of their putative ally Forsyth. Characterized by Clay as a tool of the administration, Forsyth set out to prove his independence by introducing a resolution authorizing the president to seize East Florida. Monroe and Adams opposed this provocative measure which, ironically, would have given formal sanction to what they planned to do anyway. Fortunately for the administration, Forsyth's proposal quickly disappeared from the House agenda.[3]

The British government also welcomed the defeat of Clay's measure. American recognition would have placed Castlereagh in a difficult position: to do nothing would be undeniable proof to the continental powers that Great Britain ultimately favored South American independence, yet substantive steps to punish the United

States for its actions would have jeopardized Anglo-American reconciliation, the cornerstone of Castlereagh's policy. Hence, Castlereagh was undoubtedly relieved when Bagot wrote: "It appears evident that it is not the intention of the Government, nor, I think, the disposition of the country in general, to take at present any step which can be considered as a direct acknowledgement of the independence of those colonies, or as tending to change, in fact, the neutral position" of the United States.[4]

While Adams labored to defeat Clay's efforts in the House, Andrew Jackson had embarked on a mission that proved decisive in the making of the Transcontinental Treaty. Fifteen years of diplomatic wrangling had failed to secure the Floridas for the United States. Jackson now acted to accomplish the deed by an exhibition of murder and plunder known as the First Seminole War.

The Seminole War was but one part of the American policy aimed at removing or eliminating native Americans from the Southeast. The removal process had begun during the Creek War of 1812-13. The Treaty of Fort Jackson imposed by Jackson near the end of the war resulted, in the words of Robert Remini, in the "virtual annihilation" of the Creek nation. Under its terms, 23 million acres were taken from the tribes. Ironically, the treaty was negotiated with those Creeks who had been allied with Jackson during the war; the Creek chiefs (including Hillis Hadjo, known as Francis the Prophet) and their followers who resisted Jackson had fled into Florida. Nonetheless, Jackson justified his punitive treaty on the grounds that the entire Creek nation must pay for the acts of those who had fought the United States.[5]

Between 1816 and 1818, Jackson negotiated five more cessions of land from the Cherokee, Choctaw, and Chickasaw tribes of the Southeast. Using bribery and intimidation to obtain the signature of recalcitrant chiefs, he made the deep South (with the exception of Florida) safe for cotton cultivation and the slavery that went with it.[6]

Yet Florida remained beyond the grasp of Americans. During the War of 1812 the British had used the peninsula as a base from which to attack the southern U.S. frontier. Even more outrageous from the American perspective was the use of Florida as a haven for Indians and runaway slaves. In 1815 several hundred blacks and mestizos had occupied an abandoned British garrison at Prospect Bluff on the Apalachicola River. Together with houses extending for several miles along the river, the "Negro Fort" (as the abandoned British post became known) was the largest slave refuge in the history of North

America until it was destroyed by an American gunboat in April 1816.[7] The destruction of the Negro Fort, however, did not end the threat posed to American domination of blacks and Indians; the Florida peninsula remained an asylum for those fleeing either the wrath of Jackson or slavery.

Creek chiefs who had escaped into Florida after the Creek War of 1813-15 claimed that the Treaty of Fort Jackson by which they had been dispossessed of their land was void. In the first place, they had not signed the agreement. Second, Article IX of the Treaty of Ghent stipulated that lands lost by Britain's allies during the war would be returned to them. Moreover, the chiefs had been encouraged in their claims by British agents Edward Nicholls and George Woodbine, who had signed an agreement assuring that their lands would be returned. In 1815, Chief Hillis Hadjo, escorted by Nicholls, had gone to London to plead with the English to make good their commitments.[8]

But Jackson had no intention of returning the lands obtained by the Treaty of Fort Jackson. Although the United States government instructed him in June 1815 to begin to return captured lands, the general ignored the directive, and the eviction of the tribes continued. The Madison administration, fearful of provoking the wrath of Jackson's supporters (including many who stood to own the newly acquired land), let the issue drop. Great Britain, eager to reconcile its differences with the United States, did not press the matter on behalf of its putative Indian allies.[9] In short, the process of Indian removal that had begun during the Creek War gained speed after the end of hostilities between the United States and Great Britain. That many Creeks, assisted by their Seminole and free black allies, were as yet unresigned to being uprooted from their ancestral homelands assured the outbreak of another war.[10]

The incident that precipitated the First Seminole War began as a direct result of the attempt to implement the Treaty of Fort Jackson. A small band of Seminoles living in the village of Fowltown just north of the Florida border refused to vacate their lands when ordered to do so by General Edmund P. Gaines. On 21 November 1817 a detachment of soldiers under the command of Gaines stormed the settlement, killed several of the villagers, drove off the rest, and burned Fowltown to the ground. Ironically, the Seminoles living in Fowltown had neither signed the Treaty of Fort Jackson nor sided with the Creeks who fought Jackson during the Creek War. Nonetheless, they suffered the fate of summary removal.[11]

Fowltown marked the beginning of the Seminole War; the Indians soon retaliated. On 30 November the Seminoles attacked a supply

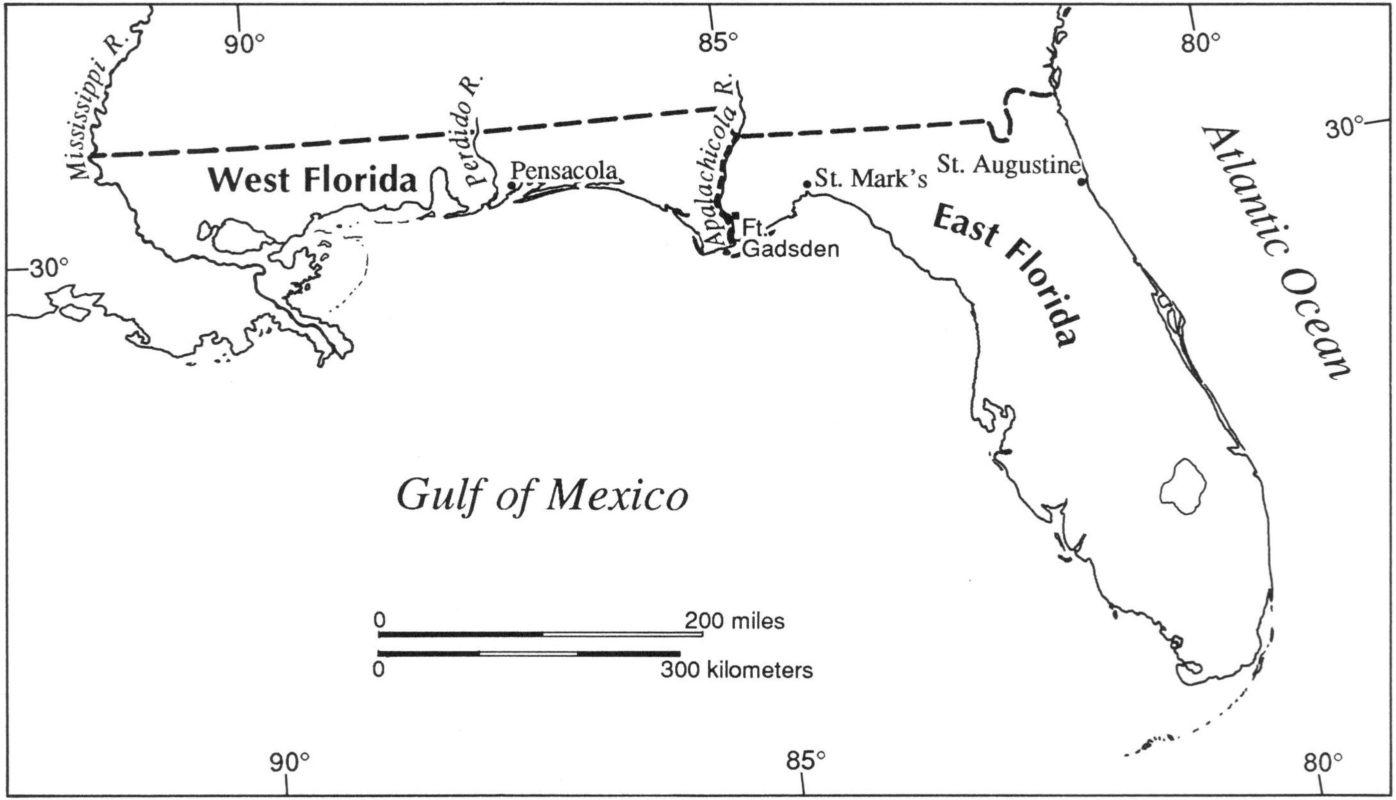

Map 3. The Floridas

Was John Behind + his

boat under the command of Lieutenant R.W. Scott as it ascended the Apalachicola River, and of some fifty passengers (including women and children) only about ten escaped with their lives. On 16 December, Secretary of War John C. Calhoun ordered Gaines to punish the Seminoles, pursuing them into Florida if necessary. On 26 December, Calhoun ordered Jackson to assume command of the forces under Gaines, instructing him to "adopt the necessary measures to terminate" the conflict. Two days later Monroe wrote to Jackson that the "movement . . . against the Seminoles . . . will bring you on a theatre where you may possibly have other services to perform. Great interests are at issue. . . . This is not a time for repose . . . until our cause is carried triumphantly thro'." [12]

Jackson had already recognized the opportunity at hand. Upon hearing of the attack on the Scott party, he had (without authorization) called out the Tennessee militia and prepared to march south. [13] On 6 January (before he had received either Calhoun's or Monroe's message) he wrote to the president, arguing that "the whole of East Florida [should be] seized and held as an indemnity for the outrages of Spain upon the property of our citizens; this done, it puts all opposition down, secures to our citizens a complete indemnity, and saves us from a war with Spain. This can be done without implicating the government; let it be signified to me through any channel (say Mr. Rhea) that the possession of the Floridas would be desirable . . . and in sixty days it will be accomplished." [14]

Monroe denied having read until a year later Jackson's letter outlining his bold plan to take East Florida from Spain, yet the president's contention that he had not authorized the seizure of Florida must be viewed skeptically. Jackson knew that when Monroe spoke of the "great interests" at stake and of "other services" the president did not refer to the problems with the Seminoles. Significantly, neither Calhoun's orders nor Monroe's letter specifically instructed Jackson to avoid engaging the Spanish. Given Jackson's reputation for not shirking conflict, the omission of direct orders not to seize Spanish posts is perhaps the strongest proof that the administration wanted benefits of a Jackson rampage in Florida without having to shoulder the blame for sanctioning aggression against another country. [15] Moreover, given Monroe's involvement in previous attempts to seize the Floridas (as secretary of state in 1811, he had ordered the Mathews mission into East Florida, only to disavow the expedition when public criticism became too intense), it is not unreasonable to assume that he would tacitly authorize another invasion of the peninsula. [16]

In any case, by mid-March, Jackson and a force of nearly 5,000 Tennessee volunteers, American troops, and Creek allies had moved into East Florida, descending the Apalachicola River as far south as the site of the destroyed Negro Fort, where Jackson ordered an American garrison built. He met minimal opposition; the Seminoles and their allies (numbering perhaps a thousand warriors in the entire province) fled his advance, and the Spanish were too weak militarily to offer any resistance to Old Hickory. Nonetheless, Jackson embarked on a campaign of terror, devastation, and intimidation, laying waste the Seminole villages of Miccosukee and Boleck's Town and capturing the Spanish garrisons at St. Mark's and Pensacola, the capital of West Florida. Unable to engage the Seminoles in battle, he destroyed their sources of food in a calculated effort to inflict starvation on the tribes, who sought refuge from his wrath in the swamps.[17]

While Jackson did not kill as many Seminoles as he might have liked, he did, through a combination of luck and trickery, capture several important enemy leaders. Creek chieftains Hillis Hadjo and Himmilemmico were taken after being lured aboard an American naval vessel flying the British flag. At St. Mark's, Jackson discovered Alexander Arbuthnot, a seventy-year-old Scottish trader who had befriended the Seminoles and who had been given power of attorney by them in their dealings with whites. And at Boleck's Town, Jackson had captured Robert C. Ambrister of the Royal Marines, an abolitionist, adventurer, and ally of the Seminoles who had wandered into Jackson's camp at night. On the person of Ambrister's companion was a letter from Arbuthnot to his son, warning him and the Seminoles not to resist Jackson's overwhelming force.

The court-martial of Arbuthnot and Ambrister—"unprincipled villains," as Jackson called the two Britons—had a predetermined outcome. Arbuthnot stood trial first. Charged with "exciting and stirring up the Creek Indians" as well as "acting as a spy, aiding and abetting the enemy," he undertook his own defense. While not denying that he had supplied Boleck's people with ten kegs of gunpowder, he claimed that that amount was no more than was necessary for hunting—a reasonable argument. The letter to his son warning of Jackson's advance was written, he claimed, to protect his personal property from destruction. Finally, Arbuthnot threw himself upon the mercy of the court, "persuaded that sympathy nowhere more abounds than in a generous American breast."[18]

In fact, Arbuthnot's greatest "crime" was befriending the Seminoles. Through his honest dealings he had gained the tribes' trust to such a degree that they had extended to him power of attorney.

Arbuthnot had not instigated the Seminole War—the attack upon Fowltown in November had done that. He had only warned the Seminoles not to trust the words or treaties of the Americans. Nonetheless, the military jury found him guilty and sentenced him to be hanged.[19]

Ambrister came next. This veteran of the Napoleonic Wars had in fact come to Florida with the intent of leading the Seminoles in battle against the Americans. Yet he too was guilty primarily of encouraging the Seminoles to stand up for their rights in the face of United States expansionism along the southern frontier—an unpardonable crime in the eyes of Jackson.[20] After first sentencing Ambrister to be shot, the jury reconsidered and reduced his penalty to fifty lashes and a year's hard labor. Jackson set aside this reconsideration, reimposed the first sentence on Ambrister, and affirmed that of Arbuthnot. He wanted the execution of the two Britons to serve as "an awful example" to the Seminoles.[21] Here lay the true meaning of the execution of the two men. Jackson, indeed most Americans, could not accept the fact that Seminole attacks on border settlements might be legitimate acts of self-defense against an expansionist neighbor. Instead, Jackson maintained the fiction that there were "good Indians" (those who submitted to American demands) and "bad Indians" (those who did not), the latter usually having been led astray by evil white men.[22] In this way Arbuthnot and Ambrister functioned as scapegoats for a nation incapable of confronting its own acts of injustice. Never mind questions of jurisdiction and impartiality (the jury was hardly composed of peers of the condemned men): for a few short weeks in 1818, Andrew Jackson was the law in Florida. On the morning of 29 April, Arbuthnot was hanged from the yardarm of his own schooner, and Ambrister faced a firing squad.

Jackson did not stay to witness the executions. Early on 29 April the general and 1,200 men marched west toward Pensacola, the capital of West Florida. He informed Calhoun of his plans, charging that the Spanish garrison there harbored four or five hundred Seminoles warriors. Pensacola, he wrote, "must be occupied by American force."[23]

Meanwhile, an incident occurred in Georgia that in retrospect seems an inevitable outgrowth of Jackson's indiscriminate violence in Florida. On orders from the governor of Georgia, a company of militiamen under the command of Major Obed Wright descended upon the Creek village of Chehaw and slaughtered a dozen men, women, and children, including the chief. Wright's men then burned the village to the ground. Tragically, nearly all the men of the Chehaw village were away at the time of the attack—serving under Jackson in Florida. In fact, these villagers had fed Jackson's half-starved troops during their march from Tennessee to Fort Scott. Now their town had been destroyed by an unauthorized act of wanton destruction and murder, made possible by the Indian-hating hysteria the Seminole War had unleashed. Jackson was outraged by the incident and wrote to the governor of Georgia demanding Wright's prosecution.[24] The general prided himself on what he considered an ability to treat native Americans with fairness; moreover, he realized that the massacre threatened his efforts to "pacify" the tribes of the region. Yet Jackson must share the guilt for the Chehaw massacre because he contributed to an atmosphere that legitimated the destruction of villages and the slaughter of native Americans. As for Wright, a Georgia jury eventually found him innocent of any wrongdoing.[25]

On 24 May, Jackson and his army seized Pensacola, driving the Spanish territorial governor and his men to nearby Fort Barrancas. After a brief siege the garrison surrendered. Jackson then declared Pensacola a United States revenue district and deported the Spanish governor and his troops to Havana. The capture of West Florida was complete. Jackson wrote to a friend: "All that I regret was that I had not stormed the works, captured the governor, put him on trial for the murder of Stokes and his family [Americans settlers killed by the Seminoles], and hung him for the deed."[26]

Jackson had not found the hundreds of Seminole warriors whose supposed presence had justified the attack on Pensacola. In fact, the general produced no substantive evidence whatever of the presence of any Seminoles near Pensacola, with the exception of about a hundred old men, women, and children whom the Spanish governor had sent north with an American officer for resettlement.[27] The alleged presence of hostiles was an excuse to allow Jackson to capture Pensacola, as he stated he would do in his letter of 6 January. His stationing of two hundred men at St. Mark's, the establishment of a garrison at the Negro Fort (which he renamed Fort Gadsden), and his orders to General Gaines (subsequently countermanded by Calhoun) to seize St. Augustine, are further evidence that from the very beginning Jackson planned to seize both East and West Florida from Spain. In his 6 January letter, Jackson had promised to deliver both Floridas within sixty days. From the time he entered the province, it actually took him seventy-nine.

During the spring of 1818, reports of Jackson's exploits, often unverified, trickled northward. Adams watched nervously. At this critical stage, neither he nor Calhoun nor Monroe sent Jackson any further orders clarifying his mission or warning him not to seize the Spanish posts. Onís, lacking confirmation of the rumors of Jackson's depredations, for the time being chose to ignore them and left Washington for his summer home in Bristol, Pennsylvania. Monroe, too, departed the capital for a vacation at his farm in Loudon County, Virginia. Adams remained in Washington, bathing frequently in the Potomac to escape the stifling heat.

In mid-June, Onís received word from the governor of Pensacola of the capture of St. Mark's, and immediately dispatched a strongly worded letter of protest to Adams, describing Jackson's actions as "enormous vexations, unexampled in history." Yet he chose to believe that the administration had not sanctioned the invasion, expecting that once all the facts were in, St. Mark's would be restored to Spain.[28] Onís's faith in American good intentions was undiminished even by reports a week later of the capture of Pensacola. Again he wrote for clarification of the administration's position.[29] Only when he received direct word from the governor of Pensacola confirming the capture of the town and the full dimensions of Jackson's actions did Onís return to Washington, rousing Adams from his bed on 8 July with the charge that "peace [has] been violated, and rights trampled under foot." Onís correctly asserted that neither he nor the governor of West Florida had been notified of the war against the Seminoles. He concluded that "the war against the Seminoles has been merely a pretext for General Jackson to fall, as a conqueror, upon the Spanish provinces . . . for the purpose of establishing there the dominion of this republic upon the odious basis of violence and bloodshed"— strong language from a diplomat, yet a painfully precise description of how the United States first came to control the province of Florida.

In spite of everything, however, Onís still refused to believe that the administration "authorized this hostile, bloody, and ferocious invasion of the dominions of Spain." He quoted from Monroe's address to Congress on 25 March that "if, in the course of the [Seminole] war, it should be necessary to enter into the Spanish territory, the authorities of Spain are to be respected and their territory evacuated the moment the war is at an end." That statement, combined with the administration's repeated assurances of pacific intentions toward Spain, led Onís to conclude that "General Jackson has acted contrary to the orders of the president." The Spanish minister awaited the speedy return of St. Mark's and Pensacola and the punishment of Jackson.[30]

Onís was not alone in his astonishment at Jackson's exploits.

Newspaper editorialists were mixed in their response to Old Hickory's bold moves. In general, editors sympathetic to the administration applauded the action, while those in opposition condemned it as a breach of the Constitution.[31] Few could acknowledge that it had actually been either the administration's or Jackson's intent to seize the Floridas. In Washington, Adams awaited Monroe's return, commenting that "the storm is rapidly thickening."

On 15 July, Monroe's cabinet met to decide how to handle the Jackson affair. All present considered that Jackson had exceeded his orders and that his actions must be disavowed—all, that is, except John Quincy Adams. He contended that "there was no real, though an apparent, violation of the instructions, that the proceedings were justified by the necessity of the case, and by the misconduct of the Spanish commanding officers in Florida." Adams argued that although only Congress had the right to declare war, the executive could "authorize hostilities . . . defensively." Calhoun came out strongly in favor of disavowing the general. Both Calhoun and Crawford had personal reasons for wishing Jackson to be publicly rebuked: each man saw in Jackson a rival to his own presidential hopes. But it is also clear that Calhoun, Crawford, and Monroe feared that the repercussions of the invasion could bring down the administration. After five long hours of debate, Adams "obtained an adjournment of the question" without any final decision.[32]

Calhoun's intense desire to disavow Jackson's actions deserves close scrutiny. It is a fascinating case of "what did the secretary of war know and when did he know it?" The legitimacy of Calhoun's anti-Jackson stand hinges on the plausibility of his belief that the general did in fact willfully exceed his orders, and the likelihood that Jackson's "Rhea letter" of 6 January requesting covert approval for a conquest of the Floridas was unknown to Calhoun and Monroe. Yet this scenario seems doubtful. First, as Bemis asserts, "it is certain that the Secretary of War, if not the President himself, well knew the contents of Jackson's letter of January 6 as soon as it was received in Washington."[33] This virtual certainty, combined with Calhoun and Monroe's open-ended instructions of 26 and 28 December and their subsequent failure to clarify the mission to Jackson, makes his alleged violation of orders dubious. Are we to believe that Calhoun's razor-sharp mind "forgot" about the letter of 6 January during the extended cabinet debate on the matter? Moreover, if Monroe and Calhoun sought only a narrowly punitive cross-border raid, why did they replace the competent Gaines with Jackson, a man notorious for boldness? Finally, it is clear that the acquisition of the Floridas and the removal of the Indians from the Southeast were at the top of Calhoun's (and the South's) priorities. Calhoun's readiness at the first sign of controversy to disavow Jackson's indisputable success in the Floridas appears retrospectively to have been an act of utter cynicism. If Calhoun and Monroe were truly afraid of Jackson's potential as a military usurper of civilian authority, they would not have placed him at the head of a column marching into the Floridas with orders to "adopt the necessary measures to terminate the conflict." The evidence suggests that Calhoun was using Jackson's alleged violation of orders as a means to neutralize a potential political rival. Small wonder that Jackson would go to his grave regretting that he had not had the chance to hang John C. Calhoun.[34]

The cabinet met again the following day, concerned that public and world opinion demanded Jackson's censure yet uncertain as to the form that censure should take. Crawford feared that outright disavowal might prompt Jackson's resignation from the army and bring the wrath of the general's huge public following down on the administration. It became clear that the challenge was to devise a way to restore the captured posts to Spain without seeming to disavow Jackson's actions—a formidable task. Again the cabinet adjourned undecided.[35]

On 17 July, Adams repeated his argument that Jackson had acted defensively, appealing "first to the facts, then to the laws of nations, and lastly to the Constitution" to defend his opinion.[36] Slowly, a response began to take shape. Monroe decided to send a "friendly letter" to Jackson, complimenting the general for valiant service to his country yet explaining the "constitutional grounds upon which Pensacola would be restored to Spain."[37] Left undetermined was what language Adams would use to answer the Spanish protest. On 20 July, Adams arrived at "a new point of view": that the governor of West Florida had threatened to drive Jackson out of the province by force and that the general seized Pensacola as "his only alternative . . . to prevent the execution of the threat." Even Adams recognized the absurdity of this explanation: "I admitted that it was necessary to carry the reasoning upon my principles to the utmost extent it would bear to come to this conclusion—But if the question was dubious, it was better to err on the side of vigor than on the side of weakness—on the side of an officer who had rendered the most eminent service to his nation than on the side of our bitterest enemies."[38]

Adams's formulation of the Jackson affair is interesting for two reasons. First, the question was not "dubious." Jackson's invasion of the Floridas—either done without orders, as Calhoun alleged, or done with the tacit authorization of the president, as seems more likely—was a significant transgression of the executive's constitutional prerogative. Only by constructing a tenuous rationalization did Adams make the issue "dubious." It was less a question of deciding between "an officer who had rendered the most eminent service to his nation" and "our bitterest enemies" that it was a choice between endorsing a significant expansion of executive warmaking power and adhering to the founding principles of the American Constitution. Yet given Adams's critique of congressional warmaking powers and the stakes involved in the Jackson affair, it is not surprising that he strongly supported the actions of Old Hickory.

Adams summed up the situation in his diary entry of 21 July: "The administration were [sic] placed in a dilemma from which it is impossible to escape censure by some, and factious recriminations by many. If they avow and approve Jackson's conduct, they incur the double responsibility of having committed a war against Spain, and of warring in violation of the Constitution without the authority of Congress. If they disavowed him, they must give offense to all his friends, encounter the shock of his popularity, and have the appearance of truckling to Spain. For all this I should be prepared. But the mischief of this determination lies deeper. (1) It is weakness and a confession of weakness. (2) The disclaimer of power in the executive is a dangerous example; and of evil consequences. (3) There is injustice to the officer in disavowing him, when in principle he is strictly justified."[39]

At this point, Adams had convinced himself that his tortuous defense of Jackson was not only expedient but true. How can one explain this delusion? The answer lies in Adams's personal stake in the outcome of the negotiations with Spain and his awareness of the crucial part Jackson's actions played in bringing Onís to terms. Adams's long experience as a diplomat made him aware that to censure Jackson, whatever the constitutional grounds for doing so, invited further intransigence at the bargaining table, where power, not principle, was the ultimate determinant. Although Jackson had gone farther in "chastising" the Seminoles than Adams would have liked, to disavow the general now would undermine and perhaps erase the gains Adams had made at the bargaining table since the previous December. Moreover, Adams knew that empire building required an executive with broader warmaking powers than the Constitution allowed. In that sense the Jackson affair stood as an important precedent from which there could be no retreat.

Equally if not more important than the constitutional issues involved were the compelling personal reasons Adams had for defending Jackson. Adams's hopes for the presidency hinged on the success of the negotiations with Spain. His reputation as an ardent expansionist, first established when he supported the Louisiana Purchase, had been essential to his success as a Republican. Now he hoped to complete the work of Jefferson by defining the boundaries of Louisiana in the most expansive way possible. If Adams could deliver a favorable treaty, he could present himself as the "man of the whole nation" and indisputably the next president. To disavow Jackson would be to renounce his only leverage in dealing with Onís—the threat of military force. Without this threat Spain might never agree to cede the Floridas or to formalize a western boundary favorable to the United States. Adams knew that such an outcome would dash his hopes for the presidency by making him appear to be an ineffectual secretary of state.

In defending Jackson, Adams was acting in what he perceived to be his own and the nation's self-interest. He had not taken part in the decision to order Jackson into Florida; that had been done by Monroe and Calhoun.[40] Nevertheless, events now gave Adams the largest personal interest in seeing that Jackson was defended. Adams's determined defense of the Seminole War campaign saved the general from probable censure and disgrace. It is impossible to know how this would have affected Jackson's future political career, but one can safely say that it would not have helped it. Ironically, it did not occur to Adams that Jackson might someday be a rival for the presidency.[41] Had Adams been able to see into the future, perhaps he would have chosen a different course.[42]

The July cabinet meetings revealed the dominant influence Adams had on the other members of the administration. He had found the words to defend what was seemingly indefensible and then, by tenacious argument, had convinced his colleagues of the efficacy of his explanation. Few times in his long public career were his rhetorical skills more severely challenged or more impressively demonstrated.

Accordingly, his note to Onís of 23 July, the result of a week's worth of cabinet haggling, in essence defended Jackson's conduct. Although Adams claims to have "given in" to the views of the other cabinet members, the note represents the substantive triumph of his position. He began by calling Onís's attention "to a series of events which necessitated and justified the entrance of United States troops" into Florida. He charged that "the treacherous, unrelenting, and exterminating character of Indian hostilities" along the Georgia-Florida border violated Pinckney's Treaty of 1795, which obligated Spain to restrain such activities. Adams denied that the Seminoles had any just motive for their actions: "The permanent and unvarying policy of the United States with regard to all of the Indian tribes within their borders is that of peace, friendship, and liberality." He asserted that "for many years" the United States had not fought "with any Indian tribe, unless stimulated by the influence of foreign incendiaries."[43]

Having justified the mission to chastise the Seminoles, Adams undertook to defend the capture of St. Mark's and Pensacola. He charged that the governor of Pensacola was guilty of giving "succor" to the Seminoles, as well as endangering Jackson's men by exacting "exorbitant duties" on American supply boats ascending the Apalachicola River. Adams claimed that a "large body" of Seminoles "were overtaken, surprised, and defeated" by Jackson "within one mile of Pensacola." These facts, combined with the governor's "threatening" letter denouncing Jackson's "aggression against Spain," made necessary the capture of St. Mark's and Pensacola.[44]

These charges had no basis in fact. Jackson produced no evidence (Adams's claims to the contrary) that the governor of Pensacola aided any Seminoles beyond the few refugees who were escorted to Georgia. Far from being charged "exorbitant duties," the supply boat had in fact been given special permission by the governor to pass through Spanish territory and had been charged with the standard rates.[45] No record exists of Jackson's having engaged any "large body" of Seminoles near Pensacola, or anywhere else in Florida during the entire campaign. In fact, the terrified tribes fled Old Hickory's overwhelming force. This leaves the governor's "threatening letter" to Jackson as the sole remaining justification for the seizure of the posts—a hollow threat indeed, when one considers the disparity between the Spanish and American forces.

Adams's argument is a classic example of blaming the victim, whereby the aggrieved party is held responsible for provoking the aggressor. Adams concluded his audacious communiqué by demanding the punishment of the Spanish colonial officials "who, the President is persuaded, have then acted contrary to the express orders of their sovereign." As a post-script, Adams casually added that Pensacola would be returned to any duly authorized Spanish official, and that St. Mark's, "being in the heart of Indian country," would be delivered to any Spanish force sufficiently strong to hold it.[46] Thus the administration solved the problem of how to return the captured posts without seeming to disavow Jackson.

As a historical document, Adams's 23 July note to Onís stands as a monumental distortion of the causes and conduct of Jackson's conquest of Florida, reminding historians not to search for truth in official explanations of events. Yet as a diplomatic instrument, the note worked extremely well. It served notice to Onís that Monroe and Adams would meet public criticism of Jackson's aggression with a vigorous, self-righteous counterargument. Onís could not use the situation to gain easy advantage in the court of international opinion. This would prove to be crucial, for even as the cabinet deliberated what to do about the Jackson affair, the negotiations reached a critical turning point.

On 8 July, the day Onís returned to Washington to protest formally the invasion of Florida, he told Adams of new instructions he had just received from Madrid giving him greater latitude to compromise than he had been given to date. The Spaniard asserted, however, that the Jackson affair erected a new obstacle to a settlement.[47] On 10 July, Adams met with Baron Jean Guillaume Hyde de Neuville, France's minister to the United States, who bore an important message: Spain was willing to cede the Floridas in exchange for a compromise on the claims question and a western boundary beginning at the Sabine River (the present Louisiana-Texas boundary). Hyde added that it was not necessary to answer the Spanish protest over the invasion of Florida for a "month or two," or "perhaps not at all if in the meantime we could come to an arrangement of the other differences." Adams termed the proposal of a western boundary at the Sabine "impossible"; but the meeting made clear that rather than provoking war with Spain or interrupting the negotiations, Jackson's actions might serve as a lever to extract further concessions from Madrid.

On 11 July, Adams and Onís met again in what would prove a landmark session in the negotiations. Onís began with a muted protest of the invasion but added that the events in Florida need not interrupt the negotiations. He followed with a new western boundary proposal: along the course of either the Mermento or Calcasieu Rivers (about 100 miles west of the mouth of the Mississippi), north along the Arroyo Hondo, between Los Adaes and Natchitoches, to the Red River, and along its course to the Missouri. From there, Onís proposed a boundary running along the Missouri to its source, or a line to be determined by joint commission. This offer represented an important Spanish concession; theretofore Madrid had clung to a western boundary approximating the Mississippi River. Adams recognized that the offer represented a significant change in the Spanish position, and he responded with an equally surprising counteroffer: a western boundary beginning at the Bahia de San Bernardo in Texas (the mouth of the Colorado), along the course of the river to its source, then north to the Missouri and following that river to its source, and from there *a line directly to the Pacific coast.*

This "suggestion," as Adams termed it, was the first mention of a transcontinental boundary. Previously, the administration's claims had extended no farther west than the front range of the Rockies. Onís, taken aback by this startling new proposal, accused Adams of wanting to dispossess Spain of all territories claimed in the Northwest by Juan de Fuca. Adams termed this charge "foolishness" (*delirio*), pointing to the conflicting claims of Great Britain and Russia to the region and asserting that the United States had the strongest right to the Columbia River because it had established settlements at its mouth and therefore needed to open communications to the interior.[48]

This critical conversation between Adams and Onís ended without agreement, yet both parties knew that the negotiations had entered a new phase. Onís returned to Bristol to await formal reply to his protest; the honor of the king of Spain required that his minister not appear to continue negotiating while American troops occupied Florida. The negotiations did continue, however, through the good offices of Hyde de Neuville.

The French minister, a respected member of the diplomatic corps, friend to both Adams and Onís, and frequent dinner host to Mrs. Adams, played a crucial role in the negotiations from this point on. On 16 July, the same day the cabinet gathered to discuss the Jackson affair, Adams made an oral offer of a western boundary to Hyde de Neuville, to be communicated by him to Onís. The new offer, "agreed to at the president's," differed significantly from that made by Adams to Onís only five days earlier. It began by following the Trinity River in Texas "from its mouth to its source, then a line due north to the Red River, following the course of that river to its source, then crossing the Rio del Norte [Rio Grande], and following the course of it, or the summit of a chain of mountains northward and parallel to it; then stop, or take a line west to the Pacific" (see map 4).[49] Although still transcontinental, this new line to the Pacific began at a point several hundred miles south of the line Adams had suggested on 11 July. One cannot be certain why Monroe and Adams arrived at such dramatically different terms over a period of five days. Perhaps, as Samuel Flagg Bemis suggests, Onís misunderstood Adams's offer of 11 July.[50] Perhaps the offer of 11 July was designed as a ploy to keep Onís from storming out of the negotiations and withdrawn once it became clear that he would not do so. In any event, Hyde de Neuville soon departed for Bristol with both the administration's reply to the Jackson protest and a new boundary proposal.

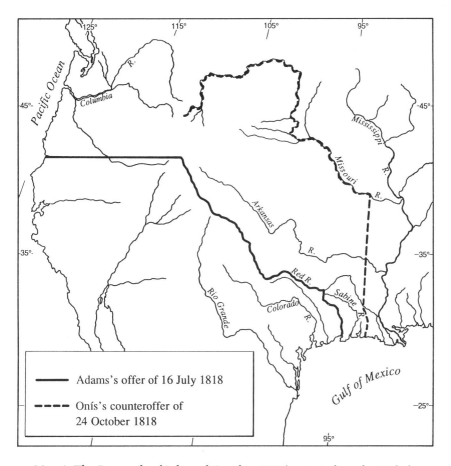

Map 4. The Proposals of July and October 1818 (projected on the Melish map of 1818)

One might wonder why Onís, confronted by overt aggression against the possessions of his country, would continue to negotiate with Adams. The simple fact is that he had no choice. To break off the talks now, with Jackson in Florida and no European powers emerging to assist Spain, would invite the Americans to take possession not only of the Floridas but of Texas as well. Spain was in danger of losing, without compensation, all the territories the United States coveted. Onís urged Pizarro that he be allowed to make the best deal possible, noting that Spain's bargaining position "certainly won't be better for a long time."[51]

The map of Spanish North America showed Onís an empire besieged. Jackson's invasion was only the latest assault. American troops still occupied Amelia Island. In Texas, Bonapartist exiles under the command of Henri L'Allemand were plotting to seize the province, preparing one more in a long line of guerrilla attacks on the Gulf Coast region.[52] Galveston remained occupied by the Lafitte gang, whose privateers harassed Spanish shipping, hindering resupply efforts. Onís recognized that Spain could not defend its interests militarily and that no European power had shown any inclination to do so. Spain stood alone in its dispute with the United States, and Onís had sufficient experience as a diplomat to know that no matter how humiliating, he must continue the negotiations or invite further American aggression. This explains the infinitely understanding tone of his letters of protest, as he contrived to give the administration every benefit of the doubt regarding the invasion of Florida. In an implacably difficult position, Onís swallowed hard and prepared to make the best deal he could.

The breakthrough on the western boundary question also explains the zeal with which Adams defended Jackson in the July cabinet meetings. While the administration debated what to do about events in Florida, Adams had already gotten a taste of a potentially monumental transcontinental boundary which whetted his already substantial appetite for a treaty with Spain.

During July 1818 the focus of the negotiations shifted from the acquisition of the Floridas (Spain's cession of them being already assured) to the delineation of a transcontinental boundary between Spanish possessions and the United States. The question remains, why did Monroe and Adams now propose a boundary to the Pacific? All previous demands had extended no further west than the front range of the Rockies. Was it because, as Bemis suggests, Monroe and Adams had not previously understood the relationship between the Anglo-American Northwest boundary question and the Spanish-American dispute in the Southwest? [53]

This explanation does justice neither to Monroe and Adams nor to the facts of the situation. The president and his secretary of state, with nearly fifty years of diplomatic experience between them, could not have overlooked the implications of defining a western boundary with Spain east of the Rockies while still contending with Great Britain and Russia for control of the Northwest. Moreover, the record reveals that Monroe and Adams's diplomacy had linked the two questions from the start. Biddle's reoccupation of Astoria (accomplished in August 1818) was the first step. The Yellowstone Expedition of 1818-19 (more commonly known as the Long-Atkinson Expedition) aimed to establish American control of the upper Missouri River watershed. Conceived in late 1817 as a pet project of

Monroe and Calhoun, the thousand-man expedition's ostensibly scientific nature masked other purposes. Calhoun stated its aim to be
"the protection of our northwestern frontier and the greater extension of our fur trade."[54] Although the Yellowstone Expedition was
concerned primarily with lessening British influence in the Northwest, one must conclude that it also planned to extinguish the lingering Spanish claims to the region. Finally, in late May 1818 the
administration had instructed Richard Rush in London to begin talks
focused on resolving the Anglo-American dispute over the Northwest.[55]

Monroe and Adams were moving toward establishing a transcontinental boundary long before Adams first suggested it to Onís in July
1818. Indeed, American diplomats had yearned for a "window on the
Pacific" since the time of Jefferson (see Chapter 1). The proposal
certainly did not surprise Onís; he had long claimed that the United
States had a "grand plan" to expand to the Pacific.[56] That the transcontinental proposal was not made sooner is explained by the shrewd
negotiating strategy of Monroe and Adams and, more important, by
their fear of a negative domestic reaction.

Charles K. Webster has observed that diplomatists sometimes
reach agreement by a circuitous route, that the art of negotiation
requires knowing when to propose what is most desired.[57] A proposal
made too soon risks being bargained away; made too late, it risks
interfering with progress achieved on other issues. The challenge is to
introduce one's maximum demand only when circumstances are
most favorable to its being agreed upon. Webster's model explains
why Monroe and Adams waited until they did to propose a transcontinental boundary. To have made such a proposal in early 1818, in light
of ten years of Spanish insistence on a western boundary at the
Mississippi, would have been futile; neither Onís's instructions nor
the power relationships existing at the time between the two nations
would have allowed him to consider it. By July, however, the situation
had changed dramatically. In the wake of the Amelia Island occupation and the Jackson affair, Onís knew that the United States was
moving to assert its claims militarily. His goal in the talks had shifted
from hemming the United States in at the Mississippi to negotiating
a boundary that would ensure the security of Texas and New Mexico.
Monroe and Adams sensed that, with the pressure on, this was the
time to make their maximum demand of a transcontinental boundary, particularly when they could hold out to Onís a tantalizing
tradeoff—concession of Texas.

In short, Monroe and Adams planned to obtain a transcontinental boundary in exchange for United States claims to Texas. Although Adams later said he had opposed the eventual retreat to the Sabine River as a western boundary, the transcontinental offer of 16 July—which he and Monroe had arrived at jointly—in substance did concede Texas. That offer proposed that the western boundary begin along the Trinity River of Texas, less than seventy-five miles from the Sabine. Adams's diary of July 1818 contains no record of his objecting to the tradeoff of Texas for the Northwest. His later protestations that he did object, in light of the political climate of sectionalism in which they were made, must be viewed skeptically.[58]

The sectional controversy is a second reason why Monroe and Adams waited to propose a transcontinental boundary. Had the American public, particularly in the South and West, known in advance of the plan to exchange Texas for the Northwest, it is likely that the outcry would have prevented the Treaty of 1819. As it happened, Adams made no *written* proposal to Onís of the deal until October, and the public knew virtually nothing of it until the treaty was presented to Congress for ratification. Adams's last public boundary offer, that of 12 March, had asserted Americans claims as far south as the Rio Grande, but by July he and Monroe had conceded Texas. It is easy to understand why the two men wanted that fact kept secret as long as possible.

July 1818 was an exhausting month for John Quincy Adams. The uproar over Jackson's invasion, combined with his other official duties, consumed all his energies, leaving little time for his wife or for much-needed rest. What sleep he did get was disturbed by the stifling temperatures of a Washington summer which made it "scarcely possible to lie on the bed." The chronic weakness and palsy in his right hand worsened so that he could barely write.[59]

Adams was not alone in his distress. The pressure and anxiety created by the Jackson affair also took its toll on Monroe. Adams wrote that the president was "so much absorbed in the subject that he rebels at thinking of any other," at times stopping in midsentence to say "something about Jackson and Pensacola."[60] At the end of the month, the weary Monroe returned to his farm in Virginia for rest.

Not so Adams. He remained in Washington to monitor both domestic and international reactions to the Jackson invasion. He was pessimistic about the chances for a favorable outcome to the crisis. On 11 July, his fifty-first birthday (and, coincidentally, the first day he suggested the transcontinental boundary to Onís), Adams prayed for God's help in surmounting the "trial I am now undergoing." He prayed "above all, that 'till I die, I may not suffer my integrity to depart from me, and that whatever dispensation of Providence hereafter awaits me, I may be prepared to receive it with prudence, temperance, justice, and fortitude."[61]

Adams's prayers for the preservation of his integrity reveal the profound crisis of conscience he experienced as a result of his actions as secretary of state. Perhaps more than any other statesman of the early republic, he had believed in the Jeffersonian idea that there was but one code of morality for nations as well as individuals. This principle resonated with everything in his puritan heritage; it was central to the belief that the American Revolution marked the birth of a *novus ordo seclorum*—a new world order. As late as 1816, in response to naval hero Stephen Decatur's famous toast "My country right or wrong," Adams had written to his father that "I cannot ask of Heaven success even for my country in a cause where she should be in the wrong. . . . I declaim as unsound all patriotism incompatible with the principles of eternal justice."[62]

Now, less than two years after expressing these sentiments, Adams found himself embroiled in an ethical quagmire in which "patriotism" seemed opposed to the "principles of eternal justice." As secretary of state, he had consciously distorted, dissembled, and lied about the goals and conduct of American foreign policy to both the Congress and the public so that a slave labor-based society he loathed could expand into the Floridas. Adams had begun to discover that fulfilling one's destiny might involve compromises of one's personal integrity previously unsuspected.

In a recent study of Jefferson's foreign policy, Robert W. Tucker and David C. Hendrickson have suggested that " 'reason and morality' without reference to 'power and expediency' can subtly derange a statecraft, subvert the modest tasks of diplomacy, and end in betraying both physical security and economic interest."[63] It is a restatement of the classic "realist" perspective of American foreign policy. Yet the formulation fails to recognize that the goals of early American diplomacy, far from being "modest," were (and remain) to remake the world in America's image. The assertion of a liberal international commercial system in the face of the established mercantile order was vigorously pursued precisely because it was presumed to be based on "reason and morality" rather than "power and expediency." "Balance of power" politics lacked legitimacy because it was founded on "power and expediency" rather than "reason and morality," the touchstones of the American Revolution.

Adams, again perhaps more than any other American statesman of his time, was acutely aware that "reason and morality" were not subject to being tempered by "power and expediency." He knew well that it is the ability to resist the temptations of expediency and the lure of power that characterize a truly moral man and nation. He recognized that once a statesman and a nation ventured down the slippery slope of "power and expediency" there could be little hope of turning back. In the end, there is no dichotomy between the morality of the statesman and the morality of the nation—the two are an identity. The choices of the statesman define not just the nation's morality but that of the statesman as well. To put it another way, Adams had believed his entire life that holding public office carried with it the burden of moral leadership and that a truly moral nation could not be led by immoral men. Abigail Adams's admonitions continued to intrude on the consciousness of the secretary of state. He sensed that his defense of Jackson not only violated his own integrity but also betrayed the hope that the United States would not adopt the corrupt practices and rationales of European diplomacy. His prayers indicate his regret for the portion of his integrity that he feared was already lost.

SIX

Onís Brought to a Point

Don Luis de Onís responded to Adams's defense of Jackson's conduct by rebutting the secretary's assertions point by point. He rejected the charge that Spanish troops had failed to restrain the Seminoles from cross-border forays into Georgia, claiming that correspondence from the Spanish governor in Florida indicated instead that the tribesmen had frequently protested attacks by North Americans. He alluded to other documents that contradicted allegations of interference with the American supply convoy and of aiding and abetting Seminole warriors. Onís demanded Jackson's punishment, yet he pledged to investigate the actions of the Spanish officials in Florida and mete out suitable punishment should any wrongdoing on their part be discovered.[1]

Although he disagreed with Adams's assessment of Jackson's activities in Florida, Onís ended his note by repeating his wish for a comprehensive settlement of the Spanish-American controversy. He claimed to have "no doubt" that his new instructions from Madrid would allow for a "treaty mutually satisfactory" to both sides. Yet his official optimism masked a private pessimism that bordered on despair. He wrote to Pizarro of the difficulties in negotiating amidst the "democratic demagogues" and "rabid Jacobinism" of Washington and recommended that the talks be shifted to Madrid.[2] He warned that the mounting impatience of the administration combined with the warlike, anti-Spanish mood of the public might lead to recognition of South American independence and possibly a declaration of war against Spain by the end of the next session of Congress.[3] Onís pleaded that Spain not rely on the European powers, especially Great Britain, to assist in the dispute with the United States. Nor, he added, should too much faith be put in the so-called "good offices" of Hyde de Neuville, for he judged the French minister to be under orders to ingratiate himself and his nation with the United States government, even at the price of "sacrificing the interests of [France's] most intimate ally," Spain. Once again, Onís called for compromise with the South American states as the only solution to Spain's difficulties.[4]

In spite of his official protestations, Onís still believed that an agreement might be reached. He wrote to Pizarro that Monroe and Adams wanted a settlement before the beginning of the next session of Congress but noted three points upon which they would not compromise. First, they would accept no clause prohibiting recognition of the South American insurgent governments by the United States. Second, they would not agree to draw the Texas border any farther east than the Sabine River. Third, they were adamant that the treaty include a western boundary allowing access to the Pacific Ocean via the Columbia River.[5] A settlement along these lines would fulfill a major Spanish objective: establishment of a recognized boundary between the United States and the "borderlands" of New Spain. Unfortunately for Onís, his instructions as of early August 1818 prevented him from settling according to these terms. At that point, he was not empowered to offer a western boundary extending west of the Missouri River. Nor was he allowed to settle without extracting a pledge of nonrecognition from the United States. Onís could see the outlines of a treaty but a majority of the Consejo de Estado (primarily those members who were part of the *camarilla*) refused him powers sufficient to reach agreement. As a result, Onís attempted to stall Adams, pledging his willingness to negotiate while still lacking the authority to do so effectively.

Meanwhile, Monroe and Adams worked to paint Spain more tightly into a diplomatic corner. Even as the startling news of Jackson's execution of two Britons reverberated throughout Great Britain, negotiations were under way to resolve the remaining differences of the combatants of the War of 1812. The talks, if successful, would signal a new phase of Anglo-American reconciliation and extinguish once and for all Spanish hopes for British aid in resolving the dispute with the United States.

The spring of 1818 seemed a perfect time for Great Britain and the United States to settle the issues that had caused the War of 1812. Time and mutual interest had cooled passions sufficiently so that thorny subjects such as impressment, compensation for slaves seized by the British, and the rights of American fisherman in the waters of British North America might be resolved. Commercial questions also loomed large. The Commercial Convention of 1815 would soon expire, and the United States wanted the terms of bilateral trade modified to allow for unrestricted access to British colonial possessions in the Western Hemisphere, especially the West Indies. Finally, and most important in the context of the dispute with Spain, the United States and Great Britain needed to demarcate the Canadian-American boundary from the Lake of the Woods to the Pacific. The border separating Canada from the United States had been vaguely defined since the time of independence; the problem took on added significance now that both nations had a growing interest in the northwest coast.

In early 1818 all signs pointed to a settlement of these issues. From London, Richard Rush wrote of the conciliatory attitude of the British government generally and of Castlereagh in particular. Rush reported conversations in which the British foreign secretary indicated a willingness to compromise on the slave and boundary issues and even hinted that Parliament might consent to reopen the British West Indies trade to American merchants.[6] This last item had been for decades the great desideratum of the merchant interests of the Northeast.

Great Britain's restrained response to the impending reoccupation of Astoria by Captain Biddle provided further evidence of its conciliatory mood. Although Bagot had registered a polite protest upon hearing in November 1817 of the expedition to the northwest coast, he was mollified by Adams's assurances of the peaceful intentions of the mission. Adams pushed the issue in private talks with Bagot on 15 May 1818. Asserting that "no force was intended to be used" in the occupation of Astoria, Adams claimed that U.S. rights to the Columbia River region dated to the "purchase of a large tract of the country made from the Indians in the year 1787."[7]

In May, Adams wrote to Rush clarifying the administration's view of the Astoria situation. He claimed that Great Britain had not been informed of the Biddle expedition because of Monroe's "absence from the seat of government" when the mission began. In any event, Adams boldly asserted, Britain could not be offended by American efforts to exert control over the northwest coast in light of U.S. willingness to acquiesce in British control of other parts of the globe. He argued that it was "not consistent either with a wise or friendly policy" for Great Britain to "watch with jealousy and alarm every possibility of extension of our natural dominion in North America."[8] Castlereagh chose to overlook this high-handed assertion of American "rights"; indeed, he instructed the British commanders at Astoria to cooperate in the restoration of the post to the Americans. Rush wrote that despite the Astoria issue, his talks with the foreign secretary did not contain "a single expression not adopted to the good feelings . . . between the two governments."[9]

Under these auspices a general negotiation of all the points at issue between the United States and Great Britain began in July 1818.

Adams ordered Albert Gallatin to vacate his post as minister to France temporarily and journey to London to take charge of the talks. In making the move, Adams alluded to Gallatin's "long experience and great knowledge," but the change also indicates what little faith Monroe and Adams had in the talents of Rush, described by Rufus King as being "a soft and empty pedant."[10]

Castlereagh welcomed the prospect of cementing Anglo-American relations. The uncertainty attached to the upcoming congress of European sovereigns at Aix-la-Chapelle made him eager to resolve lingering disputes with the United States. Castlereagh did not know quite what to expect from the first conference ever held by the European powers to regulate international affairs.[11] The congress would decide whether the European alliance was to be primarily defensive in nature (as Castlereagh wished) or committed to active intervention to defend the interests of monarchy wherever it was threatened, including the Western Hemisphere.[12] Tsar Alexander of Russia, the most ardent advocate of the second view, was attempting to turn the congress into a general forum of European states along the lines of the Congress of Vienna. Essential to his plans would be securing an invitation to the conference for Ferdinand VII. If Spain's plight could be dramatized, it might create pressure on Britain to agree to take part in an armed mediation of the South American conflicts. Castlereagh, conversely, wished to confine the conference to the major European states and keep the agenda as limited as possible. He dreaded any action by the congress beyond mutual expressions of good will and a pledge to meet again.[13]

Thus, Castlereagh wanted to solidify relations with United States in order to bolster Britain's position vis-à-vis the European powers. Beginning talks with the Americans would allow Great Britain to attend the conference at Aix and vigorously oppose armed mediation efforts in the New World while being reasonably sure that the United States would not undercut that stand by recognizing one of the South American states. Castlereagh struck this note of mutual self-interest at the beginning of the Anglo-American talks when he said to Rush and Gallatin: "Let us strive to regulate our intercourse in all respects, as that each nation may be able to do its utmost towards making the other rich and happy."[14]

In Madrid, members of the Spanish ruling class eyed with great anticipation the upcoming congress at Aix-la-Chappelle. Ferdinand, encouraged by the efforts made on his behalf by his fellow monarch Alexander, still hoped that the European powers might intervene to save his New World empire from collapse. He held on to this hope

despite the opposition of Foreign Secretary Pizarro, an experienced
and savvy diplomat who knew that the Spanish empire could not be
maintained in its historic form; he wrote in his memoirs, "For me,
America was lost from the time of Cadiz (1810) . . . and in the year
1817 I had no doubts of its loss and that it was time to think of
acquiring what advantages [we could] from a separation that was now
inevitable."[15] As foreign secretary, Pizarro faced the challenge of
presiding over this inevitable decline. In 1817 and 1818 he pushed for
a policy of pacification based on colonial free trade and amnesty for
Spanish exiles to prevent the complete independence of the South
American states.

Pizarro also favored compromise in the dispute with the United
States. War with the United States would be the ultimate disaster for
Spain, endangering all of that nation's New World possessions, including Cuba. Hence, he advocated the concession of a transcontinental boundary to the United States in exchange for a secure,
recognized border for Texas. Moreover, Pizarro saw few options in
responding to Jackson's invasion of Florida. The incident served as
further evidence that Spain must either compromise or risk losing
everything. Communiqués from the Duke of San Carlos in London
confirmed his opinion that Spain could not expect British assistance
in dealing with the United States. The duke reported that Castlereagh had responded in "generalities" and with "indifference" to
the U.S. invasion of Florida.[16]

Despite the dire need for a treaty with the United States, Pizarro
still could not persuade a majority of the Consejo de Estado to grant
Onís full negotiating powers. Although the members realized that
Spain's impotence made a military response to the Jackson affair out
of the question, they would not consent to giving Onís the latitude he
needed to ensure a settlement. Indeed, the Duke of Parque, a member
of the *camarilla,* voiced his suspicion that Onís would make unacceptable concessions if given enlarged powers. He argued for the dispatch
of a second negotiator as insurance against such an outcome—a cruel
rebuke to Onís after his thirty-eight years of faithful service to the
Spanish king. Ultimately, a majority of the Consejo de Estado, to
Pizarro's frustration, decreed that Spain should continue to put its
faith in the European powers, at least until after the conference at Aix
in September. They directed Pizarro to protest formally the invasion
of Florida and suspend the negotiations until the United States condemned Jackson's conduct and restored all captured territory to
Spain. Pizarro included a concise statement of the Spanish view of
the incident in his note, which was circulated to all the courts of

Europe as well as to newspapers in the United States.[17] Onís was given no new negotiating authority as Spain continued to place its hopes on the assistance of the European powers.[18]

Back in Washington, John Quincy Adams sent instructions to the American ministers in Europe urging them to be especially vigilant in monitoring the actions of the European governments. To George Campbell, newly appointed minister to Russia, Adams wrote of the need for "observing with the most attentive assiduity" Russian relations with its European allies. Adams even suggested that Campbell cultivate clandestine sources of information within the tsarist bureaucracy, adding that Monroe relied on his "vigilance," "penetration," and "discretion."[19] To Alexander Everett at The Hague, Adams urged a "friendly intercourse with all European ministers at court" and communication of "all interesting information."[20] To both men Adams suggested "frequent and confidential" correspondence with the other American ministers in Europe in order "to extend the sphere and multiply the sources of information."

Adams, like Pizarro, knew that the success of his policies depended in large part on accurate and timely intelligence from abroad. Adams used his control of foreign intelligence to persuade the president and the Congress to support his foreign policy initiatives. Pizarro, in contrast, neither controlled the flow of foreign intelligence (he had been unaware of the Russian ship deal) nor had the full confidence of the king. These factors largely explain the difference in the effectiveness of the two statesmen.

While direct negotiations with Onís were stalled, pending the outcome of the Jackson affair, Adams endeavored to make progress toward a settlement through continued discussions with Hyde de Neuville. The French minister played a vital role in keeping the talks alive during a period in which Onís and Adams found it difficult to be in the same room together, much less reach agreement on the issues that divided their nations. In a meeting on 9 August, Hyde de Neuville reported that although Onís was "extremely anxious to preserve peace," the Spanish government would not agree to the western boundary proposals made by the United States. Adams responded strongly: "The Spanish government says, 'let there be peace,' but will agree to nothing which is necessary to secure peace."[21] Impatient and annoyed, he abruptly ended the meeting.

Adams retired to his office and brooded. Months of steadily increasing military and diplomatic pressure had failed to crack the Spanish will to resist the demands of the United States. Now the

Spanish government appeared ready to use the Jackson affair to gain sympathy and support from the European powers. But Adams had one last card, short of a declaration of war, to pressure Spain into an agreement. In early August he began to prepare to play that card.

Adams knew that recognition of South American independence by the United States was Spain's greatest fear. A North American alignment with the insurgents would extinguish all hopes for the reconquest of South America. Onís had firm instructions to break off talks with Adams should the United States open diplomatic ties with any insurgent government (see Chapter 4); this had been a major factor in preventing U.S. recognition of the insurgents. Now, however, prospects for a settlement were at best uncertain, and Spain appeared ready to procrastinate indefinitely. Therefore, with Monroe's assent, Adams began to threaten recognition in order to force concessions from Spain. Moves toward recognition would send an unambiguous signal to Madrid that the United States had lost faith in diplomacy and no longer feared the possible consequences (including a war) of an end to the talks. It was a dangerous ploy; Spain might choose to fight a war it could not win rather than capitulate to the American demands, and Adams and Monroe knew that war could be as disastrous for the United States as it would be for Spain. Nonetheless, the logic of their policy of pressure diplomacy had brought them to this point. They could not turn back.

Monroe first proposed recognizing one of the South American states in late July when he instructed Adams to suggest to Bagot "an immediate cooperation between the United States and Great Britain to promote the independence of South America."[22] Adams at that time dissuaded the president from pursuing the plan, claiming that "Great Britain was not yet prepared for such a direct proposition." Monroe temporarily abandoned his "crude" (as Adams termed it) idea. Yet by mid-August the administration showed signs of moving in the direction of recognition. At that time Adams sent to Rush in London the following dispatch: "Referring to you my late letters on the subject of South American affairs, I am now directed to enquire what part you think the British government will take in regard to the dispute between Spain and her colonies, and in what light will they view the acknowledgement of the independence of the colonies by the United States? Whether they will view it as an act of hostility to Spain, and in case Spain should declare war against us, in consequence, whether Great Britain will take part with her in it? "[23] He sent similar notes to Gallatin in Paris and Campbell in St. Petersburg.

This abrupt reversal on the South American recognition question was a bold diplomatic gambit. Adams calculated that letting the major powers of Europe (and, hence, Spain) know that the United States intended to recognize the South American patriot governments in the near future would stampede Spain into concessions rather than precipitate European intervention on Spain's behalf.

That the deadlock with Spain, rather than any substantive change in the South American struggles, caused this new policy is indicated by Adams's comments on the South American commission's long-awaited reports, delivered to Congress in November. In a cabinet meeting of 7 November, Adams commented that the divided opinions of the commissioners (each member submitted a separate report) "afforded ample reason for postponing" recognition still longer. He cited the halfhearted mediation efforts of the European allies as another "equally decisive" reason for not acting and called for letting the mediation efforts run their course before extending recognition. At that time the United States would be "at perfect liberty to recognize any of the South American republics."[24] In short, Adams wished to create in the courts of Europe the appearance that recognition was imminent while opposing domestic efforts to speed such actions.

The negotiations with Spain temporarily suspended, Adams journeyed to Quincy in early September for a brief visit with his parents. He sorely needed a vacation. The relentless duties of his office and the lack of tangible progress in the negotiations with Spain rekindled feelings of persecution in Adams that were never far beneath the surface. In late August he wrote: "The administration is assailed in various ways, both in the House of Representatives, in Congress, and in the public newspapers—assailed both insidiously and openly, and the attack in regard to its object has been concentrated exclusively upon me. The defense has been absolutely nothing. The faithful execution of my duties, to the utmost of my power, is the only answer I can give to censure." Here again is a familiar theme in the writings of John Quincy Adams—that silent martyrdom is the only response to public criticism. Responding to an accusation by Harrison Gray Otis that Monroe was "influenced entirely" by Adams, he wrote, "Mr. Otis has always chosen to see me as a rival. He never misses an opportunity to give me a backhand thrust—and as yet I have never returned it."[25]

Adams used his vacation in Quincy to renew his sagging body and spirit. Heavy rains confined him to his parents' house, allowing him the leisure of reading the classics, one of his favorite pastimes. The life of the philosopher still appealed to Adams. "If the study of Plato were my proper business, I should be wasting my time with something else," he wrote. He was less impressed with the philosophy of Socrates. The notion that all things are produced by their contraries Adams denounced as "an absurdity." Yet he was taken by one aspect of Socratic thought—"the spiritual, simple, uncompounded nature of the soul, and the inference from it that the soul is therefore not subject to death." His month-long stay in Quincy allowed him time for such reflections. "I feel an attraction for these places more powerful than any other spot upon Earth," he wrote. Sadly, his career of public service had allowed him but two brief visits home in a decade.[26]

Upon his return to Washington, Adams prepared to renew direct talks with Onís. The "honor" of the king of Spain had now been preserved by the promise to return Pensacola and St. Mark's, and Adams anticipated rapid progress in the negotiations. Boosting these hopes was Onís's announcement that he was empowered to exchange ratifications of the Commercial Claims Convention of 1802, long held hostage to the other disputes dividing the two nations.

Hence, Adams and Monroe were deeply disappointed by Onís's new proposal of 24 October. A reexamination by his government of a "multitude of authentic papers and documents," the Spaniard began, again proved the "incontestable evidence of all the rights hitherto sustained by the crown of Spain." Onís repeated nearly word for word his historical argument of the previous March asserting Spain's sovereignty over Texas and Florida. He then moved to specific treaty points: the Floridas to be ceded in exchange for a western boundary beginning at the gulf of Mexico and running north along the Arroyo Hondo line to the Red River, then directly north to the Missouri and following the course of that river to its source high in the Rockies (see Map 3). Onís added that both the Missouri and the Mississippi were to remain open to Spanish navigation. Moreover, he called for the United States to "declare that they deeply regret the violation of Spanish territory" by Jackson and agree to pay for all damages done to Spanish citizens and property by his invasion.[27]

Adams and Monroe were enraged. Although the proposed northwest boundary following the Missouri River closely resembled that suggested by Adams the previous March (see Chapter 2), the president and secretary of state were now determined to extend the western boundary all the way to the Pacific. Onís's offer denied access to the ocean except for a narrow corridor north of the source of the Missouri, through the high mountains of present-day Glacier National Park.[28] Moreover, Onís proposed to draw the Texas boundary even farther east than the Sabine River—especially insulting in light of the major concession the administration had made in July by agreeing to retreat from the Rio Grande to the Sabine. Monroe termed the proposal "altogether inadmissible" and told Adams that "it was time to bring to Onís to a point, and if he would not agree to reasonable terms, to break off the negotiation."[29]

The president was losing patience with diplomacy. The seizure of Amelia, the invasion of Florida by Jackson, and the steadily improving relations with Great Britain made it clear to him that the United States could bring Spain to terms with military force. Monroe told Adams that "he now thought it of much less consequence then it was a year ago whether we made any adjustment with Spain at all," and that "Onís's instructions were such that he would either sign no treaty at all or sign one upon our own terms."[30] The president directed Adams to prepare "a final offer" for Onís.

Adams delivered this "final" offer on 31 October in the form of an ultimatum. He dismissed Onís's historical argument as irrelevant to the American "right . . . to the river Mississippi and all the waters flowing into it," a right he declared to be "henceforth . . . not subject to refutation." Rejecting demands that the United States apologize for the Jackson affair, Adams moved to the critical western boundary question. He proposed a line beginning at the Sabine River and extending north to 32 degrees north latitude, then directly north to the Red River and following that stream to its source in the Sangre de Cristo Mountains of Colorado. From the summit of those mountains the boundary would extend from to the 41st parallel and then directly to the Pacific (see Map 5). Adams concluded his note with a thinly veiled threat: "The president is deeply penetrated with the conviction that further discussion of the points at issue between our governments cannot terminate in a manner satisfactory to them. From your answer to this letter, he must conclude whether or not a final adjustment of all our differences is now to be accomplished, or whether all hope of such a desirable result is, on the part of the United States, to be abandoned."[31]

This hard-line response did not surprise Onís. He had known that his proposal of 24 October would provoke Monroe and Adams, but his instructions still allowed little room for compromise. His 16 November reply to Adams's ultimatum differed little from the position outlined in the 24 October note. He responded to Adams's warning with a weak plea: "The only discretionary power left me is to request of the president . . . that the negotiations . . . may be submitted to the decision of the great monarchs now assembled at Aix-la-Chapelle."[32] There was no chance that Monroe would agree to that.

Map 5. The Proposals of October and November 1818 (projected on the Melish map of 1818)

Adams also informed Hyde de Neuville that the president had reached the end of his patience. In a meeting with the French minister on 4 November he said that the administration "had retreated to the wall" and that Onís could only answer "yes" or "no" to the proposal of 31 October. Adams added that "the president was more indifferent now than he had been a year ago to the issue of this negotiation; that we knew we should obtain more by delay than we now offered to accept, and that we might quietly wait for the operation of time."[33] Adams ended the discussion on that note, confident that Hyde de Neuville would report all to Onís.

The ultimatum of 31 October and Adams's tough talk to Hyde de Neuville initiated yet another phase in the negotiations between the United States and Spain. Spain had previously enjoyed the luxury of procrastination, relying on the support of the European powers and the weakness of the United States to guarantee the status quo until a treaty favorable to Spanish interests could be obtained. In that context, Madrid had had little to fear from the interruption of negotiations. Now the balance between the two nations had shifted, and it was the United States that anticipated advantage in breaking off the talks.

Monroe had concluded that the negotiations were reaching a climax. Either an agreement would be made soon, or war would be the likely result. A cabinet meeting of 7 November, devoted to the formulation of the annual message to Congress, reflected the president's new outlook. Monroe had come around to Adams's view that the rebel forces at Amelia Island should be linked to the provocations of the Seminoles as part of a defense of the administration's actions in Florida. Adams, of course, had produced documents purporting to show the connection between the two incidents.[34] Yet the main reason for Monroe's "new view" of affairs was his realization that he needed a comprehensive, coherent justification of American actions in Florida in order to prevent a backlash against the administration either in Congress or in the courts of Europe. If war with Spain was a possibility, now was the time to seize the moral high ground. A strongly worded, unequivocal statement of the American position (however little it corresponded to fact) might even prevent conflict by justifying to the European nations the seizure of Amelia Island and the invasion of Florida.

To Adams, the draft message to Congress that took shape in early November represented the complete triumph of his analysis of the situation: "It certainly does countenance much more strongly the ground that I took in favor of Jackson's proceedings at the cabinet meetings in July than I was able to obtain then."[35] For months, Monroe and the rest of the cabinet had resisted Adams's bold, audacious recommendations. They had refused full support of Jackson's unauthorized conquest of the Floridas—not, perhaps, because of constitutional or ethical considerations but because of the possible repercussions in congress and abroad. Now the president and the rest of the cabinet (with the exception of Crawford) recognized that having come this far, they had no choice but to defend Jackson's illegal campaign wholeheartedly. To do anything less would risk incurring the wrath of the general and his many supporters and, more important, would give Onís hope of turning the affair to Spain's advantage. The president outlined this new hard-line position in his annual message to Congress on 16 November, and Adams sent along another mass of documents purporting to support the administration's case.[36]

On 8 November, Adams began work on an even more important message—a letter to Erving in Madrid explaining the administration's position and designed to be circulated to all the courts
of Europe. Adams described it as "a succinct account of the late
Seminole War from its origin, . . . in such a manner as completely
to justify the measures of this government relating to it, and as far
as possible the proceedings of General Jackson." He recognized
the importance of his assignment; his letter would be crucial in
influencing perceptions of American actions. "The task is of the
highest order," he wrote in his diary. "May I not be found inferior
to it!"[37]

Although the letter to Erving is usually described as Adams's
defense of Jackson, it is much more; it is also a defense of Jacksonianism, of American expansionism, and of Manifest Destiny. Even
though the last term had not yet been coined, its spirit thrived in the
personage of Jackson and those who admired him. It became Adams's
task, as the presumed "man of the whole nation," to give voice to that
spirit and to embellish Jackson's own defense of his actions with all
the logic, evidence, and force that could be mustered.[38] In defending
Jackson, Adams was implicitly defending Indian removal, slavery, and
the use of military force without congressional approval—all of
which he would, as a congressman, later oppose. Even in 1818 there
was a large gap between Adams's private feelings and his public
position on slavery. Yet at this stage of his career his intense desire to
wrest a treaty from Spain that would give him a claim to the presidency dictated that he defend Jackson (whom Adams would later
describe as "a barbarian"). It proved a crucial act of expediency in the
life of a man renowned for his devotion to principle.

To defend Jackson's invasion seemed difficult. Whether authorized
or unauthorized by the executive, the campaign was an act of war
without congressional approval and therefore a violation of the Constitution. To avoid meeting head-on criticism of that sort, Adams
constructed what he termed a "narrative of dark and complicated
depravity" which placed Jackson's actions in the larger context of a
struggle in the swamps of Florida of American "good" versus British,
Spanish, Indian, and black "evil." As narrator, Adams could choose
the events marking the "beginning" and "end" of the story, could
introduce evidence that supported his case (and disregard that which
contradicted it), and, perhaps most important, establish the emotional context of the drama by the terms he used to describe the
players.[39] Adams realized that the bare facts of Jackson's actions
might be excused by the public and Congress if he could place those
actions in the context of the mythic American struggle against the

wiles of foreign intrigues and the "uncivilized" natures of "inferior" races.[40]

Adams labored diligently on what would be one of the most famous state papers of his long life of public service, drafting and redrafting the message, endeavoring to show that the problems in Florida had their roots in British provocations during the War of 1812. Indeed, Monroe feared that Adams's indictment of Great Britain and vigorous defense of the execution of Ambrister and Arbuthnot would offend Castlereagh. The president also worried that his secretary of state had "gone too far" in defending Jackson and that the letter should be aimed at "shielding and supporting him" without tying the administration directly to his actions. Adams resisted any weakening of his text, persuading Monroe to submit his criticisms to the full cabinet before making any final decision.[41] After three weeks of intense drafting and debate, Monroe had made only minor revisions of the text, and Adams prepared to send it to Erving. The letter, dated 28 November, took the form of instructions to the minister, and documents purporting to support Adams's argument accompanied the dispatch.[42]

Adams framed his letter to Erving in the shape of a reply to Spanish Foreign Secretary Pizarro's diplomatic protests of the invasion. Noting the intentions of the American government to return Pensacola and St. Mark's to Spain, he charged that Pizarro's notes were "doubtless intended to be understood as a menace of war." Accordingly, Adams claimed it necessary to give the American side of the matter or, as he put it, "to remind the Government of the Catholic Majesty of the incidents in which the Seminole War originated" and the reasons Jackson was "impelled, from the necessity of self-defence" to invade Florida.[43] Thus the document began by casting the United States in the role of the party threatened by aggression, not as the aggressor.

Adams claimed that the Seminole War had its origins in the machinations of Great Britain in Florida during the War of 1812. Nicholls and Woodbine were guilty of encouraging "all the runaway negroes, all the savage Indians, all the pirates, and all the traitors to their country . . . to join their standard, and wage an exterminating war" against the United States.[44] Even worse, Nicholls and Woodbine encouraged the Seminoles and Red Sticks (the American term for the defiant Creeks) to believe "that they were entitled, by virtue of the Treaty of Ghent, to all lands which had belonged to the *Creek* nation within the United States in the year 1811, and that the government of Great Britain would support them in that pretension." British treachery had been compounded by allowing the abandoned post at Prospect Bluff (the Negro Fort) to be "occupied by banditti" and used "as a post from which to commit depredations, outrages, and murders, and as a receptacle for fugitive slaves and malefactors."[45] An American gunboat had destroyed the Negro Fort, Adams claimed, only after first being fired upon.

Adams placed direct responsibility for the Seminole War on Alexander Arbuthnot, whom he described as "the firebrand by whose touch this negro-Indian war against our borders had been rekindled." Because of Arbuthnot's "infernal instigations," including his "reviving the pretence" that the Creeks were entitled to lands lost in the Treaty of Fort Jackson, the "peaceful inhabitants" of the United States were "visited with all the horrors of savage war." Only after "repeated expostulations, warnings, and offers of peace" by the United States had been met with "renewed outrages" by the Indians was Jackson ordered to punish the "mingled hordes of lawless Indians and negroes" responsible.[46] That these "hordes" of outlaws sought refuge across the border in Florida made the penetration of Spanish territory "indispensable."

Adams's explanation of the causes of the Seminole War was made plausible by the generally correct (if overstated) nature of the facts cited. Yet more significant are the facts omitted: that the struggle between the tribes of the Southeast predated the arrival of the British in the Floridas, that the Treaty of Fort Jackson had not been signed by the chiefs who led the resistance in the Floridas; and that the United States government in 1816 had attempted to restore to the Creeks the lands taken under the Treaty of Fort Jackson, giving up its efforts only after Jackson's defiance and western opposition made them futile.[47] To castigate Arbuthnot and the other Britons for encouraging the Indians to assert a claim that even the United States government at one point had acknowledged is dubious to say the least.

The characterization of the seventy-year-old Arbuthnot, widely known as a kindly and genial old man, as the instigator of the Seminole War is an extraordinary example of scapegoating.[48] To blame him for the Seminole War was to deny that the Indians had either the justification or the inclination to resist the encroachment of Americans on their lands. Adams no doubt had taken his cue from Jackson in placing responsibility for the war on Arbuthnot, yet Adams himself seems to have believed the myth that hostilities between the United States and native Americans invariably had their roots in the agitation of evil white men. He wrote to Onís in July 1818 that "for many years" the United States had not fought "with any Indian tribes unless stimulated by the influence of foreign incendiaries." [49] It was a self-justifying rationale typical of the era of Manifest Destiny.

Adams's letter includes grisly descriptions of the murder of Americans by Indians during the course of the frontier skirmishing.[50] But his references to Indian atrocities against American settlers are not balanced by any recognition of American attacks on Indians, a tendency reflected in the press as well. The impression created is one of a steady series of unprovoked assaults on peaceful settlers. Yet much of the border violence was part of an ongoing cycle of mutual retaliation between whites and Indians in which both sides kept close tally of the "score."[51] Governor D.B. Mitchell of Georgia later testified to Congress that "truth compels me to say, that before the attack on Fowltown, aggressions . . . were as frequent on the part of whites as on the part of Indians."[52]

Perhaps most significant in Adams's exposition of the causes of the Seminole War is his omission of the act that historians acknowledge as the immediate cause of the conflict—the attack on Fowltown.[53] Adams, well aware of the incident, no doubt left it out because it did not contribute to his argument. Its omission confirms that his explanation of the Seminole War is a conscious exercise in selective truth where "facts" are included only insofar as they provide evidence for a prior conclusion.

Adams's letter to Erving differs significantly from his initial response to Spain of 23 July. That note had defended Jackson on the grounds that Spain had violated its treaty obligations by failing to control the Seminoles. The 28 November letter, in contrast, creates a cosmology in which Jackson's invasion is the only possible result of the actions of the British in the Floridas during the War of 1812, the "Negro Fort" episode, the use of Amelia Island by South American privateers, and the depredations of the Seminoles. Spain's failure to restrain the Seminoles according to the terms of Pinckneys' Treaty of 1795 is mentioned only in passing.

This selective, anecdotal approach to the "facts" of the Seminole War bears some similarity to the methods the Puritan historians used in retelling the story of the founding of New England.[54] Adams's text, like the historical works of Cotton Mather and Edward Johnson, is a sacred history designed to inspire and persuade rather than dispassionately recount. Sacred histories of America by their nature omit events uncongenial to the theme of the nation's providential and just development.[55] For Adams to refer to the dubious legitimacy of the Treaty of Fort Jackson and the attack on Fowltown would have cast doubt on the essential justice of the American case. It would also have made understandable the Seminole and Creek border attacks and would have demonstrated the moral ambiguity of the American position. Adams was seeking not the philosopher's truth but rather the truth of the prophet who overcomes contradiction by the certainty with which he reveals the divine plan.[56] Indeed, the self-righteous, uncompromising tone of his letter resonated with the nation's mood and heritage in a way that a fair-minded explanation of the Seminole War would not have done.

Reflecting the Puritan historians too is Adams's designation of opponents of American destiny in unflattering and inaccurate terms: "banditti," "savages," "outlaws," "malefactors" were all used to describe the inhabitants of Spanish Florida. Though obviously questionable as fair-minded descriptions of the blacks and Indians, they were very effective in setting the emotional tone of the letter and the desired context of good versus evil.[57] As Francis Jennings has noted, "to call a man a savage is to warrant his death."[58]

Having "justified" the invasion of Florida, Adams next addressed the issue of the seizure of the Spanish forts. The taking of St. Mark's was necessary, he said, because there was a threat of the fort's imminent capture by "hostile Indians." The "laws of neutrality and of war, as well as prudence and humanity," dictated Jackson's seizing the fort. Adams claimed no need for "citations from the printed treatises on international law to prove the correctness of the principle. It is engraved," he said, "in the common sense of mankind." In similar terms he defended the capture of Pensacola. The "enmity" of the Spanish governor in refusing passage of an American supply vessel up the Escambia River without payments of "excessive duties," the sheltering of the "savage enemies" of the United States within the garrison at Pensacola, and the threatening letter from the Spanish governor demanding that Jackson leave Florida all made the town's capture "indispensably necessary."[59] Adams claimed that both St. Mark's and Pensacola had been seized "not in the spirit of hostility to Spain, but as necessary measures of self-defence."

The record contradicts this version of the events leading to the seizure of St. Mark's and Pensacola. Adams's claims to the contrary, no evidence introduced at the trial of Ambrister and Arbuthnot proved the contention that the fall of St. Mark's was imminent.[60] Moreover, no evidence was ever found to to show that the allegation of several hundred warriors in Pensacola was anything but an excuse by Jackson to seize the town.[61] The supply barge supposedly assessed "excessive duties" was in fact given special permission to pass through Spanish territory and paid the standard rate.[62] This left only the Spanish governor's "threatening letter" to Jackson as justification for the seizure of Pensacola.

Adams's most important task in his letter to Erving was to justify the executions of Arbuthnot and Ambrister without further inflaming those in England who had called for retaliation for their slain countrymen. Adams resorted to international law and the law of the jungle to do so. According to him, Arbuthnot and Ambrister, along with Nicholls and Woodbine, were part of a conspiracy to goad the Indians into waging "savage, servile, exterminating war against the United States." Therefore, Jackson was authorized to use unusually harsh methods in dealing with his two captives; in fact, he could "have hung them both without the formality of a trial." Quoting Emmerich de Vattel to support his position, Adams defended the executions of the two Britons for its "salutary efficacy for terror and example." He added "It is thus only that the barbarism of Indians can be successfully encountered."[63]

Adams's vigorous defense of Jackson's bloodthirsty tactics is ironic in light of his initial horror at them. When informed by Crawford in May of the court-martial of Ambrister and Arbuthnot, Adams had expressed reservations: "They hung some Indian prisoners, as it appears, without due regard for humanity. A Scotchman by the name of Arbuthnot was found among them, and Jackson appears half inclined to take his life. Crawford some time ago proposed to send Jackson orders to give no quarter to any white man found with the Indians. I objected to it then, and this day avowed that I was not prepared for that mode of warfare," he had written.[64] Now he embraced such methods. Adams's aggressive defense of the Seminole War violated another deeply felt belief of the Adams family, that of standing for the peaceful resolution of international disputes. Changing the warlike practices of European diplomacy had been a major aspect of the revolutionary vision, and no one had adhered to that ideal more than the Adamses. John Adams took great pride in having kept the nation out of full-fledged hostilities with France during the "Quasi-War" of 1798-1800, even though his stand probably cost him reelection. John Quincy, too, firmly believed that the republican revolution must reject war as a tool of policy if it hoped to remake the world. Yet at the helm of American foreign policy, Adams was now resorting to the force, fraud, and hypocrisy characteristic of the European order that the republican revolution presumed to transcend. This new, more aggressive republicanism was reflected in the Erving letter: "The right of the United States can as little compound with impotence as with perfidy."

Accordingly, Adams refused the Spanish demand that Jackson be punished for his actions: "The President will neither inflict punishment, nor pass censure upon General Jackson, for that conduct, the motives for which were founded in the purest patriotism." Indeed, Adams placed a large share of the responsibility for the Seminole War on Spain for failing "to restrain *by force* the Indians of Florida from hostilities against the United States."[65] He suggested that the conduct of its colonial officials be investigated for assisting "these hordes of savages in the very hostilities against the United States which it is their official duty to restrain," claiming that such an investigation was necessary to preserve the "honor" of Spain.[66]

Adams finished his letter to Erving with a demand as audacious as it was astounding: that the Spanish government punish its colonial officials for their "misconduct" and that Spain pay "a just and reasonable indemnity to the United States for the heavy and necessary expenses which they have been compelled to incur by the failure of Spain to perform her engagements to restrain the Indians." Adams made explicit the penalty for further Spanish "misconduct": "If the necessities of self-defence should again compel the United States to take possession of the Spanish forts and places in Florida . . . another unconditional restoration of them must not be expected."[67]

Thus did John Quincy Adams, using half-truths, falsehoods, and powerful rhetoric, transform the officially unauthorized conquest of foreign territory into a patriotic act of self-defense and the United States from aggressor into aggrieved victim. Ironically, this "greatest state paper" (as Samuel Flagg Bemis termed it) of Adams's career is almost completely contradicted by the historical record. In this light, the letter to Erving must be characterized as propaganda, designed to create a perception of reality wholly in conflict with fact. Yet its tone and seemingly irrefutable logic make it convincing reading even now. It was an impressive linguistic feat, one accomplished in large measure by the self-righteous, uncompromising tone in which Adams lectured the Spanish government. In demanding that Spain pay for the costs of the American invasion, he was perhaps heeding the words of Tacitus, his favorite historian, who observed that "crime once exposed had no refuge but in audacity."[68]

The Erving letter is a prime example of John Quincy Adams serving his country in the way he knew best. He had never defended his nation as a soldier in the field, nor had he contributed to its strength through financial contributions. Like Cicero, Adams was an orator, a man who knew how to use language to maximum political effect. All his life he had honed that ability—by his endless study of the classics, tedious translations of ancient authors, and voluminous composition of correspondence both public and private. Now, at a moment of national crisis, his skill was called to the fore. The Erving letter demonstrated that even if the pen is not necessarily mightier than the sword, it can be a powerful and essential legitimator of the sword's use.

Even as John Quincy Adams composed his letter to Erving, he suffered another severe personal crisis. "Ominous words" arrived from Quincy on 30 October that Abigail had fallen seriously ill. Only a month earlier, he had left his mother in good health. Now her death appeared imminent. Despite the bad news, Adams was "compelled reluctantly" to carry on his duties during this crucial phase of the negotiations, uncertain whether his beloved mother was dead or alive. On 2 November he received the dreaded news: Abigail had died on the morning of 28 October, a victim of typhus. Ironically, the sense of duty to country that Abigail had instilled in John Quincy kept them apart at her death. As he confronted Onís with an ultimatum designed for the greater glory of the United States, his mother went to her final resting place without the presence of her prized son.[69]

Her loss provoked unusually heartfelt reflections in Adams's diary: "My mother was an angel upon earth. She was a minister of blessing to all human beings within her sphere of action. Her heart was the abode of heavenly purity. She had no feelings but of kindness and beneficence; yet her mind was as firm as her temper was mild and gentle. She had known sorrow but her sorrow was silent. She was acquainted with grief, but it was deposited in her own bosom. She was the real personification of female virtue, of piety, of charity, of ever active and never intermitting benevolence. Oh God! could she have been spared a little longer! My lot in life has been almost always cast at a distance from her. I have enjoyed but for short seasons, and at long, distant intervals, the happiness of her society, yet she has been to me more than a mother. She has been a spirit from above watching over me for good, and contributing by my mere consciousness of her existence to the comfort of my life. That consciousness is gone, and without it the world feels to me like solitude."[70]

In this dejected state, Adams strove to honor his mother's memory by concluding a treaty with Spain.

SEVEN

The Origins of Empire

John Quincy Adams began his diary for 1819 by paraphrasing from the golden verses attributed to Pythagoras:

> Let not thine eyelids close at parting day
> Till, with thyself communing, thou shalt say,
> What deed of good or evil have I done
> Since the last radiance of the morning sun?
> In strict review the day before thee pass,
> And see thyself in truth's unerring glass.
> If, scorning self-delusion's fraudful ways,
> Her solemn voice of reproving Conscience raise,
> With keen contrition, aid divine implore
> Each error to redeem, and wrong no more.
> Or, should that faithful guardian witness bear
> That all thy action should have been just and fair
> Rejoice, and Heaven invoke with soul sincere
> In spotless virtue's path to persevere.

With these lines as a guide, Adams endeavored finally to bring Onís to terms.

The Erving letter had international repercussions. That the United States publicly held Great Britain partly responsible for the Florida affair astounded the European diplomatic community. Even more astounding was Castlereagh's acquiescence, in the face of fierce criticism by the British press, to the American actions. He defended his position by stating that the "unauthorized practices" of Ambrister and Arbuthnot "deprived them of any claim" to protection by their government. The foreign secretary instructed Bagot to make no further protest of the incident.[1]

That Castlereagh chose to ignore the execution of two Britons (one a Royal Marine) by an American general is an interesting study in the nature of international diplomacy. Had Castlereagh so desired, he could have used the incident as an excuse to take strong action against the United States. Nations have gone to war over less; the

British public certainly favored some sort of retaliatory measure.[2] Yet Castlereagh would not jeopardize his policy of reconciliation with the United States merely to avenge the murders of two British adventurers. Indeed, he had done nothing in response to the unilateral reoccupation of Astoria by the United States, a more tangible threat to British interests. Adams knew that Castlereagh valued reconciliation with the United States more than he did the lives of two wayward Britons; his understanding of Castlereagh's priorities explains why Adams, unlike Monroe, saw no danger in implicating Great Britain in his letter to Erving.

The Erving letter had an even greater effect in the United States, where debate over the legality of the Florida invasion neared a crescendo. Once again, members of Congress led by Henry Clay prepared to challenge the administration, this time over the constitutionality of Jackson's campaign. Adams viewed the "agitation, misapprehension, and conflict" in partisan terms. He saw the debate as a way for Crawford supporters in the Congress to discredit Jackson and thus eliminate a potential rival for the presidency.[3] The Erving letter was intended to counter criticism of Jackson and the administration. Its publication in the 28 December issue of the *National Intelligencer* neatly coincided with the release of yet another mass of documents, this time intended to support Adams's interpretation of the Seminole War.

The letter helped to shape the terms of the debate over Jackson's conduct. Adams's vitriolic, uncompromising defense of the general gave administration supporters the language they needed to respond to the opposition's charges of unconstitutionality and Bonapartism. Adams had couched the issue in terms of patriotism and self-defense, fixing most of the blame on Spain. This left critics in the uncomfortable position of appearing to defend Spain at a critical time in the negotiations. For the moment, they delayed formally raising the issue in the Congress, as House and Senate committees prepared their own reports on the matter.

Ironically, the Erving letter had little effect on the Spanish government, the party for whom it was ostensibly intended. By the time it arrived in Madrid in early 1819, a major shakeup had already occurred in the Consejo de Estado. In mid-September Foreign Secretary Pizarro and Finance Minister Garay were relieved of their duties by the king and ordered to leave Madrid, victims of the machinations of the *camarilla*.[4] The Marquis de Casa Yrujo, who had been minister to the United States during the Jefferson administration, replaced Pizarro. Erving did not welcome the change of ministers. Though he had made little progress in his discussions with Pizarro, he had come to respect the integrity and intellect of the Spaniard. Conversely, he was suspicious of Yrujo, from whom he expected "no good." Erving wrote to Adams that he would be "very happy indeed" if he could "only keep [Yrujo] from undoing" what progress had been made in the talks.[5]

Despite Erving's fears, Yrujo moved quickly to give Onís greater negotiating powers. Instructions dated 10 October authorized Onís to agree to a transcontinental boundary extending along the Missouri to its source and then directly to the Pacific. The instructions suggested the Sabine as the Texas boundary but allowed Onís to retreat to the Colorado River of Texas if necessary to forestall invasion by the United States. Instructions dated 23 October gave him even greater latitude. They not only permitted the minister to agree to a north-western boundary as far south as the Columbia River but also authorized him to "construct, discuss, and conclude the agreement according to the circumstances, without necessity of further consultation" with Madrid.[6] In other words, Onís now had full powers to make the best deal he could without consulting the home office. These new instructions signaled that the Spanish government was finally ready to make the necessary concessions in order to reach agreement with the United States.

Significantly, this major change in direction had occurred two month before the arrival of Adams's letter to Erving. The cold realities of international politics, not the bluster of John Quincy Adams, had dictated to the Spanish government this new willingness to compromise. At the conference at Aix-la-Chapelle, Spanish hopes for direct allied support in suppressing the South American revolutions had been crushed once and for all. In what has been termed his "greatest diplomatic triumph," Castlereagh had secured, among other things, allied agreement that there be no armed mediation of the South American struggles.[7] Tsar Alexander, in contrast, had been unable even to get Ferdinand invited to the conference; in its aftermath the tsar instructed Dmitri Pavlovitch Tatistscheff to inform the Spanish government that it should give up all hopes for armed intervention by the allies.[8]

The outcome at Aix made undeniable to the Spanish government what had been clear to Onís (and Pizarro) for some time—that Spain could not expect allied help in resolving its disputes with either the South Americans or the United States. Spain must go it alone in dealing with its problems in the Western Hemisphere: hence the willingness of the Consejo de Estado (and the *camarilla*) to give Onís greater flexibility in negotiating with Adams. The illusion entertained by members of the *camarilla* that the United States could be contained at or near the Mississippi River had been replaced by a strategy calling for Onís to erect a secure barrier between the United States and the Spanish borderlands of the Southwest, even if it meant extending a boundary to the Pacific. Ironically, Pizarro, who had long advocated such a strategy, was not around to see it finally adopted.

In Washington, Onís received more bad news in mid-December 1818 when word arrived of a treaty concluded by Gallatin and Rush with Great Britain. The agreement, known as the "Convention of 1818," resolved many (though not all) of the outstanding disputes between the two nations. Its most significant aspect concerned the Canadian-American boundary. The negotiators agreed that from the Lake of the Woods to the Rockies the boundary should be the 49th parallel. The vaguely defined Oregon territory west of the mountains they declared "free and open" to both American and British citizens for a period of ten years. Thus did the United States establish partial control of the Pacific Coast in a treaty that A.L. Burt called "one of the major agreements in the history of Canadian-American relations."[9]

Onís recognized that the terms of the Convention of 1818 made substantial Spanish concessions in the Northwest inevitable. The United States had not acquired a stake in the region from Great Britain only to give it away to Spain. When word arrived of the new treaty with Great Britain, however, Onís had not yet received his enlarged powers, and he fretted that the United States might attempt to force Spain's hand by recognizing one of the South American states.

This now seemed a distinct possibility. In a conversation with Hyde de Neuville on 12 December, Adams had expressed his hope that France might act in concert with the United States in recognizing the government of Buenos Aires. He explained the abrupt reversal of American policy to the startled Frenchmen by noting that "the fact of the independence of Buenos Aires appears established, [and] we think it necessary to be recognized."[10] This talk of recognition panicked Hyde de Neuville. One of his prime objectives was to forestall recognition in order to prevent a rupture in the Adams-Onís talks which might lead to war, for a Spanish-American war could involve the other powers of Europe, sweeping France away in the maelstrom. On 28 December, Hyde de Neuville, in a state of "great agitation," again met with Adams to discuss South American affairs.

If Onís would agree "within three of four months" to a treaty on Adams's terms, he inquired, would the administration refrain from recognizing Buenos Aires? Adams coyly replied that the administration "would give no such pledge," adding that "events were placing the affairs of South America quite out of our control." He tantalized Hyde de Neuville (and, indirectly, Onís) by commenting that had Spain "taken the pains" earlier to settle the negotiations, "there would probably be much less ardor in the country against Spain and consequently less in favor of the South Americans. Spain might have trusted to the operation of these effects. Now it might be too late."[11]

Hyde de Neuville's obvious distress pleased Adams; it signaled that his strategy of using recognition as a means of putting pressure on Onís was working. The August dispatches to the American ministers requesting them to feel out the reactions of the European governments to plans for recognition had been the first step in this policy. The reports of the South American commission had heightened speculation about recognition. Moreover, Adams had been meeting with the new Buenos Airean envoy David Curtis DeForest, (a native of Connecticut) intimating that the United States would soon acknowledge him as consul general. Now Adams told Hyde de Neuville directly what the administration contemplated. Nor was the elaborate diplomatic dance yet over. Adams knew that Spain might not yield, that a war neither side wanted might erupt. Accordingly, the United States had to be ready actually to extend recognition. To prepare for this possibility, he drafted another letter to Richard Rush in London.

Adams told Rush that "the period is fast approaching" when the independence of Buenos Aires "will be so firmly established as to be beyond the reach of any reasonable pretensions of supremacy on the part of Spain." He instructed Rush to explain to Castlereagh and the rest of the diplomatic corps "how important it is to them, as well as to us, that the newly found states should be . . . recognized." Adams justified recognition on the basis of "the ordinary rules of the laws of nations in their intercourse with the civilized world." He ended by directing Rush to inform Castlereagh "in a most friendly manner" that the United States "has it in contemplation" to extend some form of recognition to Buenos Aires "at no remote period."[12]

Monroe suggested that Adams's draft note to Rush be reviewed by the whole cabinet. Astonishingly, the other members of the administration had no knowledge of the "intention" to recognize Buenos Aires. Adams described their reaction to his draft note as "startled," yet he defended his actions by claiming that Monroe had instructed him to say as much to DeForest.[13] Crawford, Calhoun, and Wirt were astounded that they had not been informed of this change in policy. Adams, formerly the main opponent to recognition, explained why it was now desirable. He alluded to "great changes" since the previous spring which provided "additional proof of the stability of the government of Buenos Aires." He argued that the reports of the South American commission provided further cause for recognition—in sharp contrast to his condemnation of the commission's findings in November. When Calhoun expressed reservations about acting without the support of Great Britain, Adams claimed that "deference to the British government should not be carried too far; that we should not have the appearance of pinning ourselves too closely upon her sleeve; that we should carefully preserve the advantage of taking the lead in advancing the recognition of the South American governments, and, while using persuasion with England to move in concert with us, take care to let her know that we shall ultimately act independently for ourselves."[14]

Of course, Adams was embracing recognition not because of any "great changes" in the state of South American affairs but because the hopeless state of the negotiations with Spain dictated that the time had arrived to play the recognition "card." Despairing of a peaceful settlement of the dispute, Adams pushed for legislation by Congress authorizing the president under certain contingencies to seize and retain Spanish Florida. This would add legitimacy to the threat in the Erving letter that further failure by Spain to "restrain" the Seminoles would result in the reoccupation of the province. Adams characterized as "hopeless" any prospects for a settlement unless such a law should pass: "That might bring Spain to it. Nothing else would."[15]

Adams gloomily contemplated the point to which his strategy of force and diplomacy had brought him—the brink of war. Spain had not knuckled under to American pressure; now the administration either had to follow through with its threats or face the humiliation of having its bluff called before the entire world. Neither outcome would reflect well on Adams's statesmanship. The landscape on other fronts appeared to him equally bleak: "This Government is, indeed, assuming daily more and more a character of cabal, and preparation, not for the next Presidential election but the one after—that is, working and counterworking, with many of the worst features of elective monarchies."[16]

Adams's personal relationship with the president had been strained when Monroe had confronted him with the rumor that Adams had agreed to represent the Prince Regent at the christening of the child of British minister Bagot. Adams vehemently denied the potentially politically embarrassing charge, made, according to Monroe, by a "friend" of John Quincy. He had no doubt as to the motive of the charge: "There had been a spirit at work ever since I came to Washington very anxious to to find or make occasion of censure upon me." That Monroe placed any credence at all in the rumor offended him: "It gives me, therefore, the measure of the president's feelings and opinions in reference to me; and they are not flattering." By this point, Adams doubted the extent of his influence over Monroe, perceiving "an undertow always working upon and about the president—what used in England to be called a backstairs influence—of which he never says anything to me, and which I discover only by its effects."[17]

Amid his political and diplomatic difficulties, Adams suffered from a profound sense of personal loss engendered by his mother's death. Abigail's passing ("one of the severest afflictions to which human existence is liable") marked a major passage in his life. He wrote of her death in revealing terms: "The silver cord is broken, the tenderest of natural ties is dissolved. Life is no longer to me what it was; my home is no longer the abode of my mother. While she lived, whenever I returned to the paternal roof I felt as if the joys and charms of childhood returned to make me happy. All was kindness and affection, at once silent and active as the movement of the orbs of heaven. One of the links that connected me with former ages is no more."[18]

Three days after writing these lines, on 3 January 1819, Adams went for a long walk through the snowy streets of Washington. On Pennsylvania Avenue he was met by Hyde de Neuville, who had news of great importance. The two men went immediately to Adams's office, where the nervous Frenchman reported that Onís had received "fresh instructions" from his government, for the first time authorizing a transcontinental boundary. The new Spanish minister of foreign affairs, the Marquis de Casa Yrujo, was "very peacefully disposed" and wanted a treaty, Hyde de Neuville said. Yet the French minister stressed that the South American recognition question still posed an obstacle. If Spain would come to terms, would the United States agree to forgo "premature recognition" of the South Americans?

Adams again flatly rejected any explicit guarantee. Recognition and the Spanish-American negotiations were separate issues, he said: "We could not make our conduct in respect to one of these objects conditional upon the result of the other." Nonetheless, he held out a glimmer of hope to Hyde de Neuville: "If the French government should suggest to us just and reasonable motives for postponing further a recognition of the South American revolutionary governments, all due consideration would be given to their advice, and if it was accompanied by a satisfactory adjustment of our differences with Spain, it would have great additional weight."[19] Rejecting explicit guarantees of nonrecognition, Adams made it clear that progress in the talks could lead to a de facto moratorium on recognition. In such indirect phrases are found the makings of diplomatic agreements.

Hyde de Neuville's "good offices" had, for the moment, saved the day. Yet despite his enlarged powers, Onís was not confident that an agreement could be reached. His instructions still did not comply with Adams's "ultimatum" of 31 October. Indeed, Adams responded unfavorably to Onís's 16 January proposal calling for a northwest boundary running from the source of the Missouri westward to the Columbia and along the middle of that river to the sea. The secretary of state's one-paragraph answer (dated 29 January) merely repeated the ultimatum of 31 October.[20] It was not until 24 January that Onís received from Yrujo the instructions granting him full powers. Jubilant, he was able to respond to Adams's 29 January note: "I am prepared to take upon myself the definitive settlement of the points in controversy." The time for haggling over historical claims and rights was past: "We should confine ourselves to the settlement of those points which may be for the mutual interest and convenience of both."[21] Onís was ready to make the necessary concessions to come to terms; an agreement was now plainly in sight.

Adams's bold diplomatic gambit had worked. The threat of imminent recognition of South American independence, combined with the news of the verdict at Aix-la-Chapelle, made capitulation by Onís inescapable. The recognition "card" might need to be played again, should Onís's conciliatory attitude turn out to be more apparent than real. Meanwhile, however, Adams had to dampen the flames of enthusiasm rekindled by his moves toward recognition. In particular, he had to rebuff the advances of DeForest, who had thought his acknowledgment as consul general from Buenos Aires was assured. Adams's public flirtation with the expatriate DeForest had been a useful tool in convincing Hyde de Neuville and Onís of the administration's intent to extend recognition to Buenos Aires, but now DeForest's presence was a menace to the success of the negotiation. To make matters worse, Adams found out that DeForest had been secretly working with Clay to pressure the administration into acting. On 14 January, in an attempt to embarrass the administration, Clay had steered through the House a resolution requesting that the Adams-DeForest correspondence be submitted to Congress.[22]

This sort of duplicity enraged Adams. Now that a settlement was within his grasp he was in no mood to contend with another round of the "great South American witchery," as he termed the latest congressional action. "In this affair everything is invidious and factious," he wrote. "The call [for the Adams-DeForest correspondence] is made for the purpose of baiting the administration and especially of fastening upon the secretary of state the odium of refusing to receive the South American ministers and consul generals. I am walking on a rope, with a precipice on each side of me, and without human aid upon which to rely." Blind to his own duplicity in handling the South American question, Adams characterized DeForest's notes to him as "cunning and deceptive," and moved to intimidate the Buenos Airean envoy.[23]

On 22 January, DeForest discovered the perils of crossing the path of so formidable an antagonist as Adams. The secretary of state informed DeForest that as a United States citizen he was liable to prosecution for violating the neutrality laws by his activities as an envoy for Buenos Aires. DeForest, startled by this information, asked whether his seventeen-year stay in Buenos Aires had not altered his status as an American citizen. Adams then made plain the situation: "It is unnecessary for me to give you an opinion on that point. You had better consult a lawyer upon it." Adams added that it was not his intention to make any mention of his conversations with De-Forest "unless it should be necessary in the discharge of my public duties." Then he drove his main point home: "It is in candor due to you to let you know that the recognition of yourself as consul general of Buenos Aires, should it hereafter be granted, will in no wise divest you of your character as a citizen of the United States." In other words, to continue to press for acknowledgment as consul general could lead to DeForest's prosecution for violation of the neutrality laws.[24]

Thoroughly chastised, DeForest beat a quick retreat. He was no doubt irked that Adams would threaten him with violation of the neutrality laws when so many American citizens were actively supporting the South American cause without fear of prosecution. Nonetheless, he repudiated his dealings with Clay and assured Adams that he was "entirely satisfied" with the administration's South American policy. With that, DeForest retired to his home in New Haven, never again to bother John Quincy Adams.

Having again quelled agitation for South American recognition, Adams turned his attention to the unfolding congressional investigation of Jackson. He hoped that his strong justification of Jackson in the Erving letter, combined with the general's enormous popularity, would suffice to repulse the constitutional, moral, political, and personal objections being raised regarding his conduct. Commentary both pro and con filled the pages of the nation's newspapers.

The persuasiveness of Adams's letter was bolstered by some seventy documents purporting to support its claims. A careful reading of the documents, however, reveals that they either "prove" facts that were common knowledge (such as Nicholls's presence in Florida during the War of 1812) or do not prove what Adams says they do. For example, Adams asserted that Arbuthnot's "principal object" was to "stimulate" the Indians to hostility, yet the documents that Adams makes reference to in this context give no support to his allegation.[25]

Indeed, Monroe and Adams themselves recognized the inadequacy of the documentary evidence to support their case. In his "friendly letter" to Jackson of 20 July, Monroe had alluded to circumstances in which a commanding general might exceed his orders. If the officers of a neutral nation (in this case Spain) should "forget" the obligations of neutrality and "stimulate the enemy to make war" by furnishing them arms and asylum, then an attack on the garrisons (in this case, St. Mark's and Pensacola) of a neutral nation, in the pursuit of the "enemy" (the Seminoles), would be justifiable. This is the scenario on which Adams based his defense, but Jackson's correspondence did not support this version of events. Monroe wrote to Jackson "By charging the offense to the officers of Spain, we take the ground which you have presented and look to you to support it. You must aid in procuring the documents necessary to this purpose. Those you sent . . . were prepared in too much haste, and do not, I am satisfied, do justice to the cause. This must be attended to without delay."

Monroe then described to Jackson what needed to be done to resolve the discrepancy between the administration's defense of the general's campaign and the correspondence regarding it: "The passage to which I particularly allude . . . is that [in] which you speak of the incompetency of an imaginary boundary to protect us against the enemy—the ground on which you bottom all your measures. This is liable to the imputation that you took the Spanish posts for that reason, as a measure of expediency, and not on the account of the misconduct of the Spanish officers. The effect of this and such passages . . . would be to invalidate the ground on which you stand and furnish weapons to your adversaries. . . . If you think proper to authorize the Secretary or myself to correct those passages, it will be done with care, though, should you have copies, as I presume you have, you had better do it yourself."[26] Unfortunately for Monroe, Jackson refused to participate in this crude attempt to alter his correspondence. He denied that he had exceeded his orders and would not agree to amend his dispatches, justifying his conduct by reference to the letter authorizing him to "adopt the necessary measures to terminate" the conflict. Jackson ignored Monroe's subsequent request that he write a letter acknowledging "that a difference of opinion existed between you and the Executive, relative to the extent of your powers."[27] Hence, Monroe and Adams were forced to confront the public and Congress using documents that even they recognized were inadequate to support their case.

The inconsistencies in Adams's letter and the documents accompanying them were publicly addressed in two letters to the *Richmond Enquirer* from Benjamin Watkins Leigh under the pseudonym "Algernon Sydney."[28] Leigh, a venerable Virginia Republican, disputed the premises upon which Adams had defended Jackson. He characterized Adams's letter as one "designed more to doubts and discontents at home, than to answer the complaints of the Spanish government."[29] He accused Adams of prodding Monroe into upholding Jackson's actions and called the arguments in the Erving letter "as dangerous as they are cruel and abhorrent from the national character for moderation, clemency, and justice." He demonstrated that Adams's references to Vattel in defending the execution of the two Britons were taken out of context and did not support what Adams claimed they did.[30] In addition, Leigh's review of the documentary evidence led him to charge that it did not support the claims Adams had made on its behalf. He pointed out that the documents that had been released proved that Jackson had exceeded his orders—thus publicizing the discrepancy Monroe had attempted to cover up by altering his correspondence with Jackson. Leigh called for the invasion of Florida to be "disavowed, disapproved, and reprehended by our government." The authoritative nature of the "Algernon Sydney" letters made Leigh's charges hard to refute. Ironic too, is the pseudonym under which he chose to write—that of one of the English "real whig" classical republicans of the early eighteenth century.

Adams's legalistic defense of an illegal act was thus revealed to be a fraudulent legalism. The president and the secretary of state knew this (as evidenced by their efforts to change Jackson's correspondence), and the Sydney letters made that fact and the discrepancies in the documentary evidence part of the public record. However, the letters appeared two weeks after the late December publication of Adams's letter, which then had already decisively effected public opinion. The Erving letter gave the rhetorical high ground to those who defended Jackson and the administration, labeling them as champions of international law, the rights of American settlers, and "patriotism" against those who were in the uncomfortable position of demanding what the Spanish government demanded—the punishment of Jackson. The charges that Jackson had acted unconstitutionally, raised amid fears of the rise of an American Bonaparte, rang hollow compared with Adams's sacred history of Americans struggling against foreign intriguers and native "savages" to fulfill the nation's manifest destiny. Given the American public's disposition to accept its myths as truths, Adams's letter needed only to be plausible to be believed. Moreover, it was read by a public that revered Jackson and wished to see his actions defended, particularly since those actions augmented the power of a nation in which many people had a stake.

That the documentary evidence did not "prove" Adams's contentions was no doubt unknown to most people and probably meant little to those who did know. It was far more important that his explanation of the Seminole War harmonize with the national myths of virtue, mission, and destiny than that it correspond to a set of documents. The sheer bulk and official-looking nature of the material Adams submitted allowed it to function symbolically as "evidence," quite apart from any relation those documents had to the events in question.

Matters worsened for the administration on 12 January when the House Committee on Military Affairs released its report condemning the executions of Ambrister and Arbuthnot. Shortly thereafter, Congressman Thomas W. Cobb of Georgia introduced resolutions calling for legislation prohibiting the execution of prisoners of war without the consent of the president, legislation prohibiting the invasion of foreign territory without congressional approval, and disapproval of the capture of St. Mark's and Pensacola as "contrary to orders and in violation of the constitution."[31] The House attack was orchestrated in part by Treasury Secretary Crawford, who had a long-standing feud with Jackson and who welcomed the chance to tarnish the image of a future presidential rival. Clay, also jealous of the public's magnetic attraction to Old Hickory, led the anti-Jackson forces.[32]

The House took up the question of the Seminole War on 16 January. It proved the longest, most celebrated, most controversial congressional debate to that time. Packed galleries greeted the procession of speakers, each of whom welcomed the opportunity to hold forth on a topic of such intense public interest. Clay made the most notable speech. In an alternately rambling, passionate, and eloquent address, the Kentuckian decried the subjugation of the Seminoles by the sword of Jackson and raised the specter of military leaders subverting American constitutional government. His fierce attack signaled the beginning of a feud with Jackson that lasted for decades.[33]

Cynics found Clay's lamentations on behalf of the Seminoles hard to swallow. Clearly, the constitutional and humanitarian impulses of the anti-Jackson forces were reinforced by their dislike and fear of both the general and the administration. Rufus King captured the ambiguity of the debate when he wrote that although many of Jackson's supporters (himself included) were "promoting measures which they would not approve," the credibility of the opposition left much to doubt. "I cannot join in the hue and cry with them, who with altogether different motives, are zealously, and for the first time in their lives, the champions of humanity, the teachers of the milder virtues, the accusers of the vindictive white warrior, and the protectors of the red men."[34]

Beyond the skepticism of those who saw the anti-Jackson forces as motivated by political considerations, the efforts of Jackson's opponents were doomed by the dynamics of American political discourse. Concerns over possible violations of the Constitution seemed vague and abstract compared with the tangible gains derived from Jackson's exploits, particularly now that those exploits had been given a patriotic luster by Adams. Indeed, the only way to rebut Adams's letter was to challenge its implicit assumption regarding the "destiny" of the United States to control the Southeast, as well as its assumption of the inherent evil of the blacks, Indians, Spanish, and British who stood in the way of that destiny. Yet to question such assumptions would automatically place the politician who did so beyond the realm of mainstream American political discourse, within which a belief in America's destiny and in the depravity of those who oppose it has generally been a prerequisite for election. Similarly, to criticize Jackson's invasion of Florida while not questioning America's "right" to the peninsula was to raise a procedural objection of the sort that carried little weight in the pragmatic mind of the American public.[35]

Chances that the resolutions disapproving Jackson's conduct would pass were greatly diminished by the appearance in Washington of Old Hickory himself on 23 January. He arrived from Nashville on horseback, determined to stymie the "hellish machinations" (as he termed them) of Clay and Crawford. Few dared directly to challenge Jackson, whose reputation for fits of uncontrolled anger and a propensity for dueling preceded him. The general monitored the remainder of the debate from his hotel suite, casting a formidable shadow over events.[36]

On 8 February, the House reached a verdict. It rejected the Committee on Military Affairs resolutions condemning the execution of Arbuthnot and Ambrister by votes of 62 to 108 and 63 to 107. The Cobb resolutions intended to prevent a repetition of the Seminole War were voted down 70 to 100. Jackson (and the administration) stood completely vindicated. Far from discrediting Jackson, the failed congressional attack increased his popularity with the American people. To many, the large margins by which he had been cleared confirmed the suspicion that the attack on their hero had been politically motivated. In the wake of the House vote, Jackson departed on a triumphant tour of the Northeast in which he was mobbed by an adoring public that for the most part knew little and cared less about his flouting of the Constitution. Then, as now, the American public loved bold figures on horseback who refused to be constrained by constitutional niceties. In a vivid display of *caudillismo* North American style, Jackson was feted with parades, banquets, bands, and portraiture.[37]

Adams's bold, ingenious handling of the Seminole War crisis resulted from his recognition of two basic truths. First, he remembered Madison's dictum that "all government rests on opinion"—a point particularly true in a democracy.[38] Second, Adams realized that public opinion could best be influenced by a defense of the Seminole War that powerfully articulated the basic American myths of virtue, mission, and destiny. Such a defense would make irrelevant any facts to the contrary in the minds of most people. In this sense, Adams's "great gun" helped define the art of rhetorical leadership in an imperial democracy that would be repeatedly faced with the need to find moral justification for what were essentially acts of self-aggrandizement. In the tradition of Cicero, Adams's powerful oratory had swayed the course of a nation.

John Quincy Adams anxiously watched the proceedings against Jackson unfold. He interpreted criticism of the general as an indirect assault upon himself. "There is a common object of decrying me," he wrote. "There is not in either house of congress an individual member who would open his lips to defend me . . . and as I am not there to defend myself, Clay has a free swing to assault me, which he does, both in his public speeches and by secret machinations, without scruple or delicacy."[39]

As the marathon debate on Jackson's conduct neared a climax in early February, the cabinet gathered to consider a new proposal by Onís, the first since he had signaled his intention to assume full negotiating power. Communicated to Adams by Hyde de Neuville, the proposal called for a western boundary following the Red River to the 95th degree longitude, then a line north to the Arkansas River, extending to its source. From there, Onís proposed that a line be drawn due west to the "Multnomah" (Willamette) River and follow its course to the Columbia and then to the Pacific. This line conceded much more to the United States than any of Onís's previous offers, and Monroe, weary of the negotiations, inclined toward accepting it. Adams, however, was not yet satisfied. The offer, he said, "would not be acceptable to the nation"; he added that if Onís really intended to come to terms, "we can obtain better."[40]

"Better" to Adams meant a northwestern boundary extending along the 41st parallel. He cajoled the president and other cabinet members not to be overanxious for a settlement now that Onís was on the verge of total capitulation. Adams reasoned that Onís, having conceded the principle of a transcontinental boundary, could be made to yield even more (see Map 6). He had judged Onís's mood correctly. Having secured the Texas boundary at the Sabine, the Spaniard was ready to make concessions along the northwest coast in order to ensure a treaty. He still feared that should a treaty not be signed before the end of the current session of Congress, the United States or its proxies would invade Florida and possibly Texas. The vindication of Jackson by Congress proved to Onís that the administration could act as it pleased without fear of censure. Moreover, he continued to distrust Hyde de Neuville, whose primary goal Onís suspected to be the improvement of Franco-American relations.[41]

Hence, on 9 February Onís delivered to Adams an eighteen-point projet outlining the elements of a treaty. Its major points were these:

1. Cession of East and West Florida (that is, as they were ceded by Great Britain to Spain in 1783) to the United States.
2. A western boundary beginning at the Sabine, running to the 32nd parallel, then due north to the Red River and along its course to to the 100th meridian, then north to the Arkansas and along the course of that river to the 42nd parallel, then directly west to the Multnomah River, following its course north to the 43rd parallel, and then to the Pacific.

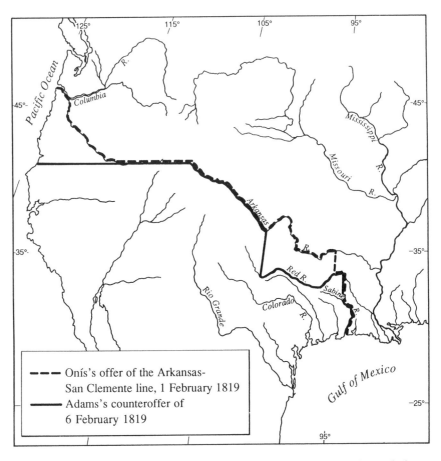

Map 6. The Proposals of 1 and 6 February 1819 (projected on the Melish map of 1818)

3. The guaranty of all land grants in Florida made by the king of Spain until 24 January 1818, the date Onís first proposed the cession of the Floridas.
4. A reciprocal renunciation of all claims, either public or private, against the other government.
5. The renewal of the treaty of limits and navigation of 1795 between Spain and the United States (Pinckney's Treaty), excepting those parts superseded by the current settlement.[42]

The projet seemed promising, but before submitting it to the cabinet for evaluation, Adams prepared a counterprojet so that the two might be considered side by side. On 11 February a long cabinet discussion found Adams once again battling the inclinations of the other members of the administration (including Monroe) to accept Onís's offer. Adams still insisted on 41 degrees as the northwestern boundary; moreover, he lobbied for the line to be drawn along the southern and western banks of the rivers (thereby excluding Spain from their navigation) rather than down the center, as is customary diplomatic practice.[43] In spite of all the concessions Onís had made, Adams still fought for more, as if every inch he could wrest from the Spaniard would add luster to his country's (and his own) greatness. He had Florida; he had a transcontinental boundary. Now he strove to make the American corridor to the Pacific as wide as possible.

Monroe instructed Adams to prepare a formal counteroffer in response to Onís's comprehensive proposal. On 13 February, Adams presented this new projet to Hyde de Neuville, terming the offer "the last we could make" (see Map 7). It varied from Onís's projet in both form and substance. First, it dispensed with the effusive expressions of good will that Onís had included, which Adams characterized as "sentimental professions of friendship and affection between the United States and the king of Spain" and "entirely superfluous." Second, Adams refused to allow Onís's presupposition that West Florida had not been part of the Louisiana Purchase. That issue had been a point of honor between the negotiators of the two sides since the beginning of the controversy, and even with victory within his grasp, Adams would not yield this symbolic triumph to Onís. He thought it "unnecessary" to say "anything directly contrary" to the past pretensions of either side.

A compromise appeared in the making on the crucial western boundary question. Adams's offer of a line from the Arkansas River to the 41st parallel and then directly to the Pacific had been countered by Onís's proposal of a line to the Pacific along the 42nd. But Hyde de Neuville stressed that on two points Onís could not yield "without humiliation": that the boundary be drawn down the center of the rivers rather than along their southern and western banks, and that Spain be allowed navigation of the rivers constituting part of the boundary. Adams rejected both demands on the grounds of practical considerations. Difficulties in charting the shifting centers of the rivers could lead to disputes over ownership of islands; and control of the waterways "was of no importance to Spain, who would never have any settlements" there, whereas "the United States would have extensive settlements upon them in a very few years," making navigation rights a moot point.[44]

Beyond these questions pertaining to the western boundary, only minor points separated the two sides. Onís objected to the $5 million

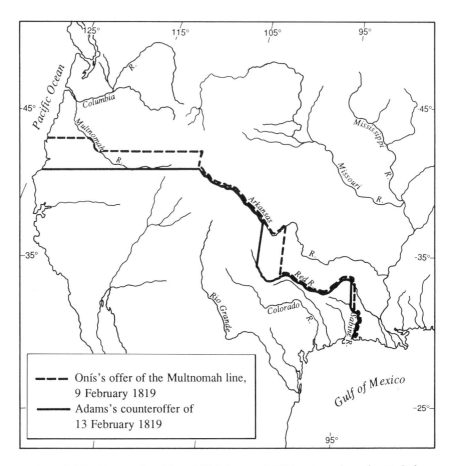

Map 7. The Proposals of 9 and 13 February 1819 (projected on the Melish map of 1818)

limit of claims by Americans against the Spanish government, to be assumed by the United States, on the grounds that Spain would appear to have sold the Floridas for that amount. He feared that the king's advisers would convince the volatile monarch that his "honor" could not be bought for so small a sum. Adams insisted on the figure to protect the government from incurring an open-ended liability for the claims of American citizens. Onís soon capitulated on this point.

On 16 February Hyde de Neuville presented to Adams a written statement summarizing the positions of two sides.[45] An agreement was tantalizingly close. The French minister reported to Adams that Onís "had agreed to all the essential points" of the latest American offer, with the exception of where to draw the river boundaries. Onís still insisted, perhaps as much for reasons of personal honor as for substantive considerations, that the boundary follow the centerline of the rivers.

At a White House reception on 18 February the mood was festive. Rumors of the impending treaty were circulating throughout the capital; conciliation filled the air; and in that spirit Monroe offered to concede the river boundary question to Onís. "I will do anything you want," said Monroe. "I have had a personal esteem for you ever since the first day I dealt with you. Have a glass of wine with me."[46] The next day, when Onís informed Adams of his conversation with Monroe, the secretary was incensed that his negotiating authority had been usurped by good feelings and good wine, even if the usurper was his boss. He went directly to the White House to lobby Monroe to retract his bit of negotiation. The president feared disrupting the prospects for a settlement over what seemed to him a minor point, but Adams persisted in his pleas—as much for the sake of his pride as for the good of his country—and finally Monroe yielded to his pugnacious secretary of state.

Adams then had to convince Hyde de Neuville that the president of the United States had not really meant what he had said to Onís at the reception. He explained to the French minister that he "was confident that Onís had not correctly understood" Monroe, and he went on to dispute the propriety of the whole exchange: "What right had Mr. Onís to speak upon the matter to the president in the drawing room at all? " Adams disingenuously declared that he would be willing to ignore such impertinence this time, "but the president himself would be much and justly displeased if he had reason to think that a complimentary expression of politeness, used by him in answer to a remark made to him by a foreign minister at a drawing room, was to be construed into an abandonment of an important principle in a pending negotiation."[47]

Onís, no doubt in disgust, yielded to Adams's view of events and agreed to take the boundaries along the southern and western banks of the rivers. On 20 February the two negotiators reached final agreement on the long-awaited treaty. Adams suggested that a formal signing ceremony be delayed for two days to coincide with birthday of Washington. At 11:00 A.M. on 22 February 1819, Adams and Onís signed in triplicate their hard-won agreement. That same day the secretary of state personally delivered the treaty to the Senate for ratification.

Adams marked the signing of the treaty with a effusive entry in his diary:

It was near one in the morning when I closed the day with ejaculations of fervent gratitude to the giver of all good. It was, perhaps, the most important day of my life. What the consequences may be of the compact this day signed with Spain is known only to the all-wise and all-beneficent disposer of events, who has brought it about in a manner utterly unexpected and by means the most extraordinary and unforeseen. . . . Let no idle and unfounded exultation take possession of my mind, as if I could ascribe to my own foresight or exertions any portion of the event. It is the work of an intelligent and all-embracing Cause. May it speed as it has begun!

The acknowledgement of a definite boundary line to the South Sea forms a great epocha in our history. The first proposal of it in this negotiation was my own, and I trust it is now secured beyond the reach of revocation. It was not even among our claims by the Treaty of Independence with Great Britain. It was not among our pretensions under the purchase of Louisiana—for that gave us only the range of the Mississippi and its waters. I first introduced it in a written proposal of 31st October last, after having discussed it verbally both with Onís and De Neuville. It is the only peculiar and appropriate right acquired by this treaty in the event of its ratification. I record the first assertion of this claim for the United States as my own, because it is known to be mine perhaps only to the members of the present administration, and may perhaps never be known to the public—and, if ever known, will be soon and easily forgotten.[48]

Thus within two paragraphs did an exultant John Quincy Adams credit both God and himself for the making of the Transcontinental Treaty.

The American people enthusiastically greeted the news of the treaty with Spain. Most newspaper reports stressed the acquisition of Florida as the most important aspect of the agreement, particularly in the South, where the "threat" posed by Spanish ownership of Florida had long been a subject of concern. Few southerners as yet perceived cession of the Texas claim as cause for alarm.[49]

It is certain that Monroe and Adams feared a negative backlash as a result of the concession of the Texas claim. In early February 1819, just weeks before reaching an agreement with Onís, Adams wrote in his diary that "There are various symptoms that if we do not come to an arrangement there will be a large party in the country dissatisfied with our concessions from the Rio del Norte to the Sabine."[50] According to Adams, Monroe shared this concern but believed that the acquisition of the Floridas, the extension of a claim to the Pacific, and the resolution of the claims question "would be such advantages to this country, that any . . . opposition founded upon our consent to take the Sabine for the western boundary would have little weight with the people."[51] Jackson, too, in conversation with Adams, reputedly argued that while "there were many many individuals who would take exception" to the retreat from the Rio del Norte, "the vast majority of the nation would be satisfied with the western boundary we propose, if we obtain the Floridas."[52]

But the point to be emphasized is that conceding the claim to Texas was not necessary to obtain the Floridas. Acquisition of the Floridas was assured as of Onís's offer of 24 January 1818. The concession of Texas was first proposed in July 1818 in exchange for a transcontinental boundary, and even so, more was conceded than was absolutely necessary. Onís's instructions of 10 October 1818 authorized him to yield as far as the Colorado River of Texas in order to make a deal. While Adams probably did not know this, it is worth comparing the secretary of state's tenacious struggle for every square inch and every watercourse in the Northwest with his passive acquiescence in the cession of the Texas claim.[53]

Samuel Flagg Bemis writes that "under Monroe's direction no determined effort was made to get Texas."[54] Indeed, Adams and Monroe saw cession of the Texas claim as a positive good. In March 1820, Adams candidly admitted to Senator Ninian Edwards of Illinois that "as an Eastern man, I should be disinclined to have either Texas or Florida without a restriction excluding slavery from them."[55] By May 1820, Monroe was even more explicit; he wrote to Jefferson that the uncertainty created by the expulsion of Spain from the continent and the formation of a new government in Mexico meant that "it would be easy to arrange the boundary in the wilderness, so as to include as much territory on our side as we might desire. No European power could prevent it. . . . But the difficulty does not proceed from these sources. It is altogether internal, and of the most distressing and dangerous tendency": that is, the issue of slavery, which Monroe traced as a point of controversy from the birth of the republic. In 1820 he perceived that the Missouri question was only the latest chapter in this controversy; the compromise by which Maine had been admitted as a free state to balance the new slave state of Missouri, he said, had gained time for "passions to subside, & for calm discussion and reflection, which have never failed to produce their proper effect in our country." To Monroe, the implications of the slavery question were clear: "From this view, it is evident, that the further acquisition of territory, to the West and South, involves difficulties of an internal nature which menace the Union itself." He counseled no more acquisitions of territory in the West or South "which is not approved, by all the members, or at least a majority of those who accomplished our revolution."[56]

Shortly thereafter, Monroe wrote to Jackson in a similar vein. "Having long known the repugnance with which the eastern portion of our Union . . . have seen its aggrandizement to the west and south, I have been decidedly of [the] opinion that we ought to be content with Florida for the present, and until the public opinion in that quarter shall be reconciled to any future change."[57] Together, the two letters unarguably demonstrate that Monroe's willingness to concede the claim to Texas stemmed from his fears of adding more potential slave territory to the Union, not as a prerequisite for securing the Floridas from Spain. It is understandable that Monroe and Adams chose not to correct the popular (and subsequent scholarly) misconception that Texas was ceded in exchange for Florida. Their relatively unchallenged cession of the Texas claim must go down as one of the greatest examples of sleight of hand in the history of American diplomacy.

Most Americans at the time did not appreciate the significance of the transcontinental boundary. In an age when it took a week to travel from New York to Washington, few recognized the importance of extending the nation's grasp to the Pacific. Rufus King's reaction was typical: "We gain the Floridas, which we want; and an immense region of territory in the west that we do not want."[58] The agreement with Spain in 1819 became known as the "Adams-Onís Treaty" or the "Florida Treaty," names that obscure its most significant aspect.

The Senate, mirroring the public's enthusiasm for the Transcontinental Treaty, ratified it unanimously on 24 February, acting so quickly that there was no time for opposition to coalesce. On that same day Senator Abner Lacock of Pennsylvania, chairman of the committee in charge of investigating the Seminole War, submitted his long-awaited report on the affair. In calm, measured terms, the report concluded that in the course of conquering Florida, Jackson had disregarded his orders, usurped the authority of Congress and the executive, and inflicted "a wound on the national character."[59] For a while it seemed that the report would reopen the controversy over Jackson's conduct. But Adams ridiculed the document by observing that Jackson's military operations in Florida were "among the most immediate and prominent causes that produced the treaty."[60] Indeed. He recognized the decisive importance of military force in the making of his diplomatic victory. Moreover, the new treaty with Spain, combined with Britain's unconcern about the execution of its subjects, made moot any criticisms of the general's methods. Neither the public nor the Senate was ready to engage in another examination of Jackson's campaign now that its benefits were obvious to all. The Senate tabled Senator Lacock's report, allowing it to expire quietly at the end of the congressional session on 4 March. Ironically, even the authors of the report voted to ratify the treaty.[61]

While Americans rejoiced at the extension of their republic, Europeans feared the birth of another New World empire. The treaty made it clear that the United States had rebounded from the War of 1812 to become a formidable actor in world affairs and nearly unassailable in the Western Hemisphere. The British press saw the agreement as powerful evidence of the ambitious, aggressive, and expansionist tendencies of the United States.[62]

John Quincy Adams brushed off all criticism of his handiwork. Why should the United States not expand its domain? The Europeans had been empire-building for three centuries. The United States could expect criticism from them, if only because of envy. "If the world do not hold us for Romans," Adams said, "they will take us for Jews, and of the two vices I would rather be charged with that which has greatness mingled in its composition."[63] To him, U.S. expansion to the Pacific meant the partial fulfillment of a divine plan. Europe, he wrote, must become "familiarized with the idea of considering our proper dominion to be the continent of North America." That the United States would expand across the continent was "as much the law of nature . . . as that the Mississippi should flow to the sea. Until Europe shall find it a settled geographical element that the United States and North America are identical, any effort on our part to reason the world out of the belief that we are ambitious will have no other effect than to convince them that we add to our ambition hypocrisy."[64] A more ringing endorsement of Manifest Destiny has never been uttered.

Adams's jubilant mood was soon shattered. On 8 March, Henry Clay informed Monroe of three large grants of land in Florida made to Spanish nobles by the king just prior to 24 January 1818, the date before which all grants were acknowledged as valid. Adams rushed to reread his dispatches from Madrid and discovered the bitter truth: in several letters the previous spring, Erving had warned of recent grants in which the king had ceded away all his remaining holdings in Florida; the minister had even included copies of the grants in one of his dispatches.[65] Inexplicably, Adams had overlooked Erving's warning that "this is, perhaps, [the king's] mode of preparing for a cheap cession of the territory to the United States."

Onís too was surprised at the turn of events. Having believed that the grants in question had been voided, he did not welcome this new obstacle to ratification of the treaty he had worked so hard to conclude. Onís had nothing to gain by obstructing the treaty. He had, after all, been the member of the Spanish government who had pushed hardest for a settlement. Historians generally have absolved him of any knowledge of the grants, ascribing them to the backstage machinations of the *camarilla*.[66] Still, Onís must have taken satisfaction at the frustration the situation engendered in his antagonist Adams.

Adams, on the other hand, took it for granted that Onís had intentionally tricked him. Nonetheless, the secretary of state took full responsibility for the error. The news of the land grants, made all the more bitter in that it was conveyed by Clay, fulfilled his "vague, general, and superstitious impression" that the treaty had been too good to be true. Amid the myriad dispatches, letters, state papers, and other correspondence that crowded upon him, Adams had overlooked messages of crucial importance. "This is at least enough to dampen all vanity and self-conceit that I could derive from it. Never will the treaty recur to my memory but associated with the remembrance of my own heedlessness."[67]

Perhaps the voice of conscience spoke to Adams as he flagellated himself for his carelessness. From the outset, he had resorted to ethically dubious tactics to bring Onís to terms. He had submitted spurious document collections to Congress. He had misrepresented the South American revolutions to the public in his "Phocion" letters. He had cynically used the threatened recognition of the South American revolutions as a wedge to gain concessions from Onís. He had exaggerated and distorted the conflict with the Seminoles in such a way as to make runaway slaves and Indians resisting dispossession of their land the aggressors. He had defended the (officially) unauthorized invasion of Florida and the execution of two British subjects. Though European (and American) practice had long divorced the morality of the statesman from that of the private citizen, John Quincy Adams had refused to believe that success in the public realm required compromising one's personal integrity or morality, yet in his diary ruminations and in his correspondence Adams fretted that his success as a statesman and national leader was being attained at the cost of his personal integrity. Now at the moment of triumph, he was deprived of victory by his own inexplicable oversight. He saw it as an act of divine retribution.

Adams's dejection worsened when it became clear that the Spanish government would not ratify the treaty. Although the King and Yrujo had received the agreement favorably, certain members of the Consejo de Estado objected on the grounds that it ceded away too much territory, that it did not protect Spanish territories from expeditions organized in the United States, and, most important, that it did not include a U.S. pledge of non-recognition of the South American governments.[68] In a weird twist, the anxiety of the king's ministers over the recognition question had been heightened by Adams's diplomatic bluff of that spring, a bluff that had pushed Onís and Yrujo toward a settlement but now led members of the Consejo de Estado to balk at its ratification.[69]

Efforts to obtain ratification by Spain were not aided by the conduct of the new minister to Madrid, John Forsyth. The Georgia congressman, had been rewarded for his loyalty to the administration with the job of replacing Erving but proved ill suited to the task. Gruff and tactless, Forsyth soon verified Adams's description of him as lacking in "experience, prudence, and sincerity." Upon arriving in Madrid he became embroiled in a dispute with Spanish officials over the handling of his baggage. He compounded his difficulties by demanding that the land grants in Florida be annulled and by sending diplomatic messages deemed too insulting to be received. Inexperienced as a diplomat and unable to speak Spanish, Forsyth extinguished the flickering hope that the treaty might soon be ratified.[70]

In July 1819, Ferdinand, swayed by his confidants, decided to withhold ratification indefinitely, using the land grant dispute as a pretext. Again, the Spanish government tried to secure British support. A new Spanish minister, General Dionisio Vives, was sent to Washington to negotiate a more favorable settlement. The whole ghastly procedure appeared ready to begin anew. Vives arrived in Washington in April 1820, demanding as preconditions for ratification that the United States strengthen its neutrality laws, guarantee the integrity of Spain's territorial possessions in the Western Hemisphere, and promise not to recognize any rebel governments.[71]

Adams had no intention of yielding to Vives's demands, but Spain's unwillingness to ratify the treaty created confusion in the minds of Monroe and Adams as to what to do next. In August 1819, Adams recorded that the cabinet was "unanimously agreed" on the necessity of asking Congress for authority to take possession of Florida with or without Spain's ratification of the treaty. In a rationale that echoed his defense of Jackson, Adams argued that the occupation of Florida by United States troops would not be "an act of hostility to Spain, but . . . an assertion of our own right, rendered necessary by a breach of faith on the part of Spain." He repeated this argument in early November as the cabinet deliberated the contents of the president's third annual message to Congress.[72]

Monroe, however, after initially agreeing with the plan to take strong action, had second thoughts. Intelligence reports from Europe indicated that France and Russia would strongly oppose a U.S. move into Florida; such a move might provoke them into active support of Spain. Monroe also worried that domestic opinion as well might oppose another military foray into Florida. Adams, too, as a result of a conversation with the Russian minister, Pierre de Polética, who stressed the tsar's desire for the "maintenance and preservation of a general peace," began to harbor doubts as to the wisdom of taking precipitate action in Florida.[73] Monroe convened his cabinet on 26 November in an attempt to reach a consensus on a course of action. That meeting again revealed the strange interpersonal dynamic of the Monroe administration. Adams entered it still committed to pushing for strong action. To his surprise (and suspicion), he found Crawford pushing for implementing the treaty unilaterally, after formerly opposing such a course. Adams now realized that to occupy Florida involved a very real danger of war; moreover, he sensed that Monroe resented being pushed in that direction: "Lately, and particularly yesterday, I saw that my advice had become irksome to the president—that he was verging on the suspicion that I was spurring him to rash and violent measures." As usual, Adams attributed this mistrust to the machinations of his rivals: "The enemies of Mr. Monroe's administration, and my enemies, have been continually laboring with the industry and venom of spiders to excite in his mind a jealousy of me. They have so far succeeded that whatever I earnestly recommend, he distrusts." Consequently, Adams abruptly reversed course and dropped his recommendation of the occupation of Florida.[74] The following day he met again with the president, who now was again leaning in favor of strong action. Adams, admitting that his reversal of the previous day had been done solely in the hope of pleasing the president, this time offered his support to whatever course Monroe chose. For once, the masterful secretary of state was reduced to the role of the fawning courtier, at a loss as to what move to recommend next.[75]

The arguments of Hyde de Neuville made clear to Adams the path to follow. The French minister pleaded with Adams to await the arrival of the new Spanish minister before taking any action to implement the treaty. Hyde de Neuville argued that forbearance by the United States in the matter would curry great favor with the

European allies, who desperately wished to avoid any conflict that might lead to a general war. Using force to implement the treaty would have the effect of making Spain the aggrieved party and perhaps compel the other European sovereigns to support its cause. Hyde de Neuville contended that ratification could be gained without the use of force if the United States would be patient.[76]

Ultimately, Monroe chose a conciliatory approach. In his message to Congress of 7 December 1819 the president requested authorization to implement the treaty, yet announced that he would make no move to do so before meeting with the new Spanish minister. Monroe contended that to refrain temporarily from asserting its claims would demonstrate the "candor, magnanimity, and honor" of the United States. He added that a short delay would cost the nation nothing.[77] In May 1820 the president again formally delayed plans to implement the treaty, this time because he wanted to assess the position of the new Spanish republican government recently established in the wake of a military revolt in Madrid.[78]

Monroe's altruistic rhetoric aside, it was European diplomatic opinion that influenced him not to take Florida by force. While military action had done much to wrest a treaty from Onís, it now promised to provoke an international backlash against the United States. Accordingly, Monroe and Adams recognized that "forbearance" was the proper diplomatic card to play. By acting with restraint, the United States stood to reinforce its role as a "responsible" actor in international affairs, secure in the knowledge that the Europeans were favorable to the treaty's eventual ratification.[79] It was the capstone of three years of astute diplomacy by Adams and Monroe.

Only on 5 October 1820, after the establishment of a new Spanish government following the military revolt, did Madrid ratify the treaty. In the end, the land grants were declared null and void. In the United States, Monroe resubmitted the treaty to the Senate for ratification. It passed, though this time there were four dissenting votes from western senators. On 22 February 1821, the "Adams-Onís Treaty" took effect.

For Adams, the two years between the treaty's initial signing and its eventual ratification were a time of self-imposed purgatory. He correctly believed that his political opponents were using his role in the land grant dispute to humiliate him.[80] He suspected that Crawford secretly wished the treaty to fail. And he perceived a rising tide of opposition to the treaty, both by westerners (led by Clay) who objected to the cession of Texas and by northerners who were spurred by the Missouri debates into opposing the entry of Florida into the

Union.[81] In January 1820, Adams wrote that "the treaty is gone forever . . . all the benefit which was hoped from it for the administration is lost."[82]

The treaty's eventual ratification provoked another revealing diary entry: "I considered the signature of the treaty as the most important event of my life. It is an event of magnitude in the history of this Union. The apparent conclusion of the negotiation had been greatly and unexpectedly advantageous to the country. It had at once disconcerted and stimulated my personal antagonists and rivals. It promised well for my reputation in the public opinion. Under the petals of this garland of roses the Scapin, Onís, had hidden a viper. . . . Clay and his admirers here were snickering at the simplicity with which I had been bamboozled by the crafty Spaniard. . . . By the goodness of that inscrutable Providence which entraps dishonest artifice in its own snares, Onís divulged his trick too soon for its success."[83] Adams (in spite of his earlier self-recriminations) could not acknowledge that the land grant dispute had been the result of his own carelessness. He preferred to believe that Onís had been out to trick him.

On the same day that the Transcontinental Treaty was ratified, John Quincy Adams submitted to Congress his *Report on Weights and Measures*, advocating the adoption of the metric system in the United States and abroad. Adams wrote of it in heroic terms: "I have no reason to expect that I shall ever be able to accomplish any literary labor more important to the best ends of human exertion, public utility, or upon which the remembrance of my children may dwell with more satisfaction." He bracketed the *Report* with the Transcontinental Treaty as "two of the most memorable transactions of my life."[84]

The painstakingly and laboriously compiled *Report* reflected a lifetime of learning. It attempted to synthesize history, philosophy, and physics into a coherent whole that illuminated the nature of human relations. The treatise had made great demands on Adams's already over-busy schedule, leaving him even less time to spend with his wife and children and preventing him from visiting his father in Quincy in the summer following his mother's death. Writing it had become almost an obsession for him, a chance to escape to the world of his imagination. On the assumption that "the associated pursuit of great objects of common interest is among the most powerful expedients for the improvement of modern man," the *Report* called for "a concert of civilized nations" to establish a uniform system of weights and measures to facilitate international commerce. Adams acknowledged that any legislated change in weights and measures would face much popular resistance, yet such a system would have more than just economic benefits. Adams envisioned its leading to "the improvement of the physical, moral, and intellectual condition of man upon earth" by strengthening the "links of sympathy between the inhabitants of the most distant regions." In a revealing parallel, he pointed to the suppression of the African slave trade as a precedent to the sort of international effort that would be required for such a project. He left no doubt as to its importance: "Uniformity of weights and measures . . . would be a blessing of such transcendent magnitude, that, if there existed upon earth a combination of power and will adequate to accomplish the result by the energy of a single act, the being who should exercise it would be among the greatest of benefactors of the human race." In essence, the *Report on Weights and Measures* was Adams's philosophical counterpart to the treaty that had been ratified that same day.[85]

William Appleman Williams describes the *Report* as "the classic document of the Age of Mercantilism. . . . [It is] a magnificent triumph of the *Weltanschauung* of mercantilism that transcends time and place."[86] Yet Adams's vision was not appreciated at the time. So great was the erudition of the piece that no one in Congress bothered to read it. Indeed, except for a member of the Royal Engineers, no one seems to have read it at all during Adams's lifetime. Even his father, perhaps in retribution for John Quincy's absence during his time of emotional need, admitted to his son that "I cannot say, and perhaps shall never be able to say, that I have read it."[87] And 170 years after the publication of the *Report on Weights and Measures*, the American people—almost alone among the nations of the world—still have not seen the wisdom in Adams's recommendation to adopt the metric system.

The American Cicero

Truth, virtue, honor, the dignity of human nature . . . are
the touchstones by which the conduct of nations as well as
individuals is to be tested.
John Quincy Adams to William Peterkin, 20 July 1821

Final ratification of the Transcontinental Treaty signaled the end of
the first phase of American continental expansionism in the nineteenth century. By establishing the previously undefined limits of the
Louisiana Purchase and adding Florida, the treaty resolved long-
standing uncertainties about the nation's borders. Moreover, the
treaty determined the course of American expansionism until the
Civil War by its claim to Oregon and the northwest coast in exchange
for an equally strong (if not stronger) claim to Texas.

The cession of the Texas in return for a transcontinental boundary
proved critically important. In effect, the "Louisiana Purchase" had
been the basis of a U.S. claim to virtually all of North America. The
Transcontinental Treaty, by defining "Louisiana" to exclude Texas,
set the stage for one of the most divisive issues in antebellum politics—Texas annexation. Proslavery leaders saw Texas as essential to
the preservation of slavery and the Union. British attempts (real or
imagined) to acquire Texas were viewed as a direct assault on southern interests. The Jacksonian pro-slavery advocate Duff Green attributed British pretensions to abolishing slavery in Texas to "the
monomaniacal ravings of John Quincy Adams" and "the fanatical
representations of the abolitionists."[1]

When seen in the context of the open-ended nature of America's
Louisiana Purchase claims, Democratic calls for the "re-annexation"
of Texas were entirely justified. Southern leaders were correct in
perceiving that the cession of the Texas claim in 1819 was an attempt
to contain slavery. Yet they were wrong to attribute the decision to
yield Texas to Adams. Historic responsibility for that decision must
be placed on Monroe.

As for the Northwest, ratification of the treaty was soon followed
by the tsar's famous ukase of September 1821 claiming exclusive

control of territory on the northwest coast as far south as 51 degrees and excluding Americans from waters within one hundred Italian miles of the shore.[2] Led by John Quincy Adams, the United States vigorously opposed this assertion of Russian imperial rights. Only after several toughly worded messages from Adams (and the financial collapse of the Russian-American Company) did the tsar repeal his edict. This led in April 1824 to an agreement between the United States and Russia allowing nearly unrestricted access for American citizens to the northwest coast and its adjoining waters.[3]

By defeating the tsar's attempt to take control of the northwest coast, Adams and Monroe legitimized the concept of noncolonization articulated in the Monroe Doctrine. Although the president's famous message to Congress of December 1823 is often characterized as a hollow threat, it must be remembered that in July 1823 Adams had stated explicitly to the Russians that the United States would contest any new colonial establishments on the northwest coast.[4] Lacking a strong naval presence in the region, the Russians chose not to challenge the United States over the issue. The agreement of April 1824 represented a Russian capitulation to American demands. Seen from this perspective, the Monroe Doctrine was less a hollow threat to the European powers than a formal announcement to Congress of a policy already in place.

Despite the establishment of an American presence on the northwest coast, the dream of a neomercantile empire centered at Astoria never materialized. The dream did not fail for lack of attention. Throughout the 1820s and 1830s a variety of entrepreneurs and interests pushed to explore the region and tap its economic potential. The most notable figure in this regard was congressman John Floyd of Virginia, who lobbied for American military occupation of the Columbia River as a first step to expanded trade with China.[5] But treacherous shoals at the mouth of the Columbia prevented Astoria from becoming a major port.[6] In addition, overzealous hunting rapidly depleted the sea otter population in the 1820s, thus eliminating a primary fur export to Canton. Finally, the expanding operations of the Hudson's Bay Company in the Oregon country limited the freedom of Americans to exploit the region during the era of "free and open occupation."[7] Only in the wake of the mass migrations of settlers in the 1840s did the United States challenge Great Britain for control of the Oregon country. It must be remembered, however, that initial U.S. interest in the region was mercantile, not agricultural. As Norman Graebner writes: "In Oregon the American territorial objective had been clear from the beginning of the boundary controversy in

1818—access to the magnificent harbor of Puget Sound through the Strait of Juan de Fuca. What had dictated the perennial American insistence on the extension of the forty-ninth parallel to the Pacific had been the realization that such a settlement would convey the necessary waterways to the United States. So clear was the national interest in the distant Northwest that Fuca Strait and Puget Sound together guided official American policy from John Quincy Adams to James K. Polk." [8] Graebner's observation on the commercial origins of U.S. interests in Oregon is sound, yet it should be said that American interest in the region dates at least from the time of the Lewis and Clark expedition or, more properly, from the 1787 voyage of Robert Gray and his ship *Columbia*.

Even though the northwest coast never proved the axis of a global trading empire, as Adams had anticipated, the United States had taken a determined first step toward acquiring a share of the wealth of the Orient. It is in this sense that the Transcontinental Treaty of 1819 may be considered to be the origin of global empire. The policy of Adams and Monroe built upon the trail learned of by Astor, blazed by Lewis and Clark, and championed by Jefferson. At the end of the trail lay a foothold on the Pacific and access to the transpacific trade. By acquiring a claim to the Oregon country, Adams and Monroe made the United States a force to be reckoned with in the imperial struggle between Russia, Spain, and Great Britain for control of the eastern Pacific Rim. Within fifty years the United States would secure clear title to Oregon, annex California, and purchase Alaska. By the turn of the twentieth century, Hawaii and the Philippines would be acquired and the principle of the "open door" firmly established with regard to China. In the twentieth century the American drive for preeminence in Asia (itself a part of the 500-year European thrust eastward) would result in a war with Japan for supremacy in Asia and the establishment of a truly global American empire. The unparalleled extent of this empire is suggested in the vision of omnipotence implicit in the U.S. role as the world's first (and, so far, only) "superpower." *Novus ordo seclorum.*

The Jeffersonian origins of the Transcontinental Treaty should not obscure Adams's critical role in making the transcontinental claim a reality. It was Adams who best perceived the nation's long-term imperial interest amid the tangled skein of diplomatic controversies confronting the United States. Adams's observation that that a transcontinental claim formed no part of either the Treaty of Paris ending the War of Independence or the Louisiana Purchase makes clear why he saw it as his great contribution to the American nation. In pursuit of this end he walked a diplomatic tightrope. He outmaneuvered opponents both at home and abroad, responded shrewdly to contingency, and tempered his diplomacy with the strategic use of force—a bravura performance in the tradition of classic European diplomacy. From the perilous circumstances facing the country when Adams took the helm of American foreign policy, the United States emerged poised to conquer a continent. It was this dramatic improvement in the nation's relative position internationally that made Adams the most successful statesman in American history—indeed, the most successful statesman of his time, a period known as the "golden age" of European diplomacy. The legacy of this statecraft would be seen in the policies of Adams protégés William Seward and grandson Henry Adams's confidant John Hay.[9]

The acquisition of Florida achieved by the Transcontinental Treaty fulfilled the long-held dream of security for the southern frontier. The famous "pistol pointed at New Orleans" finally belonged to the United States. By the early 1820s many Americans (including John Quincy Adams) saw Spanish ownership of Cuba as the next "threat" to the nation's borders and rekindled efforts to gain control of that island.[10] The slavery question and the nation's preoccupation with continental settlement, however, prevented the realization of this expansionist dream until 1898.

For the Seminoles, it must have been a sad day when they learned that their homeland now belonged to the United States and that Andrew Jackson would be the province's first American governor. Their persecution in 1818 at Jackson's hands proved but a prelude to a second war of extermination against them (1835-42) in which the remaining members of the tribe either moved west or were killed or forced to take refuge in the dense swamps of Florida. Today, the Seminoles survive in the national consciousness as the mascot of Florida State University.[11]

Final ratification of the Transcontinental Treaty in 1821 also paved the way for recognition of South American independence. Throughout the period between the initial signing of the treaty and its final ratification, recognition of Latin American independence remained hostage to U.S. relations to the European powers. Between February 1819 and February 1821, Adams continued to work to maintain a scrupulous neutrality regarding South American affairs. To Russian Minister Polética, Adams reiterated the intention of the United States to pursue a policy "entirely in harmony" with that of the European powers.[12] The secretary of state, in a manner foreshadowing his handling of the Greek question in 1823, vigorously opposed including favorable references to the South American struggles in the president's annual messages of 1819 and 1820 on the grounds that to do so would needlessly antagonize the Europeans.[13] Although Adams always refused formally to guarantee to Spain that the United States would not recognize the South American revolutionary governments, he did hint to Spanish Minister Vives that that if the treaty were ratified, the United States "probably would not precipitately recognize the independence of the South Americans."[14] Adams kept his word, waiting a decent interval before taking the step Spain had so feared. The recognition of South American independence, forecast as imminent by John Quincy Adams in January 1819, finally began in mid-1822.[15]

Throughout the period, U.S. policy toward South America paralleled that of Great Britain. Indeed, the concept of nonintervention in the Western Hemisphere, the other important principle of the Monroe Doctrine, was made viable by Great Britain's unambiguous opposition to European efforts to restore Spanish sovereignty in South America. The "Polignac Memorandum" of October 1823, in which British Foreign Secretary George Canning explicitly stated to the French minister his objections to any efforts by the European powers to intervene in South America, merely restated a policy that had been clear since the conference of Aix-la-Chapelle. Adams's genius as a diplomat is again revealed by his adamant opposition to Canning's famous offer of Anglo-American cooperation in South American affairs. Although Jefferson and Madison both advised Monroe to accept the offer as a means of ensuring British good will, Adams alone recognized that the United States had nothing to gain by allying with Great Britain and nothing to fear if it did not. Adams knew that Great Britain would continue its policy of de facto recognition of South American independence with or without the formal support of the United States.[16]

The Monroe Doctrine can be viewed as the culmination of six years (and in a larger sense, nearly fifty years) of astute American diplomacy. Adams's far-sighted, pragmatic approach to Anglo-American relations, South American affairs, continental and commercial expansionism, and the place of the United States in the world made possible the bold articulation in December 1823 of what was in effect a statement of hemispheric supremacy. It must also be said that the Transcontinental Treaty is of greater historical significance than the far more thoroughly investigated circumstances immediately surrounding Monroe's celebrated 1823 message. The success of Monroe's foreign policy (and hence the Monroe Doctrine) hinged on the treaty. Insofar as the treaty finalized the boundaries of the Louisiana

Purchase, it should be bracketed with that more heralded piece of American diplomacy as the diplomatic cornerstones of the Monroe Doctrine. Questions of authorship aside, it is undeniable that without Adams's adroit statesmanship during the preceding years, Monroe would have been in no position to pronounce his famous doctrine.

This is not to diminish the scope of Monroe's foreign policy achievements. As the nation's chief executive, Monroe deserves credit for making the Jeffersonian foreign policy a success in spite of the near-catastrophes of the Embargo and the War of 1812. In this respect, Monroe's foreign policy was more successful than that of either Jefferson or Madison. It might rightfully be claimed that the shrewdness of Adams made possible much of Monroe's success; nonetheless, Monroe deserves credit for being wise enough to know sound advice when he heard it—one of the most valuable traits for a president to have.

Recently, scholars of early American diplomacy have noted a continuity of ideas and aims in the nation's foreign policy from 1776 to the present.[17] The record of Adams and Monroe's foreign policy (and more generally the Jeffersonian foreign policy as a whole) lends support to this observation. During Monroe's presidency a number of critical precedents regarding the conduct and control of American foreign policy were established or reinforced. Most important, the executive branch of the government emerged from the Monroe presidency with substantially greater power than was envisioned by the framers of the Constitution. The expansion of presidential power represented by Jefferson's Louisiana Purchase was augmented considerably during Monroe's two terms. In several key respects it can be said that Monroe's administration marked the birth of the "Imperial Presidency."

Specifically, Congress's unsuccessful challenge to the Amelia Island occupation, failed push for South American recognition, and abortive attempt to censure Jackson's invasion of Florida demonstrated that the legislative branch would allow the executive wide latitude to conduct foreign policy. Congressional votes on these issues indicated unambiguously a reluctance to interfere with the presidential conduct of foreign affairs even if that conduct bordered on the unconstitutional. Adams, an outspoken champion of a strong executive branch, knew that an imperial foreign policy demanded a president with far more power than was prescribed by the Founding Fathers. His success in expanding the power of the executive branch over foreign affairs is one his most enduring legacies.

The power of the executive to make war was enormously strengthened during the Monroe presidency. The de facto military conquest of Florida definitively established that undeclared war would be a foreign policy tool available to the president. Unlike Jefferson, who had refrained from using force to implement the Mobile Act of 1804, or Madison, who in 1812 had disavowed the actions of Mathews in Florida, Monroe (as a result of Adams's influence) defended Jackson's seizure of Florida. In a recent work on Jeffersonian policy, Robert Tucker and David Hendrickson observe that "no chapter in American diplomacy would appear to lend itself less to the category of a morality play than the diplomacy of the Floridas."[18] Yet the military means by which the province was finally acquired does make the diplomacy of the Floridas a morality play—a drama of territory won and constitutional scruples lost. Jackson's invasion of Florida established a precedent of unilateral executive military action that would be repeated approximately two hundred times in the nineteenth and twentieth centuries. The precedent was made all the stronger insofar as Monroe lacked Jefferson's charismatic hold over Congress and the citizenry. Because of this unarguable difference between the two men, it might be said that the enlarged presidential power to conduct foreign policy acquired during Monroe's administration went primarily to the office, not to an individual.

The First Seminole War debate was the moment in which the power to make war shifted decisively in the direction of the executive. Historians have long emphasized the significance of the Louisiana Purchase in expanding the implied powers of the presidency; Adams himself noted in 1820 that it represented "an assumption of implied powers greater in itself and more comprehensive in its consequences than all the assumptions of implied powers in the twelve years of the Washington and Adams administrations put together." Then, in the aftermath of the First Seminole War debate, the executive emerged with the de facto power to make war. Hence, the Jeffersonian era marks the establishment of a presidency with the power to acquire territory and the power to make war. Although presidents have usually felt it necessary to secure support from Congress before committing troops to combat, the success of all five presidential war messages and the reluctance of legislators to cut off funds to troops already in the field indicate that congressional control of the war power has long been more symbolic than real. The power to commit troops to combat without congressional approval has proved critically important to the extension, consolidation, and protection of the constantly growing, ever farther-flung American empire. Not all presidents have chosen to use the de facto war-making power of the office, but it has been available to determined and ambitious chief executives. The inability of Congress in recent years to rein in the Imperial Presidency is seen in the impotence of the 1973 War Powers Act, which successive presidential administrations have unilaterally declared unconstitutional.[19]

Monroe's presidency also marked the definitive end of Jefferson's emphasis on "peaceable coercion" as a major tool of American foreign policy. Certainly, peaceful means would be employed whenever possible to settle foreign policy disputes, but the actions of subsequent American presidents indicate none who seriously believed that the international state system could be based on any foundation other than force and violence. In the councils of state, belief in the possibility of a world without war would be perceived as naive, sentimental, and above all, "unrealistic." Warfare, rather than becoming a relic of the past, would become a central part of the national mythology and an indispensable cultural bonding agent.[20]

Another element responsible for the steady enlargement of presidential powers in the realm of foreign affairs has been the executive's control of the amount and kinds of information available to the public and the Congress on foreign policy matters. A skillful executive is in a position to define the terms of a foreign policy debate by the release to Congress of "facts" (in the form of documents and other bits of intelligence) of his own choosing. Here again the actions of the Monroe administration were precedent-setting. The record of Secretary of State Adams's congressional dealings demonstrates that members of the executive branch have not been above selectively editing, distorting, or otherwise misrepresenting information designed for congressional scrutiny.

Related to the executive branch's ongoing informational advantage over the Congress in foreign policy matters has been the evolution of a presidential "rhetoric of empire" designed to marshal public (as well as congressional) support for its policies. It is a mode of discourse fundamentally rooted in the nation's Puritan and Revolutionary past but which first reached fruition in the rhetoric of Adams, most particularly in his 28 November 1818 dispatch to Erving. This discourse has become a durable and essential aspect of American diplomacy inherited and elaborated by successive generations of American statesmen but fundamentally unchanged over time.

The rhetoric of American empire comprises three main aspects: the assumption of the unique moral virtue of the United States, the assertion of its mission to redeem the world by the spread of republican government and more generally the "American way of life," and the faith in the nation's divinely ordained destiny to succeed in this mission. The rhetorical triad of virtue, mission, and destiny suggests the messianic dimension of the American experience in which foreign policy issues are not subject to reasoned debate but rather reduced to a choice between Right and Wrong, Good and Evil, pro- and anti-American, "us" and "them." In this rhetorical context, opponents to the advance of the American empire have been considered to be misguided, if not depraved and traitorous.

Mastery of the rhetoric of empire has given American presidents a powerful tool with which to gain congressional and public support for an imperial foreign policy. Indeed, the ability to tie specific policy goals to the universalistic myths of American nationality has been essential to presidential foreign policy leadership. Invoking the myths of virtue, mission, and destiny by appeals to blood, soil, and the flag (as Adams did in the Erving letter and as Polk would do in his war message) has proved a nearly irresistible method of gaining support for imperial ventures. Stirring narratives of long-aggrieved Americans, evil enemies, and righteous retaliation have proved persuasive to the minds of most citizens, appealing as they do to the nation's self-image. The theological aspect of these narratives has meant that facts that contradict the narrative are either explained away or ignored, as they were in the wake of Adams's Erving letter. Opponents have found themselves (as critics of Jackson did in 1819) in the position of seeming to be aiding the "enemy."

Beneath this rhetoric of empire there has consistently been an elite reluctance to trust the nation's foreign policy to the uncertainties and vacillations inherent in democracy. Indeed, it may be said that American foreign policy has been inherently undemocratic insofar as political elites have perceived (in the tradition of European *Realpolitik*) only one safe course through which to navigate the hazards of international affairs. In this view, "pluralism" may be acceptable in domestic matters but is a prescription for catastrophe in foreign affairs, where there is a far slimmer margin of error. With the nation's survival all too often at stake, the architects of American empire have generally assumed that foreign policy is too important to be left to the people's unmediated judgment. Whatever views they may have held as candidates, once in office American leaders have generally been of the conviction that the public must be shielded from a candid knowledge of the nation's foreign relations. Abstractions such as "strict construction" of the Constitution must not be allowed to interfere with the survival and success of the American global revolution. The conduct of Jefferson, Monroe, Jackson, Polk, Lincoln, Wilson, Franklin Roosevelt and others suggests that stretching the limits of constitutional authority is a prerequisite to presidential greatness. In this respect, "strict construction" is revealed to be a rhetorical device designed to rein in the presumed excesses of the political opposition, not to prevent the execution of policies deemed by the ruling clique to be vital to the nation's interest.[21] In general, it seems fair to say that America's "greatest" presidents have put more faith in their own judgment regarding how best to serve the national interest (in tacit violation of the presidential oath of office) than in adhering to the narrowly administrative role outlined for the executive in the Constitution.

In a similar way, "morality" has played a paradoxical role in the history of American foreign policy. Foreign policy goals have traditionally needed a moral rationale in order to be viable. Yet from the time of the Jefferson and Hamilton debates over foreign policy in the 1790s, American statesmen and scholars have generally believed that allowing abstract moral considerations to take precedence over tangible national interests would be the height of folly. The foreign policies of even the most "idealistic" presidents (Wilson, for example) cannot be said to have contradicted what were perceived to be the nation's concrete interests. The sheer fact of American wealth and power suggests that a disinterested altruism has not been a major factor in determining American foreign policy. Empirically, the tendency has been to equate U.S. foreign policy goals with that which is moral, and vice versa. While the universalistic rhetoric of American foreign policy has frequently masked realities distinctly less honorable than advertised, American statesmen have been of the conviction (as Adams was during the Jackson affair) that serving what they perceive to be the national interest is the greatest good.

The public's tacit acquiescence in this duplicity is explained by the fact that its desire to believe is stronger than its desire to know, and by its perception that beneath the patriotic fictions its concrete interests are being served. This being so, statesmen have been able to define morality as that which serves the American nation and, more generally, the global republican revolution. Rather than following a "double standard" as is sometimes charged, they have actually adhered to one standard throughout the nation's history: the standard of American national self-interest. The potential ethical pitfalls of this formulation are obviated by the assumption of congruity between the progress of humanity at large and the survival and success of the United States. God blesses America. Or so the thinking goes.[22]

Given John Quincy Adams's vast accomplishments as secretary of state, which dwarfed those of his predecessors Jefferson, Madison, and Monroe, it is one of the cruel ironies of American history that he was not the consensus choice for president in 1824. By the old rules, Adams deserved the chance to lead his country. Unfortunately for him, the era of selecting American presidents by consensus was over.

Throughout his term as secretary of state, Adams continued to evince a lack of interest in the presidency and an unwillingness to cultivate support for his candidacy. In 1818, he wrote to Paul P.C. Degrand: "If my country wants my services [as president], she must ask for them."[23] He spurned the backing of Pennsylvania representative Joel Hopkinson: "I will not take one step to advance or promote pretensions to the presidency."[24] And in a letter to Louisa in late 1822, Adams rejected the efforts on his behalf of newspaper editor Robert Walsh, instructing his wife to "tell him, that in his editorial capacity, I wish him to set aside all his feelings of personal regard for me, as completely as if there were no such person in existence."[25]

Beyond discouraging potential political supporters, Adams's correspondence reveals a strange ambivalence towards the presidency, similar to the ambivalence he expressed upon becoming secretary of state. In October 1822 he wrote to Louisa: "There will be candidates enough for the Presidency without me, and if my delicacy is not suited to the times, there are candidates enough who have no such delicacy. It suits my temper to be thus delicate. . . . If my friends will neither say nor write to me a single word about the Presidency, from this time forward until the election is over, I believe it would be better for me and perhaps better for them. . . . They think I am panting to be President, when I am much more inclined to envy Castlereagh [who had committed suicide] the relief he had found from a situation too much like mine. . . . If I should tell you that I dread infinitely more than I wish to be President, you would not believe me. . . . It is my situation that makes me a candidate and you at least know that my present situation was neither of my own seeking, nor of my choice."[26] The letter's open expression of a death wish is revealing, as is Adams's perception of self as a reluctant agent of destiny.

Adams's coy diffidence toward the office he believed destiny intended him to occupy is most vividly displayed in an extraordinary essay known as the "Macbeth Policy." Meant to serve as a response to Hopkinson's continued exertions on his behalf, it reveals the confused state of Adams's mind in the months prior to the election of 1824. He muses that Macbeth's remark "If chance will have me king, why chance may crown me without my stir" reveals "a remnant of virtue yet struggling in the breast of that victim of unhallowed ambition against the horrible imaginings of that policy by which he finally wins the crown and loses his life and his soul." The parallels to Adams's own life are obvious: high office is to go to those "the most able and the most worthy," not to those with the most friends in the Congress and in the press. A president is made only by the merit of his previous accomplishments, not by offers of aid to those who lend their support. Adams deemed as "essentially and vitally corrupt" an office won as the result of promises made to political backers. Hence, he felt compelled to dissuade those who would assist his candidacy because of their expectations of favors in return. Adams spurned aid in spite of the "great exertions" that he believed had been made to discredit his candidacy. "In no part of the Union, not even in my native New England, has there been an unequivocal manifestation of a public sentiment disposed to hold me up as a candidate. If that feeling does not exist, and in a force which no effort of intrigue can suppress or restrain, it would be a useless, and perhaps worse than useless, thing for a few personal friends of mine to produce it. . . . If my countrymen prefer others to me, I must not repine at their choice. . . . Merit and just right in this country will be heard. And in my case if they are not heard without my stir I shall acquiesce in the conclusion that it is because they do not exist."[27]

Adams's reluctance to take steps to promote his candidacy must be juxtaposed against his management of foreign affairs and domestic opinion as secretary of state. As the helmsman of American foreign policy, Adams maximized the interests of the nation-state he served by a policy in which the ends controlled, rather than justified, the means. Whether by linguistic persuasion, intimidation, or obfuscation, he did what was necessary (including defending the arguably unconstitutional use of military force) to advance what he perceived to be the nation's interest. Yet in the realm of presidential politics, Adams maintained a scrupulous above-the-fray attitude that neither reflected his true feelings about the office nor confronted the realities (even though he was keenly aware of them) of the political culture in which he lived. It is another of the many contradictions that composed the man John Quincy Adams.

His own words notwithstanding, when the people gave a plurality of their votes to Jackson, Adams could not "acquiesce in the conclusion." His unequivocal statement of principle in the "Macbeth Policy" makes even more astounding his shameless politicking in the months preceding the deciding vote for president in the House of Representatives. Official Washington was treated to the spectacle of the imperious John Quincy Adams visiting congressional boarding-houses and engaging in the classic art of political horsetrading. The infamous "corrupt bargain" where by he received Clay's electoral support in exchange for an appointment to head the department of state is only part of the story. Adams also schemed to swing the states of Louisiana, Illinois, and Maryland out of the Jackson camp and into his own.[28] Perhaps the greatest irony is that had Adams taken even a moderately active role in the campaign, he probably would have won the election outright; it was generally acknowledged the he was the most competent, if not the most popular, of the candidates. His rigid adherence to the Adams family myth had proved his undoing.

Samuel Flagg Bemis describes Adams's machinations to win the House presidential vote as "nothing corrupt, nothing unconstitutional."[29] George Dangerfield observes that "if corruption existed, it was a corruption that is inseparable from all political arrangements."[30] Yet even if the means by which Adams became president violated no legal statute, they made a mockery of the creed by which Adams had presumed to live. The union with the archduke of personal ambition, Henry Clay, whatever policy views the two men shared, was a sellout of all Adams purported to believe regarding the proper path to political office. In the final analysis, Adams was as ambitious and as willing to mortgage his personal integrity to feed that ambition as any of his rivals. In light of his actions, his repeated denials of ambition appear a grotesque parody of the classical republican ideal of the virtuous, unselfish, public servant. His protestations of unselfishness only add hypocrisy to his undeniable ambition.

In another sense, his actions reveal that the "classical republicanism" of revolutionary America was anachronistic in the age of Jackson. John Quincy Adams's failure to be spontaneously chosen the leader of his nation, given his capabilities, his achievements, and his character, demonstrated conclusively the irrelevance of the classical ideal that virtue and service are spontaneously rewarded. It was Adams's peculiarly bad luck to be the individual destined to dramatize this lesson. He was, it is fair to say, in a very difficult situation. To have made the major sacrifices that he did in service to his nation, to achieve the triumphs that he did, and then to concede graciously to an individual whose career he had once saved and whom Jefferson had described as "a dangerous man" was in the end too much to ask of Adams, symbolically the most principled individual in the history of American politics. In his mind, he faced an agonizing choice between preserving his personal integrity and preserving the nation to which he had dedicated his life. Perhaps he felt that having sacrificed so much else for his country, he really had *no* choice.

Louisa was disgusted at her husband's electoral schemings. His open display of a grasping ambition that she had always known existed surprised her nonetheless.[31] Henry Adams, too, would later bitterly criticize his grandfather's actions. The family historian described John Quincy as "a tool of the slave oligarchy (especially about Florida)," who "never rebelled until the slave oligarchy contemptuously cut his throat." Henry lamented that his grandfather was "abominably selfish or absorbed in self, and incapable of feeling his duty to others"; his career before 1830 had been "a sentimental folly—a bitter absurdity."[32]

Perhaps the ultimate rebuke was a line that appeared in a Jacksonian newspaper: "Expired at Washington on the ninth of February, of poison administered by the assassin hands of John Quincy Adams . . . the virtue, liberty, and independence of the United States."[33]

Having achieved the office as a result of his own machinations, Adams became one of the least successful presidents in American history. His farsighted plans for national unity and development were almost completely stymied by the opposition of both houses of Congress. His visionary program of national development, requiring as it did a strong central authority, would have been difficult for any political leader to implement. Moreover, his claim to moral leadership had been tarnished, to say the least, by the manner in which he was elected. These facts, combined with the bitterness of Jackson supporters over the "stolen" election of 1824, doomed the Adams administration from the start and spurred the formation of the Democratic party. Ironically, John Quincy Adams, whose whole public life had been devoted to preventing factionalism in American politics, contributed as much as any single individual to the rise of the second American party system by his dogged desire to become president. His defeat at the hands of Jackson in 1828 signaled the beginning of a new era in American politics.

Defeat in 1828 meant that for the second time in two generations, the American people had rejected the program, the leadership, and the values of the Adams family. Like his father before him, John Quincy found himself and his views out of step with the mainstream of American development.[34] He now knew that the destiny of his family was not to lead the nation but to serve as a symbol for all that Jacksonian America meant to change.

In the wake of his rejection by the American public and the suicide of his son George in May 1829, Adams underwent a severe personal crisis.[35] A life founded on the proposition that God's purposes on earth could be determined and acted upon by an educated, moral mind had been shattered. He experienced agonizing doubts about the existence of God and the meaning of life. All his suffering and sacrifices had led only to his defeat by a man whom Brooks Adams describes as representing to John Quincy Adams "the materialization of the principle of evil"; Adams found "to his horror that he, who had worshipped education and science, had unwittingly ministered to the demon."[36]

Adams's disillusionment was not short-lived. The triumph of Jackson and of the values of greed and avarice characteristic of Jacksonian America symbolized to him the destruction of the American experiment in liberty and republican government. The dominance of the slaveholders and the spirit of plunder that drove federal land policy sickened him. In a letter to the Reverend Charles Upham in 1837, Adams expressed his bitterness that the national patrimony of public lands was being squandered rather than used to finance the system of roads, railroads, and canals necessary for national development. Yet the "Sable Genius of the South," fearful of northern prosperity and federal authority, "fell to cursing the tariff and internal improvement, and raised the standard of free trade, nullification, and states rights. . . . The great object of my life therefore . . . has failed."[37]

It is against this backdrop of despair and doubt that Adams's return to politics via the House of Representatives seems all the more quixotic. The sane course would seem to have been retirement to the life of books and agriculture that he had always yearned for. Perhaps a lifetime of public service made politics a hard habit to break; at any rate, in spite of the opposition of Louisa and the boys, Adams took his House seat in 1831.

Perhaps he was merely fulfilling what he perceived to be his new destiny. He crafted his return to politics in Ciceronian terms, quoting the Roman statesman: "I will not desert in my old age the republic I defended in my youth."[38] In his moment of crisis Adams closely identified with Cicero. He had translated Cicero's writings as a boy and now reread them in the original Latin.[39] The Roman's steadfastness in the face of immense tribulation inspired Adams, as did Cicero's historic role as a spokesman for the past in times of political and social turbulence. He wrote to his son Charles: "Every one of the letters of Cicero is a picture of the state of the writer's mind when it was written. It is like an evocation of shades to read them. I see him approach me like the image of the Fantasmagoria—he seems opening his lips to speak to me and passes off, but his words as if they had fallen upon my ears are left deeply stamped upon my memory."[40]

Adams's career in the House is notable for the contrast it bears to his career as a national leader. Occupying a secure seat, the "man of the whole nation" became the man of his section and of his conscience, unconcerned with the divisiveness created by his antislavery stand. Indeed, he missed no opportunity to oppose the slave interests he so despised. He led the struggle to repeal the "gag rule" prohibiting congressional reception of antislavery petitions and defended before the Supreme Court a group of blacks who had mutinied on the slave ship *Amistad*.[41] Although he never publicly allied himself with the abolitionist movement, Bemis describes him as "an abolitionist at heart." It is a fair judgment. Adams's repeated attacks on the "slave-scourging republicans" made him a pariah among southerners and the target of numerous death threats.[42]

Adams's antislavery views predated his career in the House.[43] His diary for the period of the Missouri debates, while the Transcontinental Treaty remained unratified, contains an extraordinary profusion of opinion concerning the dire seriousness of the slavery question and his own uncompromising opposition to slavery and slavemasters. Believing that the problem was systemic, Adams traced the roots of the Missouri controversy to the "dishonorable compromise with slavery" sanctioned by the Constitution. He was convinced that "the bargain between freedom and slavery contained in the Constitution is morally vicious, inconsistent with the principles upon which alone our revolution can be justified."[44] He viewed Jefferson's Declaration of Independence with its promise of equality as "the precipice into which the slave-holding planters of his country sooner or later must fall."[45]

Adams described the Missouri question as "a flaming sword" that threatened the continuation of the union: "I did take it for granted that the present question [Missouri] is a mere preamble—a title page to a great tragic volume."[46] It was not his only premonition of the Civil War. In December 1819 Adams wrote that "the seeds of the Declaration of Independence are yet maturing. The harvest will be what West, the painter, calls the terrible sublime."[47] In November 1820 he eerily predicted: "If slavery be the destined sword in the hand of the destroying angel which is to sever the ties of this union, the same sword will cut in sunder the bonds of slavery itself. A dissolution of the union for the cause of slavery would be followed by a servile war in the slave-holding states, combined with a war between the two severed portions of the union. It seems to me that its result must be the extirpation of slavery from this whole continent; and, calamitous and desolating as this course of events in its progress must be, so glorious would be its final issue, that, as God shall judge me, I dare not say that it is not to be desired."[48] Adams kept this fire-eating sentiment confined (for the time being) to the privacy of his dairy, but it was the sort of apocalyptic rhetoric that would later prove unnerving in the extreme for slaveholders.

Adams's concern over the slave question had led him to doubt the wisdom of territorial expansion even as he presided over his great territorial acquisition. In April 1820 he commented to Congressman David Trimble of Kentucky: "I thought the greatest danger of this union was in the overgrown extent of its territory, combining with the slavery question." [49] Adams observed that the Missouri crisis had "operated to indispose" all sections against the Transcontinental Treaty, "the North and East because they do not wish even to have Florida as another slave state; and the South and West, because they wish to have all the territory to the Rio del Norte for more slave states." [50] Adams's comment that he "had very little attachment to the treaty" because of the acquisition of lands destined to be slave states demonstrates how keenly aware he was of the hazards of expansion to the continuation of the Union. As early as 1820, he recognized that expansion through space might not forestall the development of political conflict over time. Indeed, he sensed that territorial expansion might accelerate the disintegrative tendencies.

During the Missouri debates, Adams's diary reveals a man ready to take strong measures to prevent the spread of slavery. He lamented the failure of a provision in the Missouri Bill excluding the introduction of slaves into Missouri, a measure that foreshadowed the Wilmot Proviso of 1846.[51] He commented in March 1820 that "perhaps it would have been a wiser as well as a bolder course to have persisted in the restriction upon the Missouri, till it should have terminated in a convention of the states to revise and amend the Constitution. . . . If the union must be dissolved, slavery is precisely the question upon which it ought to break." [52] No abolitionist could have said it better. Adams speculated that Missouri's attempt to deny rights to free people of color visiting from other states required that Massachusetts refuse to recognize the rights of white Missourians visiting the Bay State; moreover, he argued that Missouri's refusal to recognize the rights of free people of color from Massachusetts meant that his home state would be justified in refusing to return fugitive slaves to Missouri slaveowners. Adams's motives are clear: "All of which I would do, not to violate, but to redeem from violation, the Constitution of the United States." [53] It is a powerful statement of the constitutional basis of antislavery.

During his tenure as secretary of state, as a candidate for president, and as president—despite his diary's passionate antislavery sentiments—Adams made no public pronouncements on the slave question.[54] His moral outrage remained unspoken, a victim of his understanding that a frank statement on the issue would spell the end of his hopes for national leadership. The slave issue most clearly reveals the contradictions Adams faced in trying to be both the "man of the whole nation" and a man true to his own conscience.

Noteworthy too, are Adams's observations regarding the dynamic of the Missouri debates. He perceived that the most energetic and impassioned orators in the slavery debates tended to be those who argued in defense of slavery. If there were "but one man" who "could arise with the genius capable of comprehending, a heart capable of supporting, and an utterance capable of communicating those eternal truths that belong to this question, to lay bare in all its nakedness that outrage upon the goodness of God, human slavery, now is the time, and this is the occasion, upon which such a man would perform the duties of an angel upon earth!"[55] Here Adams was envisioning the messianic, redemptive role which his conscience wanted him to play but which political expediency prohibited. Adams yearned for a time in which he would be no longer the statesman but rather the prophet, free to speak whatever his conscience suggested was right. Eventually, he did play the role of antislavery critic with such virtuosity as to earn the nickname "Old Man Eloquent."

Congressman Adams's defense of the rights of slaves was paralleled by his increasing sympathy for the cause of the Indians of the Southeast. He described American Indian policy as "among the heinous sins of this nation, for which I believe God will one day bring [it] to judgement."[56] The prominence of the slaveholder and speculator in the opening of new lands in the Southeast led Adams to be one of the most outspoken opponents of the Indian removal policy. He condemned the Second Seminole War as a violation of both the rights of Indians and the nation's honor.[57] This erstwhile defender of the rights of southern frontiersmen now believed that it would be better to allow the Southeast to remain in the hands of the Indians than to expand a civilization whose organizing principle was slave labor. Adams hoped that his stand might somehow aid "that hapless race of native Americans, which we are exterminating with such merciless and perfidious cruelty."[58] The language echoes that of the Erving letter, but now Adams saw justice to be on the side of the Indians, not the white frontiersmen. It hardly seems necessary to note that it was Adams who had changed between the 1810s and 1830s, not the situation on the southern frontier. Ultimately, Adams recognized the tragic hopelessness of the Indian question. In 1841 he turned down the chairmanship of the House Committee on Indian Affairs. Powerless to stop the extermination of native Americans, he wrote that the position would be nothing but "a perpetual harrow upon my feelings."

Adams's defense of the rights of slaves and of Indians led him to reject what he perceived to be the racially based foundations of Manifest Destiny. By modern standards, Adams was a racist—he firmly believed in the cultural and moral superiority of the white race—yet he differed with the dominant temper of his times (and with former associates such as Calhoun) in his conviction of the natural rights of all people, regardless of skin color. He refused to accept the proposition that black people had no rights that any white man was obliged to recognize. To Adams, slavery was a moral cancer on the body politic which forfeited America's pretensions to leadership of the cause of human freedom. He viewed the virulent, pseudoscientific racism that swept both North and South during the decades preceding the Civil War as a monstrous distortion of the promise of the republican revolution. In a landmark speech on 25 May 1836, Representative Adams denied that the Constitution prohibited Congress from interfering with slavery in the South. Anticipating Lincoln's doctrine of emancipation under martial law, he stated: "From the instant that your slaveholding states become the theater of war, civil, servile, or foreign, from that instant the war powers of Congress extend to interference with the institution of slavery in every way which it can be interfered with."[59]

Adams's stirring advocacy of human freedom won him wide rebuke; one gentleman from Alabama promised "to cut your throat from ear to ear." Undaunted by this and other threats, Adams endured congressional trial for censure in what was yet another effort to "stop the music of John Quincy Adams." He knew that the nation was not yet ready to take the great moral leap of the imagination required to end slavery: "To open the way for others is all that I can do. The cause is good and great." His pro-freedom convictions are perhaps best expressed in the last two lines of a poem he wrote in 1827 on the first anniversary of his father's death:

> Roll, years of promise, rapidly roll round
> Till not a slave on this Earth be found

Adams wanted to inscribe the lines on his father's tomb; he refrained from doing so at the prompting of friends who feared the inflammatory symbolism of such an act.[60]

Closely linked to Adams's antislavery stand was his uncompromising opposition as a congressman to the acquisition of Texas. This too
was a reversal from the position he had taken as secretary of state and
as president. Then he had fought hard to acquire Texas; he repeatedly
claimed to have been the last cabinet member to acquiesce in the
retreat to the Sabine River during the negotiations with Spain, and as
president he had pushed for annexation of the province.[61] Now he
resisted such efforts with every weapon at his disposal. Adams knew
what many historians since his time have obscured, that American
politics in the 1830s and 1840s was fundamentally a struggle between
those who viewed slavery as wrong and those who saw it as right. It
was less a "conspiracy" of the "slaveocracy" than it was a moral,
philosophical, and political debate between incommensurable world
views. Adams, like Lincoln to follow, knew that the Union could not
long endure half slave and half free, that it must become all one thing
or the other. He characterized the Texas revolution of 1836 as a
criminal revolt by slaveholders and speculators. He feared that annexation of Texas would be followed by the absorption of Cuba and the
increasing dominance of the slave interests in the halls of Congress.
In 1843 he proposed to the House Committee on Foreign Affairs that
the free states would be under no obligation to acquiesce in any Texas
annexation treaty—a stand that verged on John Calhoun-style nullification.[62] The classical lens through which he viewed events
prompted Adams to compare Tyler's defeated Texas annexation treaty
of 1844 to the Catiline conspiracy, thwarted by Cicero, in 63 B.C.
Annexation of Texas, he said, would be "robbery of Mexico."[63]

Adams's resistance to Texas annexation naturally led him to oppose the Mexican War vehemently. Despite his age and physical
frailty, he was the spiritual leader of the antiwar faction in the House,
being one of only fourteen members to vote against a declaration of
war. He urged American officers to resign their commissions rather
than fight in what he considered to be an "unrighteous war." He
called for the unilateral withdrawal of American forces from Mexico
and peace without territorial indemnity. Predictably, this stand gen-
erated charges of treason and disloyalty. Adams's intense opposition
to the spirit and tactics of Manifest Destiny during this period makes
all the more ironic his earlier role in generating and advancing the
expansionist fever. As secretary of state, Bemis writes, Adams "had
all but coined the magic making phrase 'Manifest Destiny.'"[64]

Adams (along with Calhoun) was convinced that Polk had provoked a confrontation on the Texas border and then presented the
issue to Congress and the public as an act of aggression by Mexico. It

is not surprising that Adams recognized Polk's duplicitous diplomacy; it was similar to his own defense of the First Seminole War. Both he and Calhoun knew well how easy it was to stampede the Congress into supporting executive actions of dubious legitimacy. Adams, who had disdained the constitutional objections to Jackson's foray into Florida, now found himself the one futilely opposing the shibboleths of patriotism and self-defense with abstract constitutional principles.

Adams also led the fight to obtain the release of all the documents in the president's possession relating to the conduct of the war. Polk, citing concern for the national interest, had released only a portion of the relevant material. Adams knew better than anyone that a sanitized documentary version of reality created the illusion without the substance of executive consultation with the Congress. His appeal for all the documents reveals how far he had come since his term as secretary of state: "I think the House ought to sustain, in the strongest manner, their right to call for information upon questions in which war and peace are concerned. They ought to maintain their right, and maintain it in a very distinct manner, against this assertion on the part of the President of the United States." [65]

Adams's apostasy reached its apex in a letter he wrote on 26 December 1847 to another old republican and antiwar spokesman, Albert Gallatin. The letter, one of the last Adams ever composed, decried Polk's war message as a "direct and notorious violation of the truth." He lamented that the congressional power to make war had been usurped by the executive branch: "It is now established as an irreversible precedent that the President of the United States has but to declare that war exists . . . and the war is essentially declared." [66] The former archdefender of an enlarged executive warmaking power now perceived—too late—the danger to liberty and republicanism that such power implied. He seems not to have acknowledged his part in establishing the precedent, however.

Adams's opposition to slavery and the Mexican War did not prevent him from continuing to champion the expansion of commercial relations with Asia and the acquisition of Oregon. Bemis writes that "nobody was interested in events in China more than Adams." He maintained close ties with those New Englanders involved in the China trade such as T.H. Perkins, Bryant and Sturgis, and the Cushings. He steadfastly supported Great Britain during the Opium War and welcomed the Treaty of Wanghia of 1844. [67] Having committed the United States to an East Asia policy in 1819, he was happy to see the growth of American commerce in that part of the world.

Concerning the Oregon question, Adams was an unyielding 54-40 man. His plea for no territorial indemnity from Mexico did not prevent his lobbying for all of the Oregon country. Adams posited a natural American right to the Northwest; he defended his stand in Congress by alluding to the biblical passage commanding humanity to "be fruitful and multiply . . . and have dominion over the fish of the sea, and over the fowl of the air, and over every living thing that moveth on earth." [68] In contrast to his critique of the Mexican War, he heartily approved Polk's confrontational approach to Britain in the Northwest. Adams feared that Great Britain wished to maintain Oregon as "a wilderness for the savage hunter" and to "stunt our natural growth." He even advocated war should Great Britain prove utterly resistant to American pleadings.[69] Hence, he understood Polk's meaning when, referring to Oregon, he said, "The American continents, by the free and independent condition which they have assumed and maintain, are henceforth not to be considered as subject for future colonization by any European power." Adams's own "Monroe Doctrine" had come to fruition.

His support of Polk's Oregon policy points out the contradictions in Adams's opposition to expansion in the Southwest. The president's expansionism merely reassembled the alliance of northeastern mercantile and southern slaveholding interests that had been served by the Transcontinental Treaty. "Polk's aggressive diplomacy" was essentially the continuation, both in tactics and aims, of Adams's aggressive diplomacy of a quarter-century earlier. The charges of hypocrisy leveled against Adams for his congressional record on the Indians, slavery, and expansion into the Southwest were entirely justified. His "principled" stands on these issues enraged his opponents, who were unwilling to let him walk away from such a well-defined past.

The most significant aspect of John Quincy Adams's "second career" as a congressman is the degree to which it was a repudiation of the achievements of his first career as "the man of the whole nation." On Indian removal, on slavery, on expansionism in the Southwest, on the warmaking powers of the executive he had flipflopped. Only on those issues that had always been in the interests of his home state— the acquisition of Oregon and the extension of the China trade—did he demonstrate the steadfastness characteristic of the true "man of principle" he presumed to be.

Adams's second career was as much marked by divisiveness as his first career had been marked by appeals to unity. His conduct as a congressman was confrontational and provocative. The man who had written to his father in 1811 that "union is to me what balance is to you" came to welcome the prospect of civil war.[70] To Adams, the evil of slavery had so tainted the noble experiment in republican liberty that he believed disunion desirable. To an audience in 1842 he speculated: "Was all this a Utopian daydream? Is the one talent, entrusted by the Lord of the harvest, for the improvement of the condition of man, to be hidden under a bushel? Is the lamp, destined to light the world, to be extinguished by the blasting breath of slavery?"[71] He described the Constitution as "a menstruous rag, and the Union is sinking into a military monarchy, to be rent asunder like the empire of Alexander or the kingdoms of Ephraim and Judah."[72] He wrote to Richard Rush in 1845 that "the polar star of our foreign relations at that time [1817-25] was justice it is now conquest. Their vital spirit was then liberty it is now slavery. . . . Liberty has yet her greatest warfare to wage in this Hemisphere. May your posterity and mine be armed in celestial panoply for the conflict."[73] The reference to his term as secretary of state being characterized by "justice" is telling: he could not consciously acknowledge his former complicity with the evil he now decried.

In the end, John Quincy Adams's destiny was fulfilled. Yet destiny proved a cruel trickster, placing Adams in a role that he had not anticipated; the ways of God had not been revealed to a man. As he neared death, Adams knew that the nation he had devoted his life to was coming apart, falling victim to the factionalism that history had predicted was fatal to republics. In October 1846 he made this entry in his diary: "If my intellectual powers had been such as have been sometimes committed by the Creator of man to single individuals of the species my diary would have been, next to the Holy Scriptures, the most precious and valuable book ever written by human hands, and I should have been one of the greatest benefactors of my country and of mankind. I would, by the irresistible power of genius and the irrepressible power of will and the favor of almighty God, have banished war and slavery from the face of the earth forever. But the conceptive power of mind was not conferred upon me by my Maker, and I have not improved the scanty portion of His gifts as I might and ought to have done."[74] His diary, intended to be a daily record of the evolution of God's chosen people, was instead a narrative of the birth, rise, and imminent collapse of their union.

The experiment in republican government consisting of a voluntary union of states was to fail, to be reconstructed as an imperial democracy consecrated in blood. The American republic was, as the lessons of history predicted, ending in tragedy. That most Americans have not perceived the life of John Quincy Adams or the history of the republic in such terms is not surprising, given the popular obsession with happy endings. As Henry Adams later wrote, "Americans have always taken their tragedy lightly."[75]

Despite a debilitating stroke in November 1846, Adams kept his House seat, a silent sentinel of the antiwar movement. On 21 February 1848, while voting against a measure recommending the decoration of Mexican War veterans, John Quincy Adams collapsed at his desk. Lapsing into a coma, he died two days later. He died without knowing that on his last full day of life, 22 February—birthday of Washington and anniversary of both the signing of the Transcontinental Treaty and its ratification—Polk sent to the Senate for ratification the Treaty of Guadelupe-Hidalgo, which ended the Mexican War, expanded the territory of the United States, and further inflamed the sectional controversy. A life that had begun at the birth of independence had ended in the shadow of civil war.

Notes

Abbreviations

Introduction

1. Bemis, *Union*, 545.   2. On the lifetime significance to Adams of the Battle of Bunker Hill, see *AFC*, 1:224.   3. H. Adams, *Education*, 451.

ONE: Destiny

1. Bemis, *Foundations*, chap. 3.   2. Ibid., chap. 5   3. Ibid., 120, 143-44.
4. Ibid., chap. 8.   5. See Perkins, *Castlereagh and Adams*. On the Rush-Bagot Treaty, see Bourne, *Britain and the Balance of Power*, chap. 1.
6. JQA to William Eustis, 13 Jan. 1817, *Writings*, 6:137.   7. Ibid., 270.
8. Quoted in Bemis, *Foundations*, 14.   9. Bemis, *Union*, 3-4.   10. AA to JQA, 20

Nov. 1783, A. Adams, *Letters*, 1:191. Edward Everett, *A Eulogy on the Life and Character of John Quincy Adams* (Boston, 1848), 15, said of the letters of Mrs. Adams that "no brighter example exists of auspicious maternal influence, in forming the character of great and good man. Her letters to [Adams] . . . might almost be called a manual of a wise mother's advice."

11. AA to JQA, 26 Dec. 1783, A. Adams, *Letters*, 1:198-99.   12. JA to AA, 29 June and 28 Aug. 1774, 17 July 1775, *AFC*, 1:113-14, 145, 252.   13. Quoted in Wood, *The Creation of the American Republic*, 208.   14. Quoted in Nagel, *Descent from Glory*, 33.   15. Akers, *Abigail Adams*, 59, writes that young John Quincy Adams's "lively conversation had helped warm his mother's lonely hours."

16. Ibid., 89.   17. AA to JQA, 12 Jan. 1780, A. Adams, *Letters*, 1:144.   18. AA to JQA, 20 March 1780, ibid. 1:147.   19. AA to JQA, June 1778, ibid., 1:123. 20. Bemis, *Foundations*, 7-8.

21. *Memoirs*, 3:169. On the religion of the Adamses, see Akers, *Abigail Adams*, esp. 127-28; Shaw, *Character of John Adams*, 33, 55, 211-12.   22. Bemis, *Foundations*, 5.   23. Akers, *Abigail Adams*, 28.   24. AA to JA, 19 Aug. 1774, *AFC*, 1:142:43. 25. Bemis, *Foundations*, 16.

26. AA to JQA, 26 Dec. 1783, A. Adams, *Letters*, 1:197-98; also see AA to JQA, June 1778, 1:122-25.   27. The influence of classical learning on the leaders of the early republic has been noted by many scholars in recent years. See Bailyn, *Ideological Origins*, Wood, *Creation of the American Republic*; Pocock, *Machiavellian Moment*; McCoy, *Elusive Republic*; Appleby, *Capitalism and a New Social Order*; Wood, *Cicero's Social and Political Thought*, 4.   28. See Wood, *Creation of the American Republic*, chap. 14.   29. Bemis, *Foundations*, 258, describes Adams, *Report on Weights and Measures*, as "a sadly neglected American classic."   30. Bemis, *Union*, chap. 23.

31. Ibid., 523; H. Adams, *Degradation*, 73-74.   32. H. Adams, *Degradation*, 30-31.   33. Bemis, *Union*, 501, describes Adams as the only nineteenth-century president who was "a notable sponsor of learning."   34. JA to AA, 29 Oct. 1775, *AFC*, 1:317-18.   35. AA to JQA, 12 Oct. 1787, A. Adams, *Letters*, 2:198.

36. Bemis, *Union*, 326; Richards, *Life and Times*, 3.   37. Brooks Adams, in H. Adams, *Degradation*, vi.   38. AA to JQA, June 1778, A. Adams, *Letters*, 1:123. 39. Quoted in Nagel, *Descent from Glory*, 30.   40. Hecht, *John Quincy Adams*, 106, writes: "It had been said by those who knew John Quincy Adams best that he loved his mother more than any other person in his life."

41. On civic humanism, see Pocock, *Machiavellian Moment*, 56-60, 505, 513-17.   42. See Musto, "The Youth of John Quincy Adams," 269-82.   43. Ibid., 281.   44. Akers, *Abigail Adams*, 73.   45. On the pain of separation for Abigail, see Levin, *Abigail Adams*, chap. 8.

46. AA to JA, 7 May 1776, *AFC*, 1:401-2.   47. See East, *John Quincy Adams*. 48. Adams retained a fondness for writing poetry all his life; his personal collection of verse, *Poems of Religion and Society*, reveals a sentimental side rarely seen. 49. JQA to LCA, 28 Aug. 1822, *Writings*, 7:298-99.   50. On the Mary Frazier affair, see Bemis, *Foundations*, 24-25; Nagel, *Descent from Glory*, 61-62; East, *John Quincy Adams*, 127-28; Shepherd, *Cannibals of the Heart*, 57; Levin, *Abigail Adams*, 275-81; Hecht, *John Quincy Adams*, 64-65.

51. JQA to Elizabeth Cranch, 1773?, *AFC*, 1:91.   52. JQA to JA, 13 October 1774, in ibid., 1:167.   53. Quoted in Nagel, *Descent from Glory*, 33.   54. On Adams's Harvard years, see East, *John Quincy Adams*, chap. 3.   55. *Memoirs*, 5:165.

56. Quoted in Nagel, *Descent from Glory*, 137.   57. Hecht, *John Quincy Adams*,

24, views self-pity as an Adams family trait.　　58. Bemis, *Union*, 197, describes Adams as being near-destitute when he left the White House in 1829.　　59. On Adams's role as a champion of internal improvements, see H. Adams, *Degradation*, 19-21; Lipsky, *John Quincy Adams*, 148-54.　　60. JQA to James Lloyd, 1 Oct. 1822, *Writings*, 7:312.

　　61. See *Messages and Papers of the Presidents*, 2:298.　　62. Bemis, *Foundations*, 127.　　63. See Lipsky, *John Quincy Adams*, chap. 9.　　64. Ibid., chaps. 9, 10. 65. Everett, *Eulogy*, 60.

　　66. See Adams, *Social Compact*.　　67. H. Adams, *Degradation*, 81.　　68. *Messages and Papers of the Presidents*, 2:311.　　69. *Memoirs*, 4:437-8.　　70. See Bemis, *Foundations*, esp. chaps. 21, 22, 27.

　　71. Quoted in LaFeber, *John Quincy Adams and American Continental Empire*, 50-51.　　72. JQA address, 4 July 1821, Adams Family Papers.　　73. See DeConde, *This Affair of Louisiana*, for the best recent interpretation of the Louisiana Purchase.　　74. Ibid., 194-96.　　75. Armin Rappaport, *A History of American Diplomacy* (New York, 1976), 56.

　　76. For a discussion of the expansion of the boundaries of Louisiana, see Marshall, *History of the Western Boundary*, chap. 1.　　77. Brooks, *Diplomacy and the Borderlands*, 4-5.　　78. Ibid., 5; DeConde, *This Affair of Louisiana*, 214.　　79. H. Adams, *History*, 3:257-58.　　80. Ibid., 268.

　　81. See Thomas Jefferson, "The Limits and Bounds of Louisiana," in American Philosophical Society, *Documents relating to the Purchase* and *Exploration of Louisiana* (New York, 1904), 5-45.　　82. Guinness, "Purpose of the Lewis and Clark Expedition," 90-100.　　83. Marshall, *History of the Western Boundary*, 10-14. 84. Ibid., 14.　　85. H. Adams, *History*, 4:284.

　　86. Marshall, *History of the Western Boundary*, 37; Brooks, *Diplomacy and the Borderlands*, chap. 1.　　87. H. Adams, *History*, 5:305-12; Pratt, *Expansionists of 1812*, 71-76. See also Isaac Cox, *The West Florida Controversy, 1798-1813* (Baltimore, Md., 1918).　　88. See Logan, *No Transfer*, on the No Transfer Resolution's role in American foreign policy.　　89. Pratt, *Expansionists of 1812*, 80.　　90. On the Mathews mission, see ibid.

　　91. Ibid., 109-10.　　92. Brooks, *Diplomacy and the Borderlands*, 33.　　93. Ibid., 63.　　94. Ibid., 65.　　95. Ibid., 66.

　　96. Bemis, *Foundations*, 280-81.　　97. See Benns, *American Struggle*, for a comprehensive examination of Anglo-American trade relations during the period. 98. On Anglo-American relations of the period, see Bemis, *Foundations*, chaps. 14, 23, 24; Perkins, *Castlereagh and Adams*; Bourne, *Britain and the Balance of Power*, chaps. 1-3.　　99. North, *Economic Growth of the United States*, 177.　　100. Schur, "Second Bank of the United States," 118-34.

　　101. Smith, *Economic Aspects of the Second Bank*, 82-83.　　102. See ibid.; Catterall, *Second Bank of the United States*; Schur, "Second Bank of the United States."　　103. Smith, *Economic Aspects of the Second Bank*, 34.　　104. Latourette, *Relations between the United States and China*, 28.　　105. Some contemporary works on the specie problem are McCready, *Trade and Commerce of New York*; Melish, *Protecting and Encouraging the Manufactures of the United States*; Carey, *Examination of the Pretensions of New England to Commercial Preeminence*; Pitkin, *Statistical View of the Commerce of the United States*.

　　106. Schmidt, "Internal Commerce," 798-822.　　107. On the American economy of the first quarter of the nineteenth century, see North, *Economic Growth of the United States*; Taylor, *The Transportation Revolution*; Turner, *Rise of the New*

West.   108. Richards, *Life and Times,* 96.   109. H. Adams, *Education,* 48.
110. Richards, *Life and Times,* 99-110.
    111. 21 Sept. 1817, *Memoirs,* 4:8.

TWO: Developing a Strategy

    1. 6 Aug. 1817, *Memoirs,* 4:3-4.   2. Bemis, *Foundations,* 247.   3. JQA diary,
8 Aug. 1817, Adams Family Papers; *Niles' Weekly Register,* Aug. 1817, 12:416.
4. Akers, *Abigail Adams,* 183-87.   5. JQA to AA, 16 May 1817, *Writings;* 6:181-82;
Ammon, *James Monroe,* 361; JQA to AA, 12 April 1817, Adams Family Papers, quoted in
Hecht, *John Quincy Adams,* 275.
    6. JQA diary, 4 Nov. 1817, Adams Family Papers.   7. On the Monroe-Adams
relationship, see Ammon, *James Monroe,* 361-62; Bemis, *Foundations,* 260-61.
8. JQA to LCA, 7 Oct. 1822, *Writings,* 7:316.   9. See Ammon, *James Monroe,* for the
most comprehensive recent biography. Also see Gilman, *James Monroe;* Morgan, *Life
of James Monroe;* Styron, *Last of the Cocked Hats.*   10. "James Monroe," 11.
    11. George Dangerfield, *The Awakening of American Nationalism, 1815-1828* (New
York, 1965), 20.   12. Ammon, *James Monroe,* 29-31, stresses Jefferson's influence on
Monroe's political philosophy and actions.   13. Ibid., viii, 19.   14. On the Amer-
ican sense of mission, see Pocock, *Machiavellian Moment,* chap. 15; Bercovitch,
American Jeremiad; Miller, *Errand into the Wilderness.*   15. Ammon, *James
Monroe,* ix, emphasizes Monroe's role as a crusader for national unity.
    16. Smith and Cole, *Fluctuations in American Business,* 4.   17. McCoy, *Elusive
Republic,* chap. 10, esp. 238-39.   18. Taylor, "Agrarian Discontent in the Mississippi
Valley," 471-505.   19. McCoy, *Elusive Republic,* 76-77. Also see Pocock, *Machiavellian Moment,* 530-31; Williams, *Contours of American History,* chap. 2 esp.
133-40. Williams writes: "Monroe's ultimate selection of John Quincy Adams as
secretary of state seems almost a routine projection of his mercantilism."
20. Grampp, "Mercantilism and Laissez-Faire," 50.
    21. McCoy, *Elusive Republic,* 85-86; Setser, *Commercial Reciprocity Policy*
183.   22. See Bemis, *Foundations,* chap. 21, on the Adamses role in the struggle for a
free global trade.   23. For the role of free trade in the revolutionary ideology, see
Stourzh, *Benjamin Franklin and American Foreign Policy,* 239.   24. Bemis, *Foundations,* 449.   25. Hutchins, *American Maritime Industries,* 221-22.
    26. Setser, *Commercial Reciprocity Policy,* 257.   27. McCoy, *Elusive Republic,*
91-93.   28. Ibid., 138.   29. Setser, *Commercial Reciprocity Policy,* 259-60.
Though the British West India trade was only marginally important to the prosperity of
the nation, it was quite significant to the fortunes of maritime New England—a fact
that perhaps explains the zeal with which its reopening was pursued.   30. Rothbard,
Panic of 1819, chap. 6.
    31. McCoy, *Elusive Republic,* 244-45.   32. Rothbard, *Panic of 1819,* 260-61. For
contemporary views on the tariff issue, see Carey, *The New Olive Branch;* Melish,
Protecting and Encouraging the Manufactures of the United States.   33. Setser,
Commercial Reciprocity Policy, 256. Williams, *Contours of American History,* 122,
writes that "most Americans considered free trade a tactic for attaining the strategic
objective of having an empire of their own."   34. North, *Economic Growth of the
United States,* 177.   35. McCoy, *Elusive Republic,* 243-45.
    36. Perkins, *Castlereagh and Adams,* chap. 10; Bourne, *Britain and the Balance of
Power,* 6-8. Tatum, *The United States and Europe,* errs in relying too heavily on public
opinion (as expressed in the press) in evaluating Anglo-American relations.   37. TJ

to JA, 25 Nov. 1816; TJ to JM, 16 Oct. 1816; TJ to Sir John Sinclair, 31 July 1816, in Jefferson, *Writings*, 15:85, 80, 55.   38. Perkins, *Castlereagh and Adams*, 226-27. 39. Parsons, *British Trade Cycles and American Bank Credit*, 327.   40. See ibid., chaps. 6, 9, 10, 14.

41. JQA to JM, 21 Jan. 1817; 20 Feb. 1817, *Writings*, 6:146, 6:160.   42. Perkins, *Castlereagh and Adams*, 222.   43. Webster, *Foreign Policy of Castlereagh*, 428-29, 444. Also see Dangerfield, *Era of Good Feelings*, 254-57.   44. Bemis, *Foundations*, 221.   45. JQA to JA, 29 May 1816, *Writings*, 6:38.

46. Adams, *Lives of Madison and Monroe*, 278.   47. Ammon, *James Monroe*, 345.   48. Brant, *James Madison*, 381.   49. Bourne, *Britain and the Balance of Power*, 9, 10.   50. *Messages and Papers of the Presidents*, 2:7.

51. Stuart, *War and American Thought*, 156-63. On Mahan's influence on American foreign policy, see LaFeber, *The New Empire*, 62-101.   52. On the federalist tendencies of the Republican party after the War of 1812, see Ammon, *James Monroe*, 367, 379; Brant, *James Madison*, 404-5. Also see Watts, *The Republic Reborn*, for the influence of the War of 1812 on republican ideology.   53. On the president's tour, see Ammon, *James Monroe*, 371-78.   54. Mitchell and Ames, *Narrative of a Tour of Observations*, 45.   55. Rufus King to JM, 14 April 1817; JM to Rufus King, 29 April 1817, Monroe Papers.

56. Ronda, *Astoria and Empire*, 260.   57. Porter, *John Jacob Astor*, 2:957-59. 58. Ibid., vol. 2, chap. 21.   59. Quoted in Grampp, "Mercantilism and Laissez-Faire," 329. On Astor's trade connections with China, see Porter, *John Jacob Astor*, vol. 2, chaps. 6, 7. On the background to the Astoria enterprise, see Ronda, *Astoria and Empire*, chaps. 1, 2.   60. Porter, *John Jacob Astor*, 2:144-48.

61. Astor to JM, 24 May, 2 Sept. 30 April 1814, Monroe Papers.   62. Porter, *John Jacob Astor*, 2:725-27.   63. Ibid., 2:725 n. 57.   64. Wishart, *The Fur Trade*, 18. 65. A more recent example of the mixing of special interest with the national interest is the U.S.-backed coup in Guatemala in 1954.

66. Porter, *John Jacob Astor*, 1:262.   67. Mitchell and Ames, *Narrative of a Tour of Observations*, 98.   68. Waldo, *The Tour of James Monroe*, 37.   69. Jeremiah Mason to Rufus King, 24 July 1817, King Papers.   70. Christopher Gore to Rufus King, 18 Jan. 1818, King Papers.

71. Porter, *The Jacksons and the Lees* (Cambridge, Mass., 1937), 1257. Brown, *The Republic in Peril*, 173-74, observes that the Federalists' opposition to the War of 1812 was tempered by their perception that conflict might ultimately work to discredit the persons and policies that led to war.   72. *Boston Columbian Centinel*, 12 July 1817.   73. William Crawford to Albert Gallatin, 27 Oct. 1817, Gallatin Papers. 74. Ammon, *James Monroe*, 429.   75. Richard Rush to JM, 24 Aug. 1817, Monroe Papers.

76. JQA diary, 6 and 10 Aug. 1817, Adams Family Papers.   77. A prime example of Adams's suspicion of the South American patriot cause is found in his letter to Alexander Everett, 29 Dec. 1817, *Writings*, 6:282-83. For a stimulating recent look at U.S.-Latin American relations, see Johnson, *A Hemisphere Apart*.   78. Stewart, "The South American Commission," 36-37.   79. JQA to James Biddle, 29 Sept. 1817, DS, Letters Sent, Military Affairs, 1800-1861. On Biddle's mission and Astor's efforts to reoccupy Astoria, see Ronda, *Astoria and Empire*, 310-15, 308-10.   80. Richard Rush to John Prevost, 25 Sept. 1817, DS, Communications from Special Agents.

81. Brooks, *Diplomacy and the Borderlands*, 151-52; Ronda, *Astoria and Empire*, 310.   82. JQA to JM, 6 Oct. 1817, Monroe Papers. Also see JQA to JM, 29 Sept. 1817, *Writings*, 6:204-6.   83. See Monroe's notes dated 31 Oct. 1817, Monroe Papers.

84. 24 Oct. 1817, *Memoirs*, 4:14.   85. Warren, *The Sword Was Their Passport*, 139-45.

86. Daniel Patterson to Benjamin Crowninshield, 28 July and 4 Aug. 1817; Beverly Chew to Richard Rush, 30 Aug. 1817, DS, Despatches from the Consul at Galveston.   87. 30 October 1817, *Memoirs*, 4:24-26.   88. On the nature of the Galveston and Amelia forces, see Warren, *The Sword Was Their Passport*, chaps. 6, 7; Bowman, "Vicente Pazos and the Amelia Island Affair," 273-95; Faye, "Commodore Aury," 611-97.   89. JQA diary, 4 Oct. 1817, Adams Family Papers.   90. JQA to JA, 5 Oct. 1817, *Writings*, 6:208-9; JQA to AA, 2 Nov. 1817, *Writings*, 6:228.

THREE: First Moves

1. White, *The Jeffersonians*, 200-15.   2. Ibid., 189-90.   3. Quoted in Bemis, *Foundations*, 58-59.   4. Henry Adams later charged that his grandfather neglected his father "for the sake of his damned Weights and Measures" (quoted in Nagel, *Descent from Glory*, 354).   5. Bemis, *Foundations*, x.

6. The candor of Adams's diary reflections was no doubt lessened by the snooping of his brother Charles in the 1790s.   7. Bemis, *Foundations*, viii, argues that Adams did not intend his diary to be published.   8. See JQA diary, 30 Nov. 1817, Adams Family Papers, for an example of Adams's daily schedule.   9. 31 August 1817, *Memoirs*, 4:7.   10. JQA to John Adams, Jr., 12 Nov. 1817, Adams Family Papers.

11. Quoted in Nagel, *Descent from Glory*, 139.   12. Bemis, *Foundations*, 116.   13. On George's death, see ibid., 178; Nagel, *Descent from Glory*, 167-68.   14. Nagel, *Descent from Glory*, 171-73.   15. See Duberman, *Charles Francis Adams*.

16. *Messages and Papers of the Presidents*, 2:11-20.   17. Ibid., 13-14.   18. 15th Cong., 2d sess., *Annals of the Congress*, 402.   19. *Philadelphia Aurora*, 15 Dec. 1817.   20. 15th Cong. 2d sess., *Annals of the Congress*, 409.

21. Ibid., 1790-97.   22. Captain Charles Morris to Benjamin Crowninshield, 8 April 1817; Daniel Patterson to Benjamin Crowninshield, 4 Aug. 1817, DS, Letters from the Consul at Galveston.   23. Captain Charles Morris to Benjamin Crowninshield, 14 March and 8 April 1817, DS, Letters from the Consul at Galveston.   24. Bemis, *Foundations*, 307-8.   25. 15th Cong. 2d sess., *Annals of the Congress*, 1804.

26. 12 Dec. 1817, *Memoirs*, 4:29.   27. Ammon, *James Monroe*, 418.   28. 6 Jan. 1818, *Memoirs*, 4:36.   29. 9 Jan. 1818, ibid., 4:37.   30. 19 Jan. 1818, ibid., 43.

31. 15th Cong. 2d sess., *Annals of the Congress*, 1803.   32. JQA diary, 3 Jan. and 1 Jan. 1818, Adams Family Papers.   33. 30 Dec. 1817, *Memoirs*, 4:32.   34. Lipsky, *John Quincy Adams*, 199-200.   35. Adams noted in his diary: "One of the most remarkable features of what I am witnessing every day is a perpetual struggle in both Houses of Congress to control the Executive—to make it dependent upon and subservient to them" (8 Jan. 1820, *Memoirs*, 4:497).

36. *Kentucky Reporter*, 8 Jan. 1818.   37. *Argus of Western America*, 3 Feb. 1818.   38. *New York Evening Post*, 12 Jan. 1818.   39. *City of Washington Gazette*, 13 Jan. 1818.   40. *Philadelphia Aurora*, 5, 12, and 19 Jan. 1818.

41. The *Washington National Intelligencer* regularly printed presidential messages and reports and in the spring of 1818 published a special issue devoted entirely to documents submitted to Congress by Adams on South American policy.   42. *National Intelligencer*, 27 Jan. 1818. Also see editorials of 9 and 12 Dec. 1817, and 14 January and 24 February 1818, defending the administration.   43. *ASPFR*, 4:437, 439.   44. Ibid., 445-50.   45. Ibid., 450-51.

46. Ibid., 451-52.   47. Whitaker, *The United States and the Independence of*

Latin America, 225-26.   48. On the crisis in the Spanish government during this period, see Anna, *Spain and the Loss of America*; Carr, *Spain*, 120-23; Tunon de Lara, *La Espana del siglo XIX*, 53-57; Fontana, *La crisis del antiguo regime*, 23-29. On the role of the Spanish military, see Woodward, "The Spanish Army and the Loss of America," 586-607; Christiansen, *Origins of Military Power in Spain*, chap. 1.
          49. Anna, *Spain and the Loss of America*, 126-28.   50. Ibid., 204-5.
          51. Del Rio, *La Mision de Don Luis de Onís*, 39-42.   52. Del Rio (ibid.) describes Onís as one of Spain's most competent diplomats of the era.   53. The "Verus" pamphlets are printed in Onís, *Memoria sobre las negociaciones*, 14-70.   54. Ibid., 11; Brooks, *Borderlands*, 99.   55. Onís to Pizarro, 14 Jan. 1818, AHN-Estado, leg. 5643, II.
          56. Anna, *Spain and the Loss of America*, 177.   57. *ASPFR*, 4:458.   58. Ibid., 459.   59. Ibid., 464.   60. Ibid., 465.
          61. Ibid., 466.   62. Ibid., 467.   63. Ibid., 468.   64. Ibid., 470.   65. See internal memorandum of April 1817, AHN-Estado, leg. 5660, II. Also see Charles R. Vaughan to Castlereagh, 16 Nov. 1815, *Britain and the Independence of Latin America*, 2:341.
          66. Pizarro to Henry Wellesley, 6 and 26 April 1817, AHN-Estado, leg. 5660, II.
          67. Confidential Memorandum, 20 Aug. 1817, *Britain and the Independence of Latin America*, 2:355-56.   68. Quoted in Brooks, *Diplomacy and the Borderlands*, 112.   69. Ibid., 112-13.   70. 27 Jan. 1818, *Memoirs*, 4:51.
          71. 3 Feb. 1818, ibid., 4:52.   72. *ASPFR*, 4:478.   73. Charles Bagot to Castlereagh, 8 Feb. 1818, *Correspondence and Memoirs of Viscount Castlereagh*, 12 vols (London, 1848-53), 11:404-6.   74. See Van Alstyne, "International Rivalries in the Pacific Northwest," 185-218, for an illuminating discussion of the geopolitical situation in that region. On the history of European colonization of the northwest coast generally, see Warren L. Cook, *Flood Tide of Empire: Spain and the Pacific Northwest, 1543-1819* (New Haven, Conn., 1973).   75. Okun, *The Russian-American Company*, 11, 50-51. Bartley, *Imperial Russia*, also stresses the ambitions of the tsar in the Western Hemisphere. Other works on the Russian influence in America include Ogden, *The California Sea Otter Trade*; Gibson, *Imperial Russia in Frontier America*; Manning, *Russian Influence in Early America*.
          76. Kushner, *Conflict on the Northwest Coast*, 8.   77. Ibid., 13.   78. Ibid., 14-15; Bemis, *Foundations*, 172-75; Ronda, *Astoria and Empire*, chap. 3.
          79. Kushner, *Conflict on the Northwest Coast*, 27.   80. Bemis, *Foundations*, 311, describes Biddle as having "a confidential and officious intimacy" with Monroe.
          81. Nicholas Biddle to JM, 12 Nov. 1817, Monroe Papers.   82. "The Political Picture of Europe, 1817", Monroe Papers.   83. William Pinknye to JQA, 11 Aug. 1817, DS, Dispatches from Russia.   84. Kushner, *Conflict on the Northwest Coast*, 31.   85. Okun, *The Russian-American Company*, 78-79.
          86. The relationship of the tsar's ukase to the Monroe Doctrine has been a topic of debate among historians. N.N. Bolkhovitinov, "Russia and Declaration of the Non-Colonization Principle," 101-127; Nichols, "The Russian Ukase and the Monroe Doctrine," 13-26; and Bartley, *Imperial Russia*, 142, all dispute the notion that the non-colonization clause was inspired by Russian expansion down the northwest coast. Yet Kushner, *Conflict on the Northwest Coast*, 33, notes that the ukase was clearly aimed at United States citizens, and the substantial private lobbying and congressional debate concerning the northwest coast make clear that the Russian "threat" played at least a part in the formulation of the noncolonization clause. Also see Kushner, "Significance of the Alaska Purchase," 295-315.   87. Kissinger, *A Word Restored*, 30-32.

Kissinger's book is still the best analysis of the European diplomatic scene during the post-Napoleonic restoration.   88. Ibid., 189.   89. Middleton, *Britain and Russia*, 39-44. Middleton argues that Anglo-Russian rivalry during the 1810s set the stage for a century of conflict between the two nations.   90. Webster, *Foreign Policy of Castlereagh*, 88-118, 411-14.

91. 31 Dec. 1817, *Memoirs*, 4:33.   92. JQA diary, 24 Jan. 1818, Adams Family Papers.   93. 28 Feb. 1818, ibid.   94. 15 Feb. 1818, ibid.   95. Quoted in Hecht, *John Quincy Adams*, 103.

96. Quoted in Shepherd, *Cannibals of the Heart*, 72.   97. Quoted in Hecht, *John Quincy Adams*, 110.   98. Shepherd, *Cannibals of the Heart*, 81-83; Nagel, *Descent from Glory*, 71-72.   99. Hecht, *John Quiny Adams*, 118.   100. Quoted in ibid., 141.

101. Nagel, *Descent from Glory*, 354, notes Henry Adams's bitter criticism of John Quincy for "dragging his wife to Europe in 1809, and separating her from her children."   102. Quoted in Shepherd, *Cannibals of the Heart*, 117.   103. Quoted in Hecht, *John Quincy Adams*, 456.   104. On the evolution of the role of the American woman in the nineteenth century, see Kathryn K. Sklar, *Catharine Beecher: A Study in American Domesticity* (New Haven, Conn., 1973).   105. Shepherd, *Cannibals of the Heart*, 76.

FOUR: "The South American Question"

1. Although the United States government formulated no clear policy concerning the South American wars of independence until after 1815, private citizens were aiding the patriots as early as 1811.   2. Griffin, *The United States and the Disruption of the Spanish Empire*, 98.   3. Stewart, "The South American Commission," 33-34; Griffin, *The United States and the Disruption of the Spanish Empire*, 121. 4. Johnson, *A Hemisphere Apart*, 81.   5. Stewart, "The South American Commission," 36; Goebel, *Recognition Policy of the United States*, 119, 120.

6. *Diplomatic Correspondence of the United States* 3:1946; JM to Albert Gallatin, 15 April 1816, ibid., 1:29.   7. Pizarro to Luis de Onís, 20 Feb. 1818, AHN-Estado, leg. 5643, quoted in Griffin, *The United States and the Disruption of the Spanish Empire*, 92. Also see Del Rio, *La Mision de Don Luis de Onís*, 128; Brooks, *Diplomacy and the Borderlands*, 133, 87-88.   8. Goebel, "British Trade to the Spanish Colonies, 1796-1820," 288-320.   9. For an analysis of the role of trade in the formulation of Great Britain's Latin American policy, see Kaufmann, *British Policy*, chap. 2; Johnson, *A Hemisphere Apart*, 41.   10. See the "Confidential Memo" of 20 August 1817, printed in *Britain and the Independence of Latin America*, 2:352-358.

11. Kaufmann, *British Policy*, 105-6. Other outstanding works on British Latin American policy are Webster, *Foreign Policy of Castlereagh*, chap. 8; Webster, "Castlereagh and the Spanish Colonies."   12. Goebel, "British Trade to the Spanish Colonies," 295-303.   13. See Goebel, "British-American Rivalry in the Chilean Trade," 190-202.   14. Kaufmann, *British Policy*, 113.   15. *Diplomatic Correspondence of the United States*, 3:1433-34.

16. Kaufmann, *British Policy*, 123; Webster, "Castlereagh and the Spanish Colonies," 95.   17. See Johnson, *A Hemisphere Apart*, 181-86.   18. Whitaker, *The United States and the Independence of Latin America*, chap. 4; Griffin, *The United States and the Disruption of the Spanish Empire*, 188.   19. James Yard, *Spanish America and the United States, or Views of the Actual Commerce of the United States*

with the Spanish Colonies (Philadelphia, 1818), 13.   20. Whitaker, *The United States and the Independence of Latin America*, 127-28.

21. Calhoun to AJ, 23 Jan. 1820, quoted in Johnson, *A Hemisphere Apart*, 156; on the importance of Cuba to U.S. Latin American policy, see Johnson, 153-56.   22. Goebel, "British Trade to the Spanish Colonies," 302-3.   23. Nicholas Biddle to JM, 11 Dec. 1817, quoted in Griffin, *The United States and the Disruption of the Spanish Empire*, 159.   24. Yard, *Spanish America*, 23.   25. Ibid., 36-37.

26. Nicholas Biddle to JM, 15 March 1818, Monroe Papers.   27. Ketcham, *James Madison*, 630-31.   28. Whitaker, *The United States and the Independence of Latin America*, 195, 329.   29. TJ to Lafayette, 14 May 1817; TJ to Baron von Humboldt, 13 June 1817; TJ to JA, 12 May 1818, Jefferson, *Writings*, 15:116, 127, 170.   30. JQA to Alexander H. Everett, 29 Dec. 1817, *Writings*, 6:280-82; JQA to Thomas Boylston Adams, 14 Nov. 1818, Adams Family Papers. Also see Whitaker, *The United States and the Independence of Latin America*, 147-48; Johnson, *A Hemisphere Apart*, 139.

31. 15th Cong. 2d sess., *Annals of the Congress*, 1481.   32. Van Deusen, *Life of Henry Clay*, 117-18.   33. *Nashville Clarion*, 24 March 1818.   34. Taylor, *The Transportation Revolution*, 139, 110.   35. Turner, *Rise of the New West*, 99-100.

36. On interregional economic flows, see Schmidt, "Internal Commerce," 798-822; Taylor, *The Transportation Revolution*, 158-59.   37. Quoted in Turner, *Rise of the New West*, 100.   38. Wade, *Urban Frontier*, chap. 1.   39. Ibid., 163. Wade quotes Sir Henry Brougham's famous remark to the House of Commons: "It is well worthwhile to incur a loss upon the first exportation in order by the glut to stifle in the cradle those rising manufactures in the United States which the war has forced into existence contrary to the usual course of nature."   40. Smith, *Economic Aspects of the Second Bank*, 83.

41. House results for the three pieces of legislation were as follows: (1) To postpone repeal of the charter of the National Bank (16 April 1818), ayes: West, 33; South, 25; Northeast, 27; nos: West, 11; South, 13; Northeast, 26. (2) To increase duties on iron (13 April 1818), ayes: West, 33; South, 11; Northeast, 44; nos: West, 13, South, 20; Northeast, 14. (3) To fund further construction of the Cumberland Road (1 April 1818), ayes: West, 29; South, 16; Northeast, 28; nos: West, 12; South, 18; Northeast, 26.   42. 15th Cong., 1st sess., *Annals of the Congress*, 2:1485.   43. Quoted in Whitaker, *The United States and the Independence of Latin America*, 112.   44. Quoted in Bemis, *Foundations*, 341.   45. 6 Dec. 1817, *Memoirs*, 4:28.

46. 28 March 1818, ibid., 4:70-71.   47. 18 March 1818, ibid., 4:64.   48. On Adams's views of democracy, see his *Oration Delivered before the Inhabitants of the Town of Newburyport, and his Social Compact*. Also see Richards, *Life and Times*, chap. 2; Lipsky, *John Quincy Adams*, 91, 106, 172-74.   49. Adams's one experience of spontaneous politicking occurred during his appearance at the groundbreaking for the Baltimore and Ohio Canal on 11 July 1828. See Bemis, *Union*, 102-3.   50. See Watts, *The Republic Reborn*.

51. When Portuguese Minister Correa de Serra accused Adams of authoring the Phocion letters, Adams responded by keeping the minister in "uncertainty," adding that "when persons used fictitious signatures in the newspapers, it was usually because they had motives for not signing their own." See 22 Nov. 1817, *Memoirs*, 4:22-23.   52. *Washington National Intelligencer*, 1 Dec. 1817.   53. Ibid. 54. Ibid.   55. Ibid., 8 Dec. 1817.

56. On the various ways North Americans learned about the independence struggles and South America generally, see Whitaker, *The United States and the Independence of Latin America*, chaps. 5, 6.   57. Ibid., 232-33.   58. JQA diary, 16 Dec.

1817, Adams Family Papers.   59. Griffin, *The United States and the Disruption of the Spanish Empire*, 147.   60. JQA diary, 23, 28, and 31 Dec. 1817, Adams Family Papers.

61. 13 January 1818, *Memoirs*, 4:40-41.   62. Quoted in Whitaker, *The United States and the Independence of Latin America*, 236.   63. Bowman, "Vicente Pazos and the Amelia Island Affair," 287.   64. Bowman, "Vicente Pazos, Agent for the Amelia Island Filibusters," 431.   65. Ibid., 432.

66. Ibid., 428-29.   67. Quoted in ibid., 437.   68. Ibid., 438-39.   69. House vote to refuse the Pazos Memorial (11 March 1818): ayes: West, 34; South, 39; Northeast, 51; nos: West, 14; South, 7; Northeast, 7.   70. Ibid., 440-41.

71. 13 Jan. 1818, *Memoirs*, 4:40.   72. 15th Cong., 1st sess., *Annals of the Congress*, 2:1874-98.   73. On 15 March, Adams consulted with Joseph Gales, copublisher of the *National Intelligencer*, regarding which documents to include in the special edition of the newspaper. See JQA diary, 15 March 1818, Adams Family Papers.   74. 15th Cong., 1st sess., *Annals of the Congress*, 2:1447.   75. Ibid., 1899.

76. Ibid., 1899-1943.   77. Ibid., 1934-39.   78. 24 March 1818, *Memoirs*, 4:67.   79. Whitaker, *The United States and the Independence of Latin America*, 244.   80. 15th Cong., 1st sess., *Annals of the Congress*, 2:1500.

81. Ibid., 1485-87, 1497.   82. Ibid., 1499.   83. Those taking the House floor to oppose Clay's measure included John Forsyth of Georgia, George Poindexter of Mississippi, and Samuel Smith of Maryland.   84. Stewart, "The South American Commission," 58.   85. 15th Cong., 1st sess., *Annals of the Congress*, 2:1610.

86. Ibid., 1642.   87. John Forsyth to Nicholas Biddle, 26 March 1818, Biddle Papers.   88. 15th Cong., 1st sess., *Annals of the Congress*, 2:1610.   89. House vote on Clay's resolution to allot funds for a minister to the United Provinces of the Rio de la Plata (30 March 1818): ayes: West, 27; South, 6; Northeast, 12; nos: West, 23; South, 37; Northeast, 55.   90. Quoted in Whitaker, *The United States and the Independence of Latin America*, 246.

91. Ibid., 247.

FIVE: Jackson's Invasion of Florida

1. James Madison to JM, 18 Feb. 1818, Monroe Papers.   2. *Richmond Enquirer*, 31 March 1818.   3. Ammon, *James Monroe*, 384; Van Deusen, *Life of Henry Clay*, 122.   4. Charles Bagot to Lord Castlereagh, 17 April 1817, quoted in *Britain and the Independence of Latin America*, 2:490.   5. On the Treaty of Fort Jackson, see Remini, *Andrew Jackson*, 225-33.

6. Ibid., chap. 21. The treaties are in the *American State Papers: Indian Affairs* (Washington, D.C., 1834), 2:1-150.   7. On the "Negro Fort," see Littlefield, *Africans and Seminoles*, 7; Peters, *The Florida Wars*, 17-26; McReynolds, *The Seminoles*, 73-78; Wright, *Creeks and Seminoles*, 183-44, 197-99; and Remini, *Andrew Jackson*, 344-45.   8. Wright, *Creeks and Seminoles*, 182-83, 193-94, 197; Remini, *Andrew Jackson*, 301-5; McReynolds, *The Seminoles*, 69-70, 73.   9. Remini, *Andrew Jackson*, 324-25.   10. Wright, *Creeks and Seminoles*, 202, notes that "in many respects [the Seminole War] represented a continuation of the Creek War." On the outbreak of the First Seminole War, see Silver, *Edmund Pendleton Gaines*, 71; Remini, *Andrew Jackson*, 344-45; McReynolds, *The Seminoles*, 80-81; and Peters, *The Florida Wars*, 49-50.

11. Remini, *Andrew Jackson*, 344-45.   12. Calhoun to AJ, 26 Dec. 1817, *ASPMA*, 1:689; JM to Jackson, 28 Dec. 1817, Monroe Papers. See also Calhoun to Gaines, 17 Dec.

1817, *ASPMA*, 1:689.   13. Bassett, *Life of Andrew Jackson*, 250-51.   14. Jackson to JM, 6 Jan. 1818, quoted in ibid., 246.   15. The existence of a so-called "Rhea letter" from Monroe to Jackson authorizing the conquest of Florida has long been a topic of debate among historians. Stenberg, "Jackson's Rhea Letter Hoax," 480-96, characterizes Jackson's story as a "fabrication." Remini, *Andrew Jackson*, 347-50, asserts that Jackson incorrectly interpreted Monroe's letter of 28 December as a response to his letter to the president of 6 January. Remini also notes the large number of historians who have accepted Monroe's innocence in waging an undeclared war in Florida, thereby ignoring the open-ended nature of the 28 December letter and his role in the Mathews affair of 1812.

16. See Pratt, *Expansionists of 1812*, 111-13.   17. On the Seminole War campaign, see Bassett, *Life of Andrew Jackson*, 240-64; Rogin, *Fathers and Children*, 193-202; Peters, *The Florida Wars*, 49-54; McReynolds, *The Seminoles*, 80-89; Remini, *Andrew Jackson*, 351-65; Silver, *Edmund Pendleton Gaines*, 72-82; and Wright, *Creeks and Seminoles*, 204-9.   18. See *Narrative of a Voyage to the Spanish Main*, 244-51, for a transcript of Arbuthnot's defense.   19. The letters used in Arbuthnot's prosecution are in ibid., 216-39.   20. See ibid., 251-67, for the transcript of Ambrister's trial.

21. Documents on the Seminole War are in *ASPMA*, 1:681-769.   22. Jackson's paternalistic attitude toward native Americans is described, if somewhat exaggerated, in Rogin, *Fathers and Children*.   23. AJ to Calhoun, 5 May 1818, *ASPMA*, 1:701-2.   24. Documents on the Chehaw massacre are found in *ASPMA*, 1:774-78.   25. Remini, *Andrew Jackson*, 360-62.

26. Quoted in Bassett, *Life of Jackson*, 263.   27. Ibid., 261.   28. Onís to JQA, 17 June 1818, *ASPFR*, 4:495.   29. Onís to JQA, 24 June 1818, *ASPFR*, 4:495-96. 30. Onís to JQA, 8 July 1818, *ASPFR*, 4:496-97.

31. Editorial comment on the seizure of Pensacola ranged from calling it "an act of war" (*Kentucky Reporter*, 24 June 1818) to the characterization of Jackson's exploits as having "proceeded from the purest motives of patriotism" (*National Intelligencer*, 28 July 1818).   32. 15 July 1818, *Memoirs*, 4:109.   33. Bemis, *Foundations*, 314 n.39.   34. Wiltse, *John C. Calhoun: Nationalist*, chap. 12, suggests that Calhoun was standing on constitutional principle in opposing Jackson. Niven, *John C. Calhoun and the Price of Union*, 69, argues that "Calhoun saw quite clearly that he could not tolerate Jackson's insubordination because it threatened civilian control of the military and the entire command structure."   35. 16 July 1818, *Memoirs*, 4:109-10.

36. 17 July 1818, ibid., 4:111.   37. 18 July 1818, ibid., 4:112.   38. 20 July 1818, ibid., 4:113-14.   39. 21 July 1818, ibid., 4:115.   40. JQA to JA, 14 Feb. 1819, *Writings*, 6:530.

41. Wiltse, *John C. Calhoun: Nationalist*, 162.   42. Lipsky, *John Quincy Adams*, 267, writes that Adams later regretted his defense of Jackson, citing diary entry of 29 April 1830, (*Memoirs*, 8:223).   43. *ASPFR*, 23 July 1818, 4:497-98.   44. Ibid., 498.   45. Remini, *Andrew Jackson*, 353.

46. *ASPFR*, 4:499.   47. 8 July 1818, *Memoirs*, 4:105.   48. Luis de Onís to Pizarro, 18 July 1818, AHN-Estado, leg. 5643.   49. 16 July 1818, *Memoirs*, 4:110. 50. Bemis, *Foundations*, 317-18.

51. Luis de Onís to Pizarro, 18 July 1818, AHN-Estado, leg. 5643.   52. The exploits of L'Allemand and other adventurers of the Spanish Gulf Coast are described in Warren, *The Sword Was Their Passport*.   53. Bemis, *Foundations*, 309.   54. Chittenden, *History of the American Fur Trade*, 2:563.   55. For details of the Long-Atkinson expedition and the reasons for its failure, see ibid., 2:562-87.

56. In a note to Pizarro the previous December, Onís had characterized the attacks

on Amelia Island as part of a larger U.S. strategy to realize "its great project of reaching the Pacific Ocean" (2 Dec. 1817, AHN-Estado, leg. 5642). In his *Memoria sobre las Negociaciones*, 43, Onís judged that American interest in controlling the Columbia River stemmed from the desire to establish a global trading empire centered at Astoria.   57. Webster, *The Art and Practice of Diplomacy*, chap. 1.   58. Bemis, *Foundations*, 339-40, asserts that Monroe made "no determined effort" to acquire Texas, and that the "imperfect claim" to Texas had been yielded in exchange for East Florida.   59. JQA diary, 12 July 1818, Adams Family Papers; 17 July 1818, *Memoirs*, 4:111.   60. *Memoirs*, 4:117.

61. 11 July 1818, ibid., 4:107.   62. JQA to JA, 1 Aug. 1816, Adams Family Papers.   63. Tucker and Hendrickson, *Empire of Liberty*, 221.

six: Onís Brought to a Point

1. Onís to JQA, 5 Aug. 1818, *ASPFR* 4:505-7.   2. Onís to Pizarro, 18 July 1818, AHN-Estado, leg. 5643, IX.   3. Ibid., 17 July 1818.   4. Ibid., 12 July 1818.
5. Ibid., 4 Aug. 1818, leg. 5643, X.

6. Rush to JQA, 5 Jan., 14 and 18 Feb., 21 March 1818, DS, Dispatches from Great Britain.   7. Bagot to JQA, 26 Nov. 1817, DS, Dispatches from the British Legation; Bemis, *Foundations*, 281-84; Burt, *The United States, Great Britain, and British North America*, (1940), 412-14; 15 May 1818, *Memoirs*, 4:94.   8. JQA to Rush, 20 May 1818, *ASPFR*, 4:853-54.   9. Rush to JQA, 19 June 1818, DS, Dispatches from Great Britain.   10. Rufus King to Christopher Gore, 12 April 1818, King Papers.

11. Webster, *Foreign Policy of Castlereagh*, 121.   12. An insightful discussion of the Congress of Aix La Chapelle is in Kissinger, *A World Restored*, chap. 12.
13. Webster, *Foreign Policy of Castlereagh*, 418-21; Bartley, *Imperial Russia*, 129.
14. Webster, *Foreign Policy of Castlereagh*, 403.   15. Anna, *Spain and the Loss of America*, 189.

16. Duke of San Carlos to Pizarro, 1 Aug. 1818, AHN-Estado, leg. 5660, I.   17. See the minutes of the Consejo de Estado, 26 and 29 Aug. 1818, AHN-Estado, leg. 5660, XIII; Pizarro to Erving, 29 Aug. 1818, *ASPFR*, 4:522-23.   18. Pizarro to Onís, 30 Aug. 1818, AHN-Estado leg. 5660, VI.   19. JQA to George Campbell, 28 June 1818, DS, Instructions to Ministers.   20. JQA to Alexander Everett, 10 Aug. 1818, DS, Instructions to Ministers.

21. 9 Aug. 1818, *Memoirs*, 4:125.   22. 27 July 1818, ibid., 4:118.   23. *Diplomatic Correspondence of the United States*, 1:74-75.   24. 7 Nov. 1818, *Memoirs*, 4:167.   25. 27 Aug. 1818, ibid., 4:127-28; JQA diary, 29 Sept. 1818, Adams Family Papers.

26. Nagel, *Descent from Glory*, 106-7, 130-31.   27. Onís to JQA, 24 Oct. 1818, *ASPFR*, 4:526-30.   28. Bemis, *Foundations*, 323.   29. 26 Oct. 1818, *Memoirs*, 4:144.   30. 29 Oct. 1818, ibid., 4:146.

31. JQA to Onís, 31 Oct. 1818, *ASPFR*, 4:530-31.   32. Onís to JQA, 16 Nov. 1818, *ASPFR*, 4:533.   33. 4 Nov. 1818, *Memoirs*, 4:161.   34. 5 Nov. 1818, ibid., 4:163-64.   35. 7 Nov. 1818, ibid., 4:165.

36. 15th Cong., 2nd sess., *Annals of the Congress*, 2136-2350.   37. 8 Nov. 1818, *Memoirs*, 4:168.   38. See Barthes, *Writing Degree Zero*, 19-29.   39. See Hayden White, "The Value of Narrativity in the Representation of Reality," in W.J.T. Mitchell, ed., *On Narrative* (Chicago, 1980), 1-25.   40. On the social construction of the "other," see Dower, *War without Mercy*; Todorov, *Conquest of America*; Drinnon, *Facing West*; Pearce, *Savagism and Civilization*.

41. 16 and 23 Nov. 1818, *Memoirs*, 4:171, 176.   42. JQA to Erving, 28 Nov. 1818, *ASPFR*, 4:539-45.   43. Ibid., 539.   44. Ibid.   45. Ibid., 540.
46. Ibid.   47. Remini, *Andrew Jackson*, 324-25.   48. On Arbuthnot, see ibid., 352; Rogin, *Fathers and Children*, 194-98; Bassett, *Life of Jackson*, 240-42; Peters, *The Florida Wars*, 48; McReynolds, *The Seminoles*, 79-80; Frank L. Owsley, "Ambrister and Arbuthnot: Adventurers or Martyrs for National Honor? " *Journal of the Early Republic* 5:3 (fall 1985): 289-308.   49. JQA to Onís, 23 July 1818, *ASPFR*, 4:497-98. For a stimulating discussion of Indian-white relations during this period, see Rogin, "Liberal Society and the Indian Question," in his *Ronald Reagan: The Movie*, 134-68.
50. *ASPFR*, 4:544. See also Rogin, *Ronald Reagan: The Movie*, 148.
51. On the border violence, see Peters, *The Florida Wars*, 54-55.   52. McReynolds, *The Seminoles*, 80.   53. Bassett, *Life of Jackson*; Remini, *Andrew Jackson*, 345-46; McReynolds, *The Seminoles*, 80.   54. Miller and Johnson, *The Puritans*, 1:81-90.   55. Ibid., 1:84; Gay, *A Loss of Mastery*, chap. 3. Gay (73) describes Cotton Mather's *Magnalia Christa Americana* as the work of a historian who "forgets inconvenient facts, refuses to call things by their right names, and defends the indefensible." Exactly the same can be said about Adams's letter to Erving.
56. Bercovitch, *Puritan Origins*, chap. 2, esp. 44-50.   57. See Dower, *War without Mercy*, chap. 1.   58. Jennings, *Invasion of America*, 12.   59. *ASPFR*, 4:541.
60. The transcript of Ambrister's trial is in *ASPMA*, 1:721-34.
61. AJ to Calhoun, 5 May 1818, *ASPMA*, 1:701-2.   62. Remini, *Andrew Jackson*, 353.   63. *ASPFR*, 4:544.   64. JQA diary, 14 May 1818, Adams Family Papers.
65. *ASPFR*, 4:542.
66. Ibid., 541.   67. Ibid., 545.   68. Tacitus, *Complete Works*, 243.
69. Nagel, *Descent from Glory*, 131, argues that Adams had ample time to come to the bedside of his dying mother but that he remained in Washington because of the negotiations.   70. 1 Nov. 1818, *Memoirs*, 4:155.

SEVEN: The Origins of Empire

1. Castlereagh to Bagot, 2 Jan. 1819, quoted in Brooks, *Diplomacy and the Borderlands*, 117.   2. See Perkins, *Castlereagh and Adams*, 289-92, for examples of British public and press opinion.   3. JQA diary, 25 Dec. 1818, Adams Family Papers.   4. Anna, *Spain and the Loss of America*, 208; Del Rio, *La Mision de Don Luis de Onís*, 138.   5. Erving to JQA, 20 Sept. 1818, DS, Dispatches from Spain.
6. Brooks, *Diplomacy and the Borderlands*, 155-57; Yrujo to Onís, 10 and 23 Oct. 1818, AHN-Estado, leg. 5660, v. 6.   7. Kaufmann, *British Policy*, 118.   8. On the conference at Aix-la-Chapelle, see ibid., 116-21; Webster, *Foreign Policy of Castlereagh*, 418-21; Kissinger, *A World Restored*, 214-31; Bartley, *Imperial Russia*, 129-33.
9. Burt, *The United States, Great Britain, and British North America*, 422, and see chap. 12 for a complete discussion of the Convention of 1818. Also see Bemis, *Foundations*, chap. 14.   10. 12 Dec. 1818, *Memoirs*, 4:190.
11. 28 Dec. 1818. ibid.,   12. JQA to Richard Rush, 1 Jan. 1819, DS, Instructions to Ministers.   13. Keen, *David Curtis DeForest*, 139-46.   14. 2 Jan. 1819, *Memoirs*, 4:207.   15. Ibid., 208.
16. 17 Dec. 1818, ibid., 4:193.   17. 24 and 25 Nov., 8 Dec. 1818, ibid., 4:178, 181, 187.   18. 31 Dec. 1818, ibid., 4:202.   19. 3 Jan. 1819, ibid.   20. Onís to JQA, 16 Jan. 1819; JQA to Onís, 29 Jan. 1819, *ASPFR*, 4:615-16.
21. Onís to JQA, 1 Feb. 1819, *ASPFR*, 4:616.   22. Keen, *DeForest*, 153.   23. 20 Jan. 1819, *Memoirs*, 4:223-24.   24. Keen, *David Curtis DeForest*, 155; JQA diary, 22

Jan. 1819, Adams Family Papers.   25. See esp. Document 49 regarding Arbuthnot's guilt.   26. JM to AJ, 20 July 1818, Monroe Papers, quoted in Bassett, *Life of Andrew Jackson*, 274-75.   27. JM to AJ, 20 Oct. 1818, Monroe Papers.   28. *Richmond Enquirer*, 7 and 12 Jan. 1819.   29. Ibid., 7 Jan. 1819.   30. Ibid., 12 Jan. 1819.   31. Bassett, *Life of Andrew Jackson*, 283.   32. Remini, *Andrew Jackson*, 370; James, *Life of Andrew Jackson*, 324; Bassett, *Life of Andrew Jackson*, 281-82.   33. Bassett, *Life of Andrew Jackson*, 283; Carl Schurz, *Life of Henry Clay* (New York, 1915), 1:159. The Seminole War debate is recorded in the *Annals of the Congress*, 15th Cong. 2d sess., 1:515-30; 1:583-1138.   34. King to Christopher Gore, 7 Feb. 1819, King Papers.   35. See Beisner, *Twelve against Empire*, on the difficulties in making a principled stand against imperialist adventures.   36. Remini, *Andrew Jackson*, 371. Jackson reportedly threatened to "cut off the ears" of Senator John Eppes of Virginia, a member of the investigating committee.   37. Ibid. Subsequent examples of "bold figures on horseback" include William Sherman, George Armstrong Custer, Douglas MacArthur, and George Patton.   38. Madison makes this observation in *Federalist* No. 49.   39. 5 Jan. 1819, *Memoirs*, 4:212.   40. 4 Feb. 1819, ibid.   41. Onís to Yrujo, 25 Nov. 1818, AHN-Estado, leg. 5644, v. 3; Onís to Yrujo, 1 Feb., 8 and 14 Jan. 1819, AHN-Estado, leg. 5645, v. 1; Onís to Yrujo, 10 and 12 January 1819, AHN-Estado, leg. 5645, v. 3.   42. Onís to JQA, 9 Feb. 1819, *ASPFR*, 4:617-19.   43. Bemis, *Foundations*, 333.   44. 15 Feb. 1819, *Memoirs*, 4:255.   45. *ASPFR*, 4:621-22.   46. Quoted in Bemis, *Foundations*, 334.   47. 19 Feb. 1819, Memoirs, 4:269.   48. 22 Feb. 1819, ibid.   49. Although no congressman actively opposed the treaty in 1819 for ceding the claim to Texas, by 1821 the issue had become a serious concern for both northerners and southerners. In 1820 Adams said privately that he opposed annexation of Texas except under terms prohibiting slavery. See Moore, *The Missouri Controversy*, 343-46.   50. 1 Feb. 1819, *Memoirs*, 4:237.   51. 2 Feb. 1819, ibid., 4:238-39.   52. 3 Feb. 1819, ibid., 4:239.   53. Brooks, *Diplomacy and the Borderlands* 156.   54. Bemis, *Foundations*, 339-40.   55. 31 March 1820, *Memoirs*, 5:54.   56. JM to TJ, May 1820, Monroe, *Writings*, 6:119-23.   57. JM to AJ, 23 May 1820, ibid., 6:126-30.   58. Rufus King to Christopher Gore, 19 Feb. 1819, King Papers.   59. The Lacock report is in *Annals of the Congress*, 15th Cong. 2nd sess., 1:256-68.   60. 24 Feb. 1819, *Memoirs*, 4:278.   61. Remini, *Andrew Jackson*, 376; Bassett, *Life of Andrew Jackson* 288-89; James, *Life of Andrew Jackson*, 365.   62. Perkins, *Castlereagh and Adams*, 294-95.   63. 16 Nov. 1819, *Memoirs*, 4:439.   64. LaFeber, *John Quincy Adams and American Continental Empire*, 36-37; 16 Nov. 1819, *Memoirs*, 4:439.   65. Erving to JQA, 10 and 26 Feb. 1818; also see Erving's dispatches concerning the land grants, 1 and 18 March, 5 and 26 April, 14 May, DS, Dispatches from Spain.   66. Brooks, *Diplomacy and the Borderlands*, 176.   67. 8 March 1819, *Memoirs*, 4:289.   68. Brooks, *Diplomacy and the Borderlands*, 179. Also see the minutes of the Consejo de Estado, 1 May 1819, AHN-Estado, leg. 5661, v. 2.   69. Brooks, *Diplomacy and the Borderlands*, 181.   70. Ibid., 177-78; 184-85.   71. Vives to JQA, 14, 19, and 24 April 1820, *ASPFR*, 4:680-84.   72. 10 Aug. 1819, 5 Nov. 1820, *Memoirs*, 4:406-8, 432.   73. 24 Nov. 1819, ibid., 4:447.   74. 26 Nov. 1819, ibid., 4:450.   75. 27 Nov. 1819, ibid., 4:451.   76. 27 Nov. 1819, ibid., 4:453-56.   77. *Messages and Papers of the Presidents*,

2:57-58.   78. Ibid., 2:71-72.   79. 31 March 1820, *Memoirs,* 5:55.   80. 1 May 1820, ibid., 5:83-84.
81. 12 and 13 March 1820, ibid., 5:65-68.   82. 8 Jan. 1820, ibid., 4:502.   83. 22 Feb. 1821, ibid., 5:289-90.   84. Ibid., 291, 289.   85. Adams, *Report on Weights and Measures,* may also be found in the Adams Family Papers.
86. Williams, *Contours of American History,* 214-15. Also see Dangerfield, *Era of Good Feelings,* 160-61.   87. Brooks Adams in H. Adams, *Degradation,* 38-52.

EPILOGUE: The American Cicero

1. Hietala, *Manifest Design,* 19-20.   2. Bemis, *Foundations,* 494-95; Kushner, *Conflict on the Northwest Coast,* chap. 2.   3. Kushner, *Conflict on the Northwest Coast,* 48-62.   4. Ibid., 54. Perkins, *Castlereagh and Adams,* 329, states that "noncolonization was laid down at this time solely because of the Russian ukase."
5. Bemis, *Foundations,* 485-88, 493-98; Coughlin, "Commercial Foundations," 22-25; Kushner, *Conflict on the Northwest Coast,* 34-39; Ronda, *Astoria and Empire,* 327-36.
6. Coughlin, "Commercial Foundations," 29 n.33.   7. Galbraith, *The Hudson's Bay Company,* 102, 113-14.   8. Norman Graebner, *Empire on the Pacific: A Study in American Continental Expansionism* (1955; Santa Barbara, 1983), viii. Graebner writes: "It was the Pacific Ocean that determined the territorial goals of all American presidents from John Quincy Adams to Polk." (xiv). He might have included Thomas Jefferson and James Monroe in that list. Graebner adds that "mercantile interests in the Pacific . . . determined the course of empire."   9. On Seward's role in American expansionism, see E.N. Paolino, *The Foundations of the American Empire: William Henry Seward and U.S. Foreign Policy* (Ithaca, N.Y., 1973). On Hay, see Kenton J. Clymer, *John Hay: The Gentleman as Diplomat* (Ann Arbor, Mich., 1975).   10. For Adams's views on the Cuban question, see LaFeber, *John Quincy Adams and American Continental Empire,* 126-31.
11. The reality of the mass television audience means that millions of Americans watch Florida State football, basketball, and other intercollegiate sports—many more than the number who know that the Seminoles were nearly exterminated or that some are alive today. Indeed, were this history widely remembered, "Seminoles" would not be used as a university team mascot.   12. 29 May 1819, *Memoirs,* 4:380.   13. 3 Dec. 1819, 20 Nov. 1820, ibid., 4:461, 5:200.   14. 1 May 1820, ibid., 5:86.
15. Bemis, *Foundations,* 359-62.
16. Canning's famous overture to the United States is well explained in Perkins, *Castlereagh and Adams,* chap. 16.   17. Tucker and Hendrickson, *Empire of Liberty,* viii; Hietala, *Manifest Design,* viii.   18. Tucker and Hendrickson, *Empire of Liberty,* 250.   19. 20 Oct. 1820, *Memoirs,* 5:364-65. On the president's war powers, see Levy, *Original Intent and the Framers' Constitution,* chap. 2.   20. On the cultural significance of war in the early republic, see Watts, *The Republic Reborn.*
21. Adams shrewdly noted in his diary: "The Virginian opposition to implied powers, therefore, is a convenient weapon, to be taken up or laid aside as its suits the purpose of state turbulence and ambition" (20 Oct. 1820, *Memoirs,* 5:365).   22. The Vietnam War represented the first time in American history that the government's patriotic narrative was successfully contradicted by an "enemy." North Vietnam's implacable resistance made the optimistic assessments of American leaders increasingly implausible: hence the creation of Lyndon Johnson's "credibility gap."
23. JQA to Paul P.C. Degrand, 16 Nov. 1818, quoted in Bemis, *Union,* 18.   24. JQA to

Joseph Hopkinson, quoted in Bemis, *Union*, 19.   25. JQA to LCA, 29 Sept. 1822, *Writings*, 7:309.
26. JQA to LCA, 7 Oct. 1822, ibid., 7:315-16.   27. "The Macbeth Policy," ibid., 7:356-62.   28. Bemis, *Union*, chap. 3, gives the most detailed account of Adams's scheming for the presidency. See also Dangerfield, *Era of Good Feelings*, 331-37.
29. Bemis, *Union*, 131.   30. Dangerfield, *Era of Good Feelings*, 344.
31. Nagel, *The Adams Women*, 214.   32. Henry Adams to Brooks Adams, 18 Feb. 1909, quoted in Nagel, *Descent from Glory*, 352-54.   33. Quoted in Dangerfield, *Era of Good Feelings*, 345.   34. Wood, *The Creation of the American Republic*, chap. 14.   35. George Washington Adams's suicide is described in Bemis, *Union*, 178-82.
36. Brooks Adams in H. Adams, *Degradation*, 77.   37. JQA to Charles Upham, 2 Feb. 1837, quoted in H. Adams, *Degradation*, 24-25.   38. Quoted in Bemis, *Union*, 210.   39. Ibid., 204.   40. Beyond his avid study of Cicero's writings, Adams's life bears a number of similarities to that of the Roman statesman. Adams's belief in the principles of natural law and universal moral equality, the rule of law, mixed government, the sanctity of private property, the rule of a natural aristocracy all reflect aspects of Ciceronian thought. See Wood, *Cicero's Social and Political Thought*, 4; Wood confirms the judgment that "among the numerous classical role models in America . . . pride of place was given above all to Cicero."
41. On the Amistad affair, see Howard Jones, *Mutiny on the Amistad: The Saga of a Slave Revolt and Its Impact on American Abolition, Law, and Diplomacy* (New York, 1987).   42. On the assassination threats against Adams, see Bemis, *Union*, 348, 375-76, 435, 438. See Richards, *Life and Times*, 131.   43. Richards *Life and Times*, 96-97, traces Adams's antislavery views to lessons he learned as a small boy from his mother's example.   44. 3 March 1820, *Memoirs*, 5:4, 11.   45. 27 Dec. 1819, ibid., 4:492.
46. 10 Jan. 1820, ibid., 4:502.   47. 27 Dec. 1819, ibid., 4:492-93.   48. 29 Dec. 1820, ibid., 5:210. Also see diary entry of 24 Feb. 1820, ibid., 4:531.   49. 13 April 1820, ibid., 5:68.   50. 30 March 1820, ibid., 5:53-54.
51. 23 Feb. 1820, ibid., 4:530.   52. 3 March 1820, ibid., 5:12.   53. 29 Nov. 1820, ibid., 5:209.   54. Bemis, *Union*, 34.   55. 11 Feb. 1820, *Memoirs*, 4:424-25. Also see 16 Jan. 1820, ibid., 4:506.
56. Lynn Hudson Parsons, "A Perpetual Harrow upon My Feelings': John Quincy Adams and the American Indian," *New England Quarterly*, Sept. 1973, pp. 339-40.
57. Ibid., 374; Richards, *Life and Times*, 148-50.   58. JQA to George Parkman, 22 June 1836, quoted in Parsons, "Perpetual Harrow," 372.   59. Quoted in Bemis, *Union*, 338.   60. Ibid., 329.
61. See Richards, *Life and Times*, chap. 6; Bemis, *Union*, chaps. 18, 21, 22.
62. Bemis, *Union*, 463.   63. 7 July 1845, *Memoirs*, 12:202.   64. Bemis, *Union*, 481; Adams's opposition to Manifest Destiny is detailed in chap. 22.   65. Quoted in ibid., 532-33.
66. JQA to Albert Gallatin, 26 Dec. 1847, Adams Family Papers.   67. Bemis, *Union*, 484-87.   68. Ibid., 490. On the ideology of America's "natural right" to Oregon, see Weinberg, *Manifest Destiny*, chap. 5.   69. JQA to Joseph Sturges, April 1846, Adams Family Papers.   70. Lipsky, *John Quincy Adams*, 127.
71. Adams, *Address to the Citizens of the Twelfth Congressional District of Braintree*.   72. 19 Feb. 1845, *Memoirs*, 12:171.   73. JQA to Richard Rush, 16 Oct. 1845, Adams Family Papers.   74. Quoted in Bemis, *Union*, 526.   75. H. Adams, *Education*, 416.

Selected Bibliography

MANUSCRIPT SOURCES
Adams Family Papers. Massachusetts Historical Society, Boston.
Archivo Histórico Nacional, Sección de Ministerio de Estado, Madrid, Spain.
Astor, John Jacob, Papers. Baker Library, Harvard University, Cambridge, Massachusetts.
Biddle, Nicholas, Papers. Library of Congress, Washington, D.C.
Crawford, William, Papers. Library of Congress, Washington, D.C.
Department of State, Records. National Archives, Washington, D.C.
Gallatin, Albert, Papers. New-York Historical Society, New York.
Jefferson, Thomas, Papers. Library of Congress, Washington, D.C.
King, Rufus, Papers. New-York Historical Society, New York.
Madison, James, Papers. Library of Congress, Washington, D.C.
Monroe, James, Papers. Library of Congress, Washington, D.C.
War Department, Records. National Archives, Washington, D.C.
Wirt, William, Papers. Maryland Historical Society, Baltimore.

NEWSPAPERS
Albany Argus
Argus of Western America
Boston Columbian Centinel
City of Washington Gazette
Kentucky Reporter
Nashville Clarion
New York Evening Post
Niles' Weekly Register
Philadelphia Aurora
Richmond Enquirer
Washington National Intelligencer

PUBLISHED CONTEMPORARY SOURCES
Adams, Abigail. *Letters of Mrs Adams, the Wife of John Adams.* Ed. Charles Francis Adams. 2 vols. Boston, 1840.
Adams, John Quincy. *Memoirs.* Ed. Charles Francis Adams. 12 vols. Philadelphia, 1874-77.
———. *The Writings of John Quincy Adams.* Ed. W. C. Ford. 6 vols. New York, 1913-17.
———. *Lives of James Madison and James Monroe.* Buffalo, 1850.

———. *Address to the Citizens of the Twelfth Congressional District of Braintree, 17 September 1842.* Boston, 1842.

———. *An Oration Delivered before the Inhabitants of the Town of Newburyport at their request, on the Sixty-first Anniversary of the Declaration of Independence, July 4, 1837.* Newburyport, 1837.

———. *Poems of Religion and Society.* Auburn and Buffalo, 1848.

———. *Report on Weights and Measures.* Washington, D.C., 1821.

———. *The Social Compact, Exemplified in the Constitution of the Commonwealth of Massachusetts.* Providence, 1842.

Adams Family Correspondence. Ed. L.H. Butterfield. 4 vols. to date. Cambridge, Mass., 1963-73.

American State Papers: Foreign Relations. Ed. under the authority of Congress by Walter Lowrie and Mathew St. Clair Clark. 6 vols. Washington, D.C., 1832-59.

American State Papers: Indian Affairs. Ed. under the authority of Congress by Walter Lowrie and Walter S. Franklin. 2 vols. Washington, D.C., 1834.

American State Papers: Military Affairs. Ed. under the authority of Congress by Walter Lowrie and Mathew St. Clair Clark. 7 vols. Washington, D.C., 1832-61.

Annals of the Congress of the United States. 15th Congress, 1854-55. Washington, D.C., 1854-55.

Brackenridge, H. M. *South America.* London, 1818.

Britain and the Independence of Latin America. 1812-1830. Ed. Charles K. Webster. 2 vols. London, 1939.

Carey, Mathew. *Examination of the Pretensions of New England to Commercial Preeminence on Which is Added a View to the Causes of the Suspension of Cash Payments at the Banks.* Philadelphia, 1814.

———. *The New Olive Branch.* Philadelphia, 1821.

Clay, Henry. *The Papers of Henry Clay.* Vols. 1-6, ed. James F. Hopkins and Mary W.M. Hargreaves. Vols. 7-8, ed. Robert Seager II. Lexington, Ky., 1961-84.

Correspondence and Memoirs of Viscount Castlereagh. 12 vols. London, 1848-53.

Diplomatic Correspondence of the United States Concerning the Independence of the Latin American Nations. Ed. William R. Manning. 3 vols. New York, 1925.

Everett, Edward. *A Eulogy on the Life and Character of John Quincy Adams.* Boston, 1848.

"James Monroe." *Analectic Magazine,* Aug. 1819, 11-19.

Jefferson, Thomas. "The Limits and Bounds of Louisiana." In American Philosophical Society, *Documents Relating to the Purchase and Exploration of Louisiana,* 5-45. New York, 1904.

———. *Writings of Thomas Jefferson.* Ed. A.A. Lipscomb. 20 vols. Washington, D.C., 1903.

McCready, John. *A Review of the Trade and Commerce of New York from 1815 to the Present.* New York, 1820.

Melish, John. *Letter to James Monroe, esq., On the State of the Country, with a Plan for Improving the Condition of Society*. Philadelphia, 1820

————. *On the Necessity of Protecting and Encouraging the Manufactures of the United States*. Philadelphia, 1818.

Messages and Papers of the Presidents. 1789-1897. Ed. James D. Richardson. 11 vols, Washington, D.C., 1875-93.

Mitchell, S. A., and H. Ames. *A Narrative of A Tour of Observations made during the Summer of 1817 by James Monroe*. Philadelphia, 1818.

Monroe, James. *Writings of James Monroe*. Ed. Stanislaus M. Hamilton. 7 vols. New York, 1896.

Narrative of a Voyage to the Spanish Main (1819). Ed. John W. Griffin. Gainesville, Fla., 1978.

Onís, Luis de. *Memoria sobre las negociaciones entre España y los Estados Unidos de America* (1820). Colonia Guerrero, D.F., Mex., 1820.

Pitkin, Timothy. *Statistical View of the Commerce of the United States*. Hartford, Conn., 1816.

Rush, Richard. *Memorandum of A Residence at the Court of London*. London, 1833.

Seybert, Adam. *Statistical Annals of the United States*. Philadelphia, 1818.

Waldo, Samuel P. *The Tour of James Monroe*. Hartford, Conn., 1818. Library of Congress rare book collection.

Yard, James. *Spanish America and the United States, or Views of the Actual Commerce of the United States with the Spanish Colonies*. Philadelphia, 1818.

Secondary Sources

Adams, Henry. *The Degradation of the Democratic Dogma*. New York, 1920.

————. *The Education of Henry Adams* (1918). Ed. Ernest Samuels. Boston, 1973.

————. *History of the United States during the Administrations of Jefferson and Madison, 1801-1817*. 9 vols. New York, 1891-96.

Akers, Charles. *Abigail Adams: An American Woman*. Boston, 1980.

Ammon, Harry. *James Monroe: The Quest for National Identity*. New York, 1971.

Anna, Timothy. *Spain and the Loss of America*. Lincoln, Neb., 1983.

Appleby, Joyce. *Capitalism and a New Social Order: The Republican Vision of the 1790's*. New York, 1984.

Arthur, Stanley C. *Jean Lafitte: Gentleman Rover*. New Orleans, 1952.

Bailyn, Bernard. *The Ideological Origins of the American Revolution*. Cambridge, Mass., 1967.

Barbier, Jacques, and Allan Kuethe, eds. *The North Amercian Role in the Spanish Imperial Economy, 1760-1819*. Manchester, Eng., 1984.

Barthes, Roland. *Writing Degree Zero*. New York, 1968.

Bartlett, C.J. *Castlereagh*. New York, 1966.

Bartley, Russell H. *Imperial Russia and the Struggle for Latin American Independence, 1808-1828*. Austin, Texas, 1978.

Basset, John Spencer. *The Life of Andrew Jackson* (1911). New York, 1967.

Becker, Jeronimo. *Historia de las relaciones exteriores españa durante el siglo XIX.* Madrid, 1924.

Beisner, Robert. *Twelve against Empire: The Anti-Imperialists, 1898-1900.* New York, 1968.

Bemis, Samuel Flagg. *John Quincy Adams and the Foundations of American Foreign Policy.* New York, 1949.

———. *John Quincy Adams and the Union.* New York, 1956.

Benns, F. Lee. *The American Struggle for the British West India Carrying Trade, 1815-1830* (1923). Clifton, N.J., 1972.

Bercovitch, Sacvan. *The American Jeremiad.* Madison, Wis., 1978.

———. *The Puritan Origins of the American Self.* New Haven, 1975.

Bolkhovitinov, N.N. "Russia and the Non-Colonization Principle: New Archival Evidence." *Oregon Historical Quarterly* 72, no. 2 (1971): 101-26.

Bourne, Kenneth. *Britain and the Balance of Power in North America.* Berkeley, 1965.

Bowman, Charles. "Vicente Pazos, Agent for the Amelia Island Filibusters, 1818." *Florida Historical Quarterly* 53, no. 4 (1975): 428-42.

———. "Vicente Pazos and the Amelia Island Affair, 1817." *Florida Historical Quarterly* 53, no. 3 (1975): 273-95.

Brant, Irving. *James Madison, Commander in Chief, 1812-1836.* Indianapolis, 1961.

Brooks, Philip C. *Diplomacy and the Borderlands: The Adams-Onís Treaty of 1819.* Berkeley, 1939.

———. "Pichardo's Treatise and the Adams-Onís Treaty." *Hispanic American Historical Review* 15 (1935): 94-99.

Brown, Roger. *The Republic in Peril: 1812.* New York, 1964.

Burt, A.L. *The United States, Great Britain, and British North America from the Revolution to the Establishment of Peace after the War of 1812.* Washington, D.C., 1940.

Campbell, Charles. *From Revolution to Rapprochement: The United States and Great Britain, 1783-1900.* New York, 1974.

Carr, Raymond. *Spain, 1808-1939.* Oxford, Eng., 1966.

Catterall, Ralph C.H. *The Second Bank of the United States.* Chicago, 1902.

Chittenden, Hiram B. *History of the American Fur Trade of the Far West.* 2 vols. Rpt., Stanford, Cal. 1954.

Christiansen, E. *Origins of Military Power in Spain, 1800-1854.* London, 1967.

Clymer, Kenton J. *John Hay: The Gentleman as Diplomat.* Ann Arbor, Mich., 1975.

Cook, Warren L. *Flood Tide of Empire: Spain and the Pacific Northwest, 1543-1819.* New Haven, 1973.

Coughlin, Magdalen. "Commercial Foundations of Political Interest in Opening the Pacific, 1789-1829." *California Historical Society Quarterly* 50 (March 1971): 15-33.

Cox, Isaac. *The West Florida Controversy, 1798-1813.* Baltimore, 1918.

Cresson, William P. *Diplomatic Portraits.* Boston, 1923.

———. *The Holy Alliance*. Washington, D.C., 1922.

———. *James Monroe*. Chapel Hill, 1946.

Crooks, David. *American Democracy and English Politics, 1815-1850*. Oxford, Eng., 1965.

Dangerfield, George. *The Awakening of American Nationalism, 1815-1828*. New York, 1965.

———. *The Era of Good Feelings*. New York, 1952.

Davis, T. Frederick. *MacGregor's Invasion of Florida. 1817*. Gainesville, Fla., 1928.

DeConde, Alexander. *This Affair of Louisiana*. New York, 1976.

del Rio, Angel. *La Mision de Don Luis de Onís a los Estados Unidos. 1809-1819*. New York, 1981.

Dower, John W. *War without Mercy: Race and Power in the Pacific War*. New York, 1985.

Drinnon, Richard. *Facing West: The Metaphysics of Indian Hating and Empire Building*. Minneapolis, 1980.

Duberman, Martin. *Charles Francis Adams, 1807-1886*. Boston, 1961.

Dyer, J. O. *The Early History of Galveston*. Galveston, Tex., 1916.

East, Robert A. *John Quincy Adams: The Critical Years*. New York, 1962.

Esteban, Javier Cuenca. "Trends and Cycles in U.S. Trade with Spain and the Spanish Empire, 1790-1819." *Journal of Economic History* 44, no. 2 (June 1984): 521-45.

Faye, Stanley. "Commodore Aury." *Louisiana Historical Quarterly* 24 (July 1941): 611-97.

Fontana, Josep. *La crisis del antiguo regime*. Barcelona, 1979.

Fuller, Hubert B. *The Purchase of Florida*. Cleveland, 1906.

Galbraith, John S. *The Hudson's Bay Company as an Imperial Factor, 1821-1869*. Berkeley, 1957.

Gay, Peter. *A Loss of Mastery: Puritan Historians in Colonial America*. Berkeley, 1966.

Gibson, James R. *Imperial Russia in Frontier America*. New York, 1976.

Gilman, Daniel Coit. *James Monroe*. New York, 1885.

Glick, Wendell. "The Best Possible World of John Quincy Adams." *New England Quarterly* 37, no. 1 (March 1964): 3-17.

Goebel, Dorothy Burne. "British-American Rivalry in the Chilean Trade, 1817-1820." *Journal of Economic History* 2, no. 2 (1942): 190-207.

———. "British Trade to the Spanish Colonies, 1796-1820." *American Historical Review* 43, no. 2 (Jan. 1938): 288-320.

Goebel, Julius L. *The Recognition Policy of the United States*. New York, 1915.

Goetzmann, William. *Army Exploration in the American West. 1803-1863*. Lincoln, Neb., 1959.

Graebner, Norman. *Empire on the Pacific: A Study in American Continental Expansionism*. Santa Barbara, 1955; rpt. 1983.

Grampp, William D. "Mercantilism and Laissez-Faire in American Political Discussion, 1787-1829." Ph.D. diss., Univ. of Chicago, 1944.

Griffin, Charles C. "Privateering from Baltimore during the Spanish American Wars of Independence." *Maryland Historical Quarterly* 34, no. 3 (1940): 2-25.

———. *The United States and the Disruption of the Spanish Empire 1810-1822* (1937). New York, 1968.

Guinness, Ralph B. "The Purpose of the Lewis and Clark Expedition." *Mississippi Valley Historical Review* 20 (June 1933): 90-100.

Hargreaves, Mary W.M. *The Presidency of John Quincy Adams*. Lawrence, Kan., 1985.

Hecht, Marie B. *John Quincy Adams: A Personal History of a Public Man*. New York, 1972.

Hietala, Thomas R. *Manifest Design: Anxious Aggrandizement in Late Jacksonian America*. Ithaca, 1985.

Hill, H.A. *The Trade and Commerce of Boston, 1630-1890*. Boston, 1895.

Hinde, Wendy. *Castlereagh*. London, 1981.

Hunt, Michael H. *Ideology and U.S. Foreign Policy*. New Haven, 1987.

Hutchins, John G.B. *American Maritime Industries and Public Policy, 1789-1914*. Cambridge, Mass., 1941.

James, Marquis. *The Life of Andrew Jackson: The Border Captain*. New York, 1936.

Jennings, Francis. *The Invasion of America: Indians, Colonialism, and the Cant of Conquest*. Chapel Hill, 1975.

Johnson, John J. *A Hemisphere Apart: The Foundations of United States Policy toward Latin America*. Baltimore, 1990.

Jones, Dorothy V. *License for Empire: Colonialism by Treaty in Early America*. Chicago, 1982.

Jones, Howard. *Mutiny on the Amistad: The Saga of a Slave Revolt and Its Impact on American Abolition, Law, and Diplomacy*. New York, 1987.

Kaufmann, William. *British Policy and the Independence of Latin America, 1804-1828*. New Haven, 1951.

Keen, Benjamin. *David Curtis DeForest and the Revolution of Buenos Aires*. New Haven, 1947.

Ketcham, Ralph. *James Madison: A Biography*. New York, 1971.

Kissinger, Henry A. *A World Restored*. Boston, 1957.

Kushner, Howard I. *Conflict on the Northwest Coast*. Westport, Conn., 1975.

———. "The Significance of the Alaska Purchase to American Expansion." In S. Frederick Starr, ed., *Russia's American Colony*. Durham, N.C., 1986.

LaFeber, Walter, ed. *John Quincy Adams and American Continental Empire*. Chicago, 1965.

———. *The New Empire*. Ithaca, 1962.

Latourette, K.S. *The History of the Early Relations between the United States and China, 1784-1844*. New Haven, 1917.

Levin, Phyllis L. *Abigail Adams*. New York, 1987.

Levy, Leonard W. *Original Intent and the Framers' Constitution*. New York, 1988.

Lipsky, George A. *John Quincy Adams: His Theory and Ideas*. New York, 1950.

Liss, Peggy K. *Atlantic Empires: The Network of Trade and Revolution, 1713-1826.* Baltimore, 1983.

Littlefield, Daniel F., Jr. *Africans and Seminoles: From Removal to Emancipation.* Westport, Conn., 1977.

Livermore, Shaw. *The Twilight of Federalism: The Disintegration of the Federalist Party, 1815-1830.* Princeton, 1962.

Logan, John A. *No Transfer: An American Security Principle.* New Haven, 1961.

McCoy, Drew. *The Elusive Republic.* Chapel Hill, 1980.

McReynolds, Edwin C. *The Seminoles.* Norman, Okla., 1957.

Manning, Clarence A. *Russian Influence in Early America.* New York, 1953.

Mares, José Fuentes. *Genesis del expansionismo norteamericano.* Mexico City, 1985.

Marshall, Thomas M. *History of the Western Boundary of the Louisiana Purchase, 1819-1841.* Berkeley, 1914.

Middleton, K.W.B. *Britain and Russia.* Port Washington, N.Y., 1947.

Mitchell, W.J.T., ed. *On Narrative.* Chicago, 1980.

Miller, Perry. *Errand into the Wilderness.* Cambridge, Mass., 1956.

———. and Thomas Johnson, eds. *The Puritans: A Sourcebook,* 2 vols. New York, 1963.

Mooney, Chase C. *William H. Crawford.* Lexington, Ky., 1974.

Moore, Glover. *The Missouri Controversy, 1819-1821.* Lexington, Ky., 1953.

Morgan, George. *Life of James Monroe.* Boston, 1921.

Morison, Samuel Eliot. *The Maritime History of Massachusetts.* Boston, 1921.

Musto, David. "The Youth of John Quincy Adams." *Proceedings of the American Philosophical Society* 113 (1969): 269-82.

Nagel, Paul C. *The Adams Women: Abigail and Louisa Adams, Their Sisters and Daughters.* New York, 1987.

———. *Descent from Glory.* New York, 1983.

Nasatir, Abraham. *Borderland in Retreat.* Albuquerque, 1976.

Nichols, Irby C. "The Russian Ukase and the Monroe Doctrine: A Reassessment." *Pacific Historical Review* 36 (Feb. 1967): 13-26.

Niven, John. *John C. Calhoun and the Price of Union.* Baton Rouge, 1988.

North, Douglass. *The Economic Growth of the United States, 1790-1860.* Englewood, N.J., 1961.

Novick, Peter. *That Noble Dream: The "Objectivity Question" and the American Historical Profession.* New York, 1988.

Ogden, Adele. *The California Sea Otter Trade, 1784-1848.* Berkeley, 1941.

Okun, S.B. *The Russian-American Company.* Trans. Carl Ginsburg. New York, 1979.

Owsley, Frank L. "Ambrister and Arbuthnot: Adventurers or Martyrs for National Honor?" *Journal of the Early Republic,* 5, 3 (Fall 1985): 289-308.

Paolino, Ernest N. *The Foundations of the American Empire: William Henry Seward and U.S. Foreign Policy.* Ithaca, N.Y., 1973.

Parsons, Burke. *British Trade Cycles and American Bank Credit.* New York, 1977.

Parsons, Lynn Hudson. " 'A Perpetual Harrow upon My Feelings: John Quincy Adams and the American Indian." *New England Quarterly* (Sept. 1973), 339-79.

Pearce, Roy Harvey. *Savagism and Civilization.* (1953) Rev. ed.: Baltimore, 1965.

Perkins, Bradford. *Castlereagh and Adams: England and the United States, 1812-1823.* Berkeley, 1964.

Perkins, Dexter. "Russia and the Spanish Colonies, 1817-1818." *American Historical Review* 28, 4 (July 1923): 656-72.

Peters, Virginia B. *The Florida Wars.* Hamden, Conn., 1979.

Pocock, J.G.A. *The Machiavellian Moment: Florentine Political Thought and the Atlantic Republican Tradition.* New York, 1975.

Porter, Kenneth Wiggins. *The Jacksons and the Lees.* Cambridge, Mass., 1937.

———. *John Jacob Astor: Businessman.* 2 vols. Cambridge, Mass., 1931.

Pratt, Julius. *Expansionists of 1812.* New York, 1925.

Rappaport, Armin. *A History of American Diplomacy.* New York, 1976.

Remini, Robert V. *Andrew Jackson and the Course of American Empire, 1767-1821.* New York, 1977.

Rezneck, Samuel. "The Depression of 1819-22: A Social History." *American Historical Review* 34 (Oct. 1933): 28-33.

Richards, Leonard L. *The Life and Times of Congressman John Quincy Adams.* New York, 1986.

Robertson, William Spence. *France and Latin American Independence.* Baltimore, 1939.

———. "Russia and the Emancipation of Spanish America." *Hispanic American Historical Review* 21, no. 2 (May 1941): 196-221.

Rogin, Michael P. *Fathers and Children: Andrew Jackson and the Subjugation of the American Indian.* New York, 1975.

———. *Ronald Reagan: The Movie and Other Episodes in Political Demonology.* Berkeley, 1987.

Ronda, James P. *Astoria and Empire.* Lincoln, Neb., 1990.

Rothbard, Murray. *The Panic of 1819: Reactions and Policies.* New York, 1962.

Schellenberg, T.R. "Jeffersonian Origins of the Monroe Doctrine." *Hispanic American Historical Review* 14, no. 1 (Feb. 1934): 1-32.

Schmidt, Louis B. "Internal Commerce and Development of the National Economy before 1860." *Journal of Political Economy* 48 (Dec. 1939): 798-822.

Schur, Leon. "The Second Bank of the United States and the Inflation after the War of 1812." *Journal of Political Economy* 68 (April 1960): 118-34.

Schurz, Carl. *The Life of Henry Clay.* New York, 1915.

Setser, Vernon. *The Commercial Reciprocity Policy of the United States, 1784-1829.* Philadelphia, 1937.

Shaw, Peter. *The Character of John Adams.* Chapel Hill, 1976.

Shepherd, Jack. *Cannibals of the Heart.* New York, 1980.

Silver, James W. *Edmund Pendleton Gaines, Frontier General.* Baton Rouge, 1949.

Sklar, Kathryn K. *Catharine Beecher: A Study in American Domesticity.* New Haven, 1973.

Slotkin, Richard. *The Fatal Environment: The Myth of the Frontier in the Age of Industrialization, 1800-1890.* Middletown, Conn., 1985.

———. *Regeneration through Violence: The Mythology of the American Frontier, 1600-1860.* Middletown, Conn., 1973.

Smith, Walter Buckingham. *Economic Aspects of the Second Bank of the United States.* Cambridge, Mass., 1953.

——— and Arthur H. Cole. *Fluctuations in American Business.* Cambridge, Mass., 1935.

Snyder, James W.A. *Bibliography for the Early American China Trade, 1784-1815.* New York, 1940.

Stenberg, Richard R. "The Boundaries of the Louisiana Purchase." *Hispanic American Historical Review* 14 (Feb. 1934): 32-64.

———. "Jackson's Rhea Letter Hoax." *Journal of Southern History* 2 (1936): 480-96.

Stewart, Watt. "The South American Commission, 1817-1818." *Hispanic American Historical Review* 7 (1927): 31-59.

Stourzh, Gerald. *Benjamin Franklin and American Foreign Policy* (2d ed. 1954). Chicago, 1969.

Stuart, Reginald. *War and American Thought from the Revolution to the Monroe Doctrine.* Kent, Ohio, 1982.

Styron, Arthur. *The Last of the Cocked Hats.* Norman, Okla., 1945.

Tacitus. *Complete Works of Tacitus.* Ed. Moses Hadas. New York, 1942.

Tatum, E.H. *The United States and Europe, 1815-1823,* New York, 1936.

Taylor, George Rogers. "Agrarian Discontent in the Mississippi Valley Preceding the War of 1812." *Journal of Political Economy* 39, no. 4 (Aug. 1931): 471-505.

———. *The Transportation Revolution.* New York, 1951.

Terrell, John. *Furs by Astor.* New York, 1963.

Thomas, Alfred B. "The Yellowstone River, James Long, and the Spanish Reaction to American Intrusions into Spanish Dominions, 1818-1819." *New Mexico Historical Review* 4 (1929): 164-87.

Todorov, Tzvetan. *The Conquest of America: The Question of the Other.* Richard Howard, trans. New York, 1984.

Tucker, Robert W., and David C. Hendrickson. *Empire of Liberty: The Statecraft of Thomas Jefferson.* New York, 1990.

Tunon de Lara, M. *La España del Siglo XIX.* Paris, 1961.

Turner, Frederick Jackson. *The Rise of the New West* (1906). Gloucester, Mass., 1961.

Van Alstyne, Richard. "International Rivalries in the Pacific Northwest." *Oregon Historical Quarterly* 46, no. 3 (Sept. 1945): 185-218.

Van Deusen, Glyndon G. *The Life of Henry Clay.* New York, 1937.

Velasco, Manuel Fernandez de Las. *Relaciones diplomaticas entre España y los Estados Unidos: Don Luis de Onís y el Tratado Transcontinental.* Mexico City, 1965.

Waciuma, Wanjohi. *Intervention in the Spanish Floridas.* Boston, 1976.

Wade, Richard C. *The Urban Frontier.* Cambridge, Mass., 1959.

Walters, Raymond. *Albert Gallatin, Jeffersonian Financier and Diplomat.* New York, 1957.

Warren, Harris Gaylord. *The Sword Was Their Passport.* Baton Rouge, 1943.

Watts, Steven. *The Republic Reborn: War and the Making of Liberal America, 1790-1829.* Baltimore, 1987.

Webster, Charles K. *The Art and Practice of Diplomacy.* New York, 1962.

———. "Castlereagh and the Spanish Colonies." *English Historical Review* 27, no. 105 (Jan. 1912): 78-95; 30, no. 120 (Oct. 1915): 631-45.

———. *The Foreign Policy of Castlereagh, 1815-1822.* London, 1925.

Weinberg, Albert. *Manifest Destiny: A Study of Nationalist Expansionism in American History.* Baltimore, 1935.

Whitaker, Arthur Preston. *The United States and the Independence of Latin America, 1808-1830.* Baltimore, 1941.

White, Hayden. *The Content of the Form: Narrative Discourse and Historical Representation.* Baltimore, 1987.

White, Leonard. *The Jeffersonians: A Study in Administrative History, 1801-1829.* New York, 1951.

Williams, William Appleman. *The Contours of American History* (1961). New York, 1973.

Wiltse, Charles M. *John C. Calhoun: Nationalist, 1782-1828.* Indianapolis, 1944.

———. *John C. Calhoun: Sectionalist, 1840-1850.* Indianapolis, 1951.

Wishart, David J. *The Fur Trade of the American West, 1807-1840.* Lincoln, Neb., 1979.

Wood, Gordon. *The Creation of the American Republic, 1776-1787.* Chapel Hill, 1969.

Wood, Neal. *Cicero's Social and Political Thought.* Berkeley, 1988.

Woodward, Margaret. "The Spanish Army and the Loss of America." *Hispanic American Historical Review* 48, no. 4 (Nov. 1968): 586-607.

Wright, J. Leitch, Jr. *Creeks and Seminoles: The Destruction and Regeneration of the Muscogulge People.* Lincoln, 1986.

———. "A Note of the First Seminole War as Seen by the Indians, Negroes and Their British Advisors." *Journal of Southern History* 34 (Nov. 1968): 565-75.

Young, James Sterling. *The Washington Community, 1800-1828.* New York, 1966.

Index

instructions to, 108, 113, 114-15, 116, 117, 156-57, 210 n 15; plans for seizure of Florida, 108, 210 n 15; court-martials and executes Ambrister and Arbuthnot, 110-11, 128, 140, 143, 144, 147, 157, 158, 160; U.S. reaction to actions of, 112-15, 138, 139, 148, 157, 158, 159, 160-61, 210 nn 31, 34; Spanish reaction to actions of, 113, 115, 116-17, 119-22, 123, 127, 131; JQA defends actions of, 114, 115-19, 126, 127-28, 131, 138-46, 147-48, 168, 170, 196, 210 n 42; JQA and Monroe personally affected by action of, 124; Congress investigates actions of, 156-60, 168-69, 213 n 36; as focus of rhetoric of empire, 184, 185

Jackson affair. *See* Jackson, Andrew: in First Seminole War
"Jackson's Rhea Letter Hoax" (Sternberg), 210 n 15
James and Thomas H. Perkins (firm), 80
James Monroe (Ammon), 203 nn 12, 15
Japan, 178
Jay's Treaty, 7
Jefferson, Thomas: and JQA, 9, 12, 18, 21, 185; and Louisiana Purchase, 22, 24-26, 27, 117; and Monroe, 39, 44, 181, 182, 183, 203 n 12; advocates free trade, 43; on Anglo-American relations, 44; relationship with Astor, 50, 51; in U.S. South American policy, 90, 180; and transcontinental boundary, 123; and Yrujo, 148; in U.S. interest in American northwest coast, 178, 214 n 8; and expansion of executive power, 181; and rhetoric of empire, 184; and slavery, 191. *See also* Jeffersonians
Jeffersonians, 19, 39, 40, 43, 125, 178, 181
Jefferson's Embargo, 181
Jennings, Francis, 143
John C. Calhoun: Nationalist (Wiltse), 210 n 34
John C. Calhoun and the Price of Union (Niven), 210 n 34
John Quincy Adams and the Foundations of American Foreign Policy (Bemis), 4, 201 n 29, 205 n 7, 206 n 80, 211 n 58
John Qunicy Adams and the Union (Bemis), 4, 201 n 33, 202 n 58
John Quincy Adams (Hecht), 201 nn 40, 57
John Quincy Adams (Lipsky), 210 n 42
Johnson, Edward, 142

Johnson, Louisa Catherine. *See* Adams, Louisa Catherine (wife)
Johnson, Lyndon, 214 n 21

Kentucky *Reporter*, 67
King, Rufus, 48-49, 52, 130, 159, 168
Kushner, Howard I., 206 n 86

Lacock, Abner, 168, 169
Lafayette, Marie-Joseph-Paul-Yves-Roch-Gilbert du Motier de, 90
Lafitte, Jean, 64, 98, 122
L'Allemand, Henri, 121
La Salle, René-Robert Cavelier de, 26, 73, 76
Law of 1811. *See* No Transfer Resolution
Lee, Henry, 52
Leigh, Benjamin Watkins, 157-58
Lewis, Meriwether, 26, 31, 49, 178
Lewis and Clark expedition, 26, 31, 49, 178
Life and Times of Congressman John Quincy Adams, The (Richards), 215 n 43
Lincoln, Abraham, 1, 184, 194, 195
Lipsky, George A., 210 n 42
Liverpool, second earl of, 45
Livingston, Robert, 23, 27
Livy, 12
Lloyd, James, 18
London *Spectator*, 12
Long-Atkinson Expedition, 122-23
Louis XIV, king of France, 26, 76
Louisiana Purchase: JQA's role in, 1, 7, 19, 26, 117; and imperialism, 3; U.S./Spanish disputes over (1804-17), 22-30; and Transcontinental Treaty, 163, 176, 180-81; and transcontinental claims, 178; and expansion of power of executive, 181, 182. *See also* boundary negotiations between U.S. and Spain; Louisiana Territory
Louisiana Territory, 25-26, 35. *See also* boundary negotiations between U.S. and Spain; Louisiana Purchase

MacArthur, Douglas, 213 n 37
"Macbeth Policy" (JQA), 186-87
MacGregor, Gregor, 64
McIntosh, John, 64
Madison, James: and JQA, 7, 160, 185; tries to acquire Florida, 27-30; and Monroe, 39, 181, 182; advocates free trade, 42, 43; military buildup by, 47; relationship with Astor, 50, 51; relationship with Onís, 71-72; and